D1607590

SOUL PAIN
The Meaning of
Suffering in Later Life

Helen K. Black
Thomas Jefferson University

Society and Aging Series
Jon Hendricks: Series Editor

BAYWOOD PUBLISHING COMPANY, INC.
Amityville, New York

Baywood Publishing Company, Inc.
26 Austin Avenue
PO Box 337
Amityville, NY 11701
(800) 638-7819
E-mail: baywood@baywood.com
Web site: baywood.com

Library of Congress Catalog Number: 2005045390
ISBN: 0-89503-304-6 (cloth)

Library of Congress Cataloging-in-Publication Data

Black, Helen K., 1952-
   Soul pain : the meaning of suffering in later life / Helen K. Black.
      p. cm. -- (Society and aging series)
   Includes bibliographical references and index.
   ISBN 0-89503-304-6 (cloth)
      1. Suffering in old age.   I. Title. II. Series.

BF724.85.S84B58 2005
55.9'3--dc21

                                                          2005045390

This book is dedicated
to the memory of

STEPHEN J. HRUSKO
1945–1999

"He ain't heavy; he's my brother."

Table of Contents

Have you entered into the sources of the sea,
Or walked about in the depths of the abyss?
Have the gates of death been shown to you,
Or have you seen the gates of darkness?
Have you comprehended the breadth of the earth?
Tell me, if you know all:
Which is the way to the dwelling place of light,
And where is the abode of darkness?
Have you entered the storehouse of the snow?

Job 38:16–22

Preface

I began work in research at the Philadelphia Geriatric Center as an interviewer on a study about childlessness. With an eye to Erikson's next to last psychosocial stage—generativity versus stagnation—the project explored how childless elders compensated for a lack of biological generativity. "Some trees bear fruit and some trees give shade," one woman explained her ease with the choices that she made in life and with circumstances that were thrust upon her. Although some men and women regretted being childless, most elders fought their regrets through introspection and an active decision to believe that the "products" of their lives were worthwhile.

Some time later, during research of elderly women's experiences of personal poverty, I understood that "objective" definitions of poverty had little to do with these ladies' subjective experiences. For most women, as long as basic needs were met, lack of finances did not mean poverty. Poverty was often interpreted as a state of mind that occurred through broken relationships or a lack of connection with significant others. To the women I interviewed, poverty was more of a personal lack than a financial one.

Sometime after that I explored the meaning of forgiveness to a sample of elderly men and women varied by race and religion. Elders did not talk about forgiveness as an abstract concept; they told complex and complicated stories of "wrongs" they had done to others or that had been done to them. Some elders thought that forgiveness might be construed as weakness and therefore rejected it. Other elders saw forgiveness as an act that was mandated by their religious beliefs, and struggled, sometimes with great resentment, to forgive.

As I looked back, the stream of research that I undertook followed a stream of life where experiences shape a life by the choices they offer and the sense of control they take away. The experiences I researched were often interpreted by elders as either dignity-giving or dignity-depriving, depending on, ultimately, the meaning each person gave to the experience. Older persons created meaning using a retrospective view of their entire lives. Childlessness, poverty and forgiveness held particular meanings in old age because each was set within the large frame of a long life. The metaphor of a shade-giving tree for childlessness showed that this elder took into account, when choosing the metaphor, her words and deeds of many decades.

I explored the experience of suffering because I wondered how an individual incorporates the emotional and spiritual fractiousness of suffering into a life already laboring under the "work" of old age. I questioned how elders create meaning for suffering at a stage in life when personal resources are lessened and time seems to be "running out." I had no difficulty in recruiting respondents for this research. As with former projects, I was moved by elders' willingness to share their experiences with me as well as their need to do so. "No one," many said, "asked me these questions before." Elders seemed pleased to tell their life stories and stories of suffering to me—the intimate stranger.

As "popular" as the subject was with elders, it was as unpopular with editors. As data was analyzed and I sought publication, one journal editor, in rejecting an article about this subject that I had sent him, accused me of adding to ageism and ageist stereotypes by discussing "negative" aspects of old age, such as suffering. "Why didn't you," he asked, "write an article about happiness?" A kindly book editor rejected the manuscript saying, "Suffering is not a social problem; it is an ongoing human problem that will never go away."

I both agreed and disagreed. In respondents' definitions and descriptions, suffering was as social and political a problem as poverty, as revealing of destructive religious absolutes as forgiveness, and as "loaded" with culturally negative connotations as childlessness. Yet, elders' accounts of suffering hinted that even with social parity among all people, suffering would remain a human experience. This observation revealed my own bias concerning the experience of suffering. I define suffering as a visceral awareness of my own or another's vulnerability to be broken at any time and in many ways. In other words, human brokenness is the ground in which suffering takes root; negative events, incidents or time periods in life unearth both the clay and the humus. And I find suffering meaningful. I understood that my response to suffering flows from my ethnic and religious background, my life experience, and my age (I am not elderly). I also recognized that the older people I interviewed dwell in culture-bound and value-laden space. Their definitions of suffering, like mine, emerge from the uniqueness of their lives as well as the profundity of their experiences. I recognized that persons interviewed for this study may not share my definition of suffering or my perception of its value, so I did not define suffering or offer my opinion of its worth during interviews—unless asked.

In writing this book, my strongest sense of accountability was to the elders whose stories I tell. I protect their identity by using pseudonyms throughout the book, and I am faithful to their words and to the voices they used to share their lives and stories of suffering. I also acknowledge that respondents expressed their suffering non-verbally as well as with words. Their languages of suffering, such as silence, gestures, cries and stories, and their definitions, portraits, and theories about suffering were varied and unique. Respondents viewed suffering as eminently human and part of the life course as well as a political outrage that thrives in "isms" that continue to exist—ageism, classism, racism, and sexism.

Literature on suffering suggests that the best way to know what suffering is or what it means to an individual is to ask. So, this book is about suffering in old age in the words of experts—elders who told me they had suffered. I could have written a book about happiness, but I chose to write about suffering. As the journal editor imagined, this book is sad in parts. But it is also humorous, hopeful, peculiar, and unpredictable. There are no stereotypes here.

Acknowledgments

It is difficult to adequately express my gratitude to the men and women who shared their life stories and stories of suffering with me. Without their willingness to talk about suffering—a word that is loaded with cultural and religious connotations, as well as memories and fears, this book could not have been written.

I also acknowledge the support (in part) of the original research by the Fetzer Institute. This study was accomplished because of their funding.

I sincerely acknowledge the intellectual encouragement of Dr. Lucy Bregman, of Temple University in Philadelphia, who read, edited, and commented upon an earlier version of this work.

I am deeply grateful to Dr. Robert Rubinstein of the University of Maryland Baltimore County, the Principal Investigator of the original study, friend and colleague who generously shared time and knowledge along the way, and also read and commented upon the final version of the manuscript.

I also thank the editor of this volume, Dr. Jon Hendricks, for seeking and finding value in this manuscript, and the anonymous reviewer who carefully read the manuscript and offered insightful comments.

CHAPTER 1

The Topography of Suffering

This book explores the experience of suffering in old age. It reports on research that elicited stories of suffering from 40 community-dwelling adults (aged 70+). Each of the major ideas (suffering and age) discussed has a unique cultural and social meaning, yet each construct holds a particular meaning in relation to the other. The goal in the original research was to tap into this "meaning in relation" by asking elders to tell their stories of suffering, and to discover the personal meaning of suffering that lies within each elder's story. My goal is to report on and interpret elders' stories for the reader.

For purposes of discussion, I define terms that are integral here, such as culture, self, suffering, personal meaning, and meaning systems. *Culture* is our native starting point; it is the shared blueprint of both the local and larger world into which we are born and take part in shaping. Culture cannot be abstracted from a society's historical reality; interaction among members is central to inheriting and bequeathing a culture (Hall, 1959; Turner, 1996).[1]

There are many definitions of "self" that reflect various disciplines. I chose a definition that resonates to elders' dual sense of living their lives as well as watching their lives unfold. That is, the self may be defined as two complementary faculties: a process that is evolving and an object that is observed (Charmaz, 1999). In this definition the self includes an abiding identity that is both actor and acted upon, watcher and watched, and subject and object of life experiences.

Suffering has been defined in medical, psychological, and religious idioms as: "the state of severe distress associated with events that threaten the intactness of the person" (Cassell, 1982, p. 640); "a threat to our composure, our integrity, and the fulfillment of our intentions" (Reich, 1987, p. 117) and, "as involving threats that constitute an alienation of our being" (van Hooft, 1998, p. 14). These definitions speak to the all-encompassing nature of suffering as a threat to an integrated existence. In the book's Preface I offered my own definition of

---

[1] References for all chapters start on page 193.

1

suffering. In the Conclusion, I will present a definition of suffering based on respondents' accounts.

Personal meaning is defined here as each person's version of the events of her own life. Personal meaning is abstracted from the shared meanings of a particular culture as well as gleaned from individual experience (Rubinstein, 1992). I analyze the personal meaning of suffering by examining elders' life stories and stories of suffering based on the uniqueness of each life story as well as common themes. Elders' religious beliefs and personal spirituality add another dimension of meaning to elders' interpretations of suffering.

Meaning systems provide the lens through which the world is experienced and interpreted. An elder's meaning system is based on her current context, personal and communal history, cultural background and traditions, and religious and spiritual beliefs. In this book, I explore how elders' meaning systems create their attributions, definitions, and theories about suffering.

I examine the literature on aging and narrative studies in this work because I am asking older persons to "tell stories" about themselves. I also examine the literature on Western religious beliefs and personal spirituality. Thus, I investigate elders' experiences of suffering under the headings of aging studies, narrative studies and religious beliefs, and personal spirituality. These rubrics share a concern with how older individuals make meaning of their experiences and their lives, how they develop and maintain a "self" through the life span, and how they accommodate and assimilate negative experiences into their lives through the stories they tell about suffering.

BACKGROUND

Discussion of suffering has a long history in human thought as well as within various academic disciplines of study (Amato, 1990). Research on suffering examines the causes, results, and manifestations of suffering under several orientations. Among them are: The experience of suffering viewed by the medical model; psychological suffering; social suffering; and suffering as a religious, spiritual or theological issue. Within these orientations, the literature narrows when research on suffering in old age is the focus. There, it centers on suffering as cognitive and physical loss in old age and the inevitable decline of the aging body and mind (Birren & Cunningham, 1985; Bradley, Fried, Kasl, & Idler, 2001; Cristofalo, Tresini, Francis, & Volken, 1999). Certainly, loss in every domain of being human occurs with more frequency and rapidity in old age. Also, elders may have fewer expectations about replacing those losses in the time they believe is left to them. Yet respondents show that although loss may be a significant component in their narratives, the word is not a synonym for suffering. The term loss is neither broad nor deep enough to collapse all of elders' experiences of suffering under it.

In the following sections, I explore the current research on suffering in old age from the medical, psychological, social, and religious viewpoints. This exploration provides a framework to show the range of contemporary research on suffering and leads the reader into how this book extends the extant literature concerning suffering in old age.

The Medical Model

In regard to suffering, the medical model is a *way of thinking* that pursues an objective physical cause for an individual's suffering (Coyne, 2001). Suffering is viewed as a symptom in the medical model, and is rationally investigated in order to find its causal framework, usually at the biological level. After putting forth a diagnosis for suffering, the health care professional will methodically discover its cause and prescribe a remedy. Other models, types or orientations toward suffering incorporate the medical model because of its emphasis on a cure (Duchan, 2001). Because suffering is usually discussed as an event within patienthood and as an outcome of illness and pain, research on suffering most often originates from a medical standpoint (Good & Good, 1981). Suffering certainly may result from illness and pain because they reveal the contingency of the body and the self at any age, i.e., that one cannot depend on one's body (Frank, 1995), its *normal* functioning, and the self that one was before illness (Black, 2001).

In the medical model, suffering is generally connected to pain. The word *pain* is used to describe the bodily consequences of injury or disease, although this word is also employed to describe emotional upset or trauma, as well as a generic term for any type of misery (Rawlinson, 1986). Episodes of pain are treated in an event- or disease-specific manner and parts of the body are the foci of treatment. In the medical model, the word suffering may be used to connote a personal reaction to pain (Kleinman et al., 1992).

Medical research acknowledges pain as a variable in human experience that can be objectively described and measured in a clinical setting (Beecher, 1957; Pan & Meier, 2000). The duration and intensity of an individual's pain determine how researchers dimensionalize it, for example, as daily or infrequently or as severe or moderate, and how pain correlates with the measurement of other variables of human experience, such as lack of mastery, negative affect, or locus of control (Lawton, 2000). Other research explores cultural notions of pain, for example, what similar pains connote to dissimilar racial, ethnic, or religious groups, whether and how pain should be expressed, and the gendered difference in the experience and expression of pain (Black, 2002; Lipton & Marbach, 1984; Zbrowski, 1969).

In gerontological health care research, experiences of pain and suffering have been quantified and dimensionalized in part to help institutionalized elders communicate their pain. For example, elders may point to a series of facial expressions on a chart to reveal the level of discomfort they feel (Pan & Meier, 2000). In the nursing home setting, a health care worker may determine an elder is suffering according to key elements or behaviors that the elders displays, such as, for example: confusion, vertigo, lack of appetite, fear, etc. (Picard, 1991; Robinson, 1993).

Metaphors of battle may be used to describe the enemy-like nature of pain (Sontag, 1978). Pain, illness, and disease are considered attacks against the person or parts of the person; medicine and medical practitioners are combatants against the attack, and doctors and medical staff become repairmen who bind the injury and suppress the pain (Zussman, 1993). Metaphors of battle are also cultural symbols that show illness as an enemy and entity imbued with a particular moral meaning (Sabatino, 1992). Pain is a hostile aggressor, the ill person is a victim, and medical practitioners are either heroes or those who lost the *war* against pain, illness, and disease. If the victim remains ill or dies, the morality at work is that the ill person, due to his/her own fault, such as engaging in risk behaviors, is blamed (Farley, 1992, p. 28; Murphy, 1987). For example, pain that results from diseases accompanying alcoholism or drug abuse are perceived differently from pain that results from arthritis (Black, 2001). An uncured illness may also point to the incompetence or negligence of the attending health professional. Either way, pain and illness are not perceived as normative. If someone had lived *better* or the doctor had done a *better* job, good health would be the outcome.

The medical model has been faulted by some for fragmenting the sufferer, reducing the patient to bodily parts, and separating person from context (Heath, 1989). Other work suggests that the focus of clinical practice should be the treatment of suffering in a general sense rather than the specificity of localized pain (Cherny, 1996). In medical literature, some practitioners have expanded their purview of research on pain and disease to welcome illness narratives, which highlight the experiential aspect of illness through a story that the patient tells about his malady (Brody, 1987; Kleinman, 1988; May, 1991). Illness narratives usually offer a multi-dimensional view of illness that includes the perspectives of the patients, their family, and the medical practitioner who treats her (Frank, 1992; Kleinman, 1988). Illness narratives contextualize the patient and hearken back to case studies and patient histories analyzed by doctors in earlier medical practice.

In Medical Anthropology a distinction is made between disease, a biological construct, and illness, or the victim's experience of the disease episode. Work on "explanatory models" and "exploratory maps" of illness experiences also has been the focus of research in medical anthropology (Kleinman, 1980; Williams & Healy, 2001). Other research in this discipline examines the "illness experience" and the meaning of such constructs as "distress," "misfortune," and "affliction."

Suffering and age are linked in the medical literature by common assumptions concerning these constructs (Bradley et al., 2001), for example: aging engenders particular types of suffering, such as debilitation, loss, and poor health, especially as poor health augurs death. These assumptions hold that age and suffering have a shared root—loss, and mental and physical decline (Belsky, 1997). Also inherent in these assumptions is that suffering and age are intertwined; there is a causal relationship between them. Certainly pain, illness, and disease may be compounded by age (Kleinman, 1996), but suffering in old age does not necessarily mean that the older person who suffers is ill, fraught with disease symptoms, or experiencing pain. According to elders described below, age, suffering, and illness may be linked, but to them suffering is an experience different from, and more encompassing than pain.

Psychological Suffering

According to the psychological view, human suffering has many and varied origins. Suffering may result from psychiatric and psychological disorders that can be classified through descriptive, diagnostic processes and treated effectively with medication (Keyes, 1985). Psychological suffering also may be rooted in an organic deficiency, neurological factors, or pathology of the brain that manifests itself in a variety of disorders such as depression or schizophrenia. Relief is offered through medicines that balance the brain's chemistry (Baltes & Smith, 1999).

In the past four decades, treatment of psychological suffering has moved toward the medical model of illness and away from psychoanalysis or talking cures. Cogent classification and description of mental disorders organizes psychological suffering and offers pharmacological remedies. Therapy is usually suggested as a companion treatment to medicine. Psychotherapy is viewed as a "relationship between therapist and client founded on human suffering," and it attempts to alleviate psychological suffering in an individual by revealing its genesis (Young-Eisendrath & Miller, 2001).

Current literature also places psychological suffering within a stress and coping framework. Research on stress and trauma, post-traumatic reaction and post-traumatic stress disorder suggests that these events have a continuing role in shaping the life that follows (Cassidy & Mohr, 2001; Simeon, Guralnik, Schmeidler, Sirof, & Knutelska, 2001). I note that persons interviewed for this study who endured events of stress and trauma did not usually seek professional help. Some remarked that "Stress is a part of life," or "Everybody's traumatized by war." In other words, these elders sought no care or cure for this type of suffering because they did not view it as an illness or they did not believe that it could be alleviated by medicines or therapy.

Psychological research sometimes categorizes suffering. For example, suffering which includes shame and guilt is often described in psychological research as "mundane." Mundane suffering is emotionally and physically experienced as self-diminishment, and is classified differently from existential suffering, such as angst, worry or fear of finitude (Schneider, 1992). Research findings offer similar suggestions for alleviating both mundane and existential suffering, such as behavior modification, that is, keeping busy, engaging in social activities and participating in church or community programs. This is incongruous advice for elders whose sense of shame or anxiety is precisely what keeps them isolated. Such a recommendation also may be inappropriate for elders who believe that it is too late for them to right wrongs done early in life (Miller, 1985). The very vulnerability of age may be a cause of shame to the elder (Lazare, 1995). As shown in both Chapters 2 and 8, two elderly men's sense of shame occurs not so much for having committed particular wrongs in life, but for *being wrong,* that is, exposed as powerless in old age (Nathanson, 2003). Likewise, angst, stress, worry, and post-traumatic reactions experienced in old age may be life threatening in an urgent and immediate sense. For the elder, end of life does not seem distant; it is one's personal horizon closing in on the self.

Research on psychological suffering in older age acknowledges that symptoms of mental illness may be overlooked or dismissed as predictable incidents, both by family and professionals, in the aging process (Schaie & Willis, 1999). Confusion and forgetfulness are symptoms of both dementia and depression. Elders' diminished energy, lack of activity, increased isolation, and decreased ability to make decisions in minor and major matters may be both the causes and the manifestations of depression. Indeed, most respondents experienced one or more of these events. A major finding of the study described here is that just as elders differentiated suffering from loss or pain, they also determined that although a depressed person could be suffering, the term depression did not adequately encompass an experience of suffering (see Chapter 7, "The Morality of Suffering").

Myths, stereotypes, and expert opinions abound concerning normative psycho-logical attitudes in old age, such as activity and disengagement theories, increased interiority and gerotranscendence (Cumming & Henry, 1961; Estes, Swan, & Gerard, 1982; Katz, 1996; Tornstam, 1994). Common sense assumptions about old age may mask psychiatric disorders. Notions about elders' clinical responses to pain or grief, such as decreased appetite, crying, or depression, may assume a pathology that may be, depending on an individual's cultural background or religious beliefs, not pathological at all.

The experience of psychological suffering within individuals of any age may spring from many sources and touch all areas of life. Current research suggests that diagnoses, co-morbidity, and interventions for mental disorder in late life should take the elders' culture, ethnicity, gender, and religious beliefs into account (Kales & Valenstein, 2002; Sajatovic, 2002). Certainly, the web of causation in elders' psychological suffering confounds the mental health worker's ability to trace suffering to a particular genesis or onset, or to predict its effect on other domains of the elder's life (Rubinstein & Lawton, 1997).

Respondents in this study said that by age 70 most individuals have experienced the loss of significant others as well as a measure of cognitive and physical decline. Elders in this sample believed that decline foreshadows death, and some wondered if death portends annihilation. Through this type of suffering and its portent of the unknown, one's being becomes at issue (Heidegger, 1962). It is perhaps here that psychological suffering exists for many elders—at the place and time where they (contrary to Freud) imagine their own deaths in the near (rather than in the distant) future.

"Social Suffering"

In the social sciences, the notion of "social suffering" has been introduced to examine "the devastating injuries that social forces can inflict on human experience" (Kleinman, 1997, p. ix). The notion of social suffering emphasizes large scale economic, political, and social structures that lead to suffering through a variety of means, such as poverty, racism, displacement, genocide, and ethnocide. Literature concerned with social suffering focuses on the macro or global level events that produce suffering in communities and in individuals (Das, 2000). Work in anthropology has attended to the effects of broad structural forces, often violent, that in different ways affect individuals' and groups' subjectivities and create suffering (Das, 1997; Kleinman, 1997; Kleinman, Das, & Lock, 1997; Scarry, 1985; Uehara, Morelli, & Abe-Kim, 2001). Social suffering has a broad causality. It is indicative of the power differentials between individuals and between groups that perpetuate social injustice (Harrison, 1985). The economy, institutional structures, and politics support, repress, contribute to, or ameliorate individual experiences and expressions of suffering (Bourdieu, 1993; Grant, 1989). The emphasis here is on large-scale categories, such as poverty and racism that affected the lives of elders I interviewed and produced suffering. The private suffering of individuals is placed under the large rubric of *social suffering* because suffering is experienced in a social milieu and is judged as suffering within the ethos of the larger public world (Das, 1997; Lipton & Marbach, 1984; Zbrowski, 1969). Individual suffering is always at root social (Soelle, 1975) because suffering, as a *lived experience,* naturally relates to "being in the world." If an individual suffers, the question must be asked: "Where has their society let them down?" (Frankl as cited in Drazen, 2003). Elders' accounts show suffering as embedded in relationships with self, others or God; the situatedness of suffering is fundamentally social.

The literature on social suffering rarely is gerontological, although the issues that social suffering examines are significant gerontologically. Social theorists conclude that suffering is never generic and always contextual (Cone, 1970). Suffering is rooted in the social attributes of age, class, gender, and race that determine who is the less powerful partner in a relationship of any type, such as the relationship that occurs between elders and family members or between residents in a nursing home and the home's administrators or direct caretakers (Grant, 1989; Tellis-Nyak & Tellis-Nyak, 1989).

Age is a powerful source of alienation in a society where worth equals production or reproduction (Martin, 1987) and the appearance of the body takes on paramount importance (Dass, 2000). If "[human beings'] characteristic function and highest asset is conception," (Langer as cited in Geertz, 1973) suffering may result from an elder's inability to conceive of a useful product. Pervasive cultural beliefs challenge the worth of those who no longer author, invent, or bring into being (Harrison, 1985; Martin, 1987). Old age, if perceived as a period of non-generativity, becomes less a stage of life than a concrete condition for suffering due to the moral status connected with being old (Dass, 2000; Harrison, 1985).

Just as the causes of social suffering are built into the structure of a society, so are its cures. Language, as the "main bearer of social structure" imputes a moral value to stages of life, such as old age, and lived experiences, such as suffering (Brodwin, 1992). For example, discussion of suffering in old age reveals generalizations and stereotypes, such as: elders are weak, sexless, passive and inflexible, and for the most part, more silent and interiorized than middle aged persons (Moss, Moss, Rubinstein, & Black, 2003; Townes, 1997; Weiss & Bass, 2002). Of course, individuals from any group are neither homogenous nor easily classified. Apart from a similarity in age (even this is problematic because of the young-old, old-old, and the rise of the third age) elders are as diverse in health, core values, belief systems, and worldview as any cohort.

The meaning of any personal experience, such as suffering, is culturally and socially imposed. To deconstruct and reconstruct the meaning of suffering in old age is a monumental task. Changing the lens through which society views an experience or stage in life, such as suffering in old age, requires dissemination of information regarding elders' experiences. Current gerontological research has challenged stereotypes about elders in all domains of their lives. I hope to add to the social metanoia, or change of heart, by looking at suffering in old age through the *new eyes* of elders who experience these constructs day by day.

Religionist View

Within the last thirty to forty years, Western religious perspectives have viewed individual and communal suffering as an outcome of social inequality. Suffering is thus linked with economic and political oppression in the historical and social arenas in which injustice occurs (Chopp, 1987; Moltemann, 1969; Soelle, 1975). In this view, the causality and ontology of suffering do not transcend the worldly domains in which they are rooted.

In the religionist view, suffering is a form of religious communication. Members use particular symbols, master narratives, myths and rituals to explore, explain and seek healing or solace for the experience of suffering. In the Western traditions, certain words are integral to suffering's language, such as "God" and "redemption." These words are based on interpretations from the primary narratives of suffering, such as the history of the Jews and the prophetic and wisdom literature revealed in the Tanak, and Jesus Christ's passion in the Christian Bible. What makes millennia-old literature current is its relevance. Both ancient and current landscapes of suffering are shaped, in large part, by economic, political, and social injustice (Bregman, 1987). Present day inequity and the Biblical injunction for social justice meet at the nexus of suffering.

The religionist view of suffering highlights individual discernment regarding the meaning of suffering, despite the emphasis on suffering's social causes. A community shares suffering because of the collective oppression of its members, but each member personally interprets the experience. Suffering results from individual choices concerning relationships with self, others, and God. Yet, suffering itself is a forum for choice; it is the "place" where one either encounters or turns away from God.

In the religionist view of suffering, it is generally futile to attempt to rationally link God's love to a personal or communal experience of surd evil, that is, the suffering of the innocent (Surin, 1986). Suffering, like God, is immediate, imminent, and profoundly personal; each incident of suffering is uniquely experienced rather than understood. The sufferer, both individually and in community, must learn to talk *not about* God but *to* God through both the particularity and ubiquitousness of suffering in order to glean meaning from the experience (Gutierez, 1987). Internal conflict is significant to faith; personal suffering holds value because it has the potential to transform the individual. Liberation is the operative word in the religionist view of suffering—not only from cultural, gender, racial, and social oppression, but also from personal fears and desires that enslave an individual. Liberation from suffering occurs through individual actors committed to social metanoia; individual epiphanies engender social change. What is important to note here is the inherent paradox of suffering because of free will. That is, suffering's value is not within the event of suffering per se; rather, individual choice determines the reaction to the experience of suffering and the struggle to alleviate it.

According to the religionist view, research into the experience of suffering belongs in the realm of practice rather than theory (Soelle, 1975). Research on suffering must always be interventionist because of its social and political causes (Schussler-Fiorenza, 1989). For the researcher, there is no standing "outside the data" of suffering; any witness to suffering demands an ethical stance. The researcher must work in solidarity with the sufferer to disclose and change the situations that cause suffering (Frank, 2001).

In regard to a religious view of suffering in old age, some literature suggests that a vital religious life complements the physical limitations of old age (Bianchi, 1982). Bodily decline may foster a spiritual quest; meaning in life may be garnered through religious meaning (Krause, 2003). For several respondents introduced later, the stresses of old age, such as grief, illness, loneliness or fear precluded, rather than fostered, religious faith, especially because religion was not important to them earlier in life. According to respondents, developing habits of religious practice in old age was difficult or unlikely if these habits had been ignored or rejected in youth and middle-age.

Currently there are several academic journals devoted to "religious" research. Some of this research explores religion and spirituality in old age, such as how gender and race influence religious belief, and how religious practice affects health, well-being, or the ability to cope with adversity or "reframe" the outcome of a negative experience (Eisenhandler, 2003; Krause, 2003; McFadden, 2003). Some studies "pre-set" the definitions of concepts being researched; researchers investigate these concepts with closed-ended questions, and responses are quantitatively measured. For example, respondents define their "perceived closeness to God," "belief in an afterlife," and "attitudes toward death or dying" by choosing one of several answers provided for them (Fetzer Institute Publication, 1999). The value of this research is its generalizability; the limitation of such research is its decontextualization (Mischler, 1985). There is little or no chance for the individual to elaborate her responses or to set them in the frame of daily life, memories or expectations. Although religious scholars (among others) have called for research on suffering that welcomes a religious or spiritual context, it has been notably absent (Sullivan, 1996).

A Response to the Above Views

The views of suffering named previously reveal the enormous breadth and depth of knowledge on human suffering. Research on suffering traverses the many domains of being human, such as (to name a few) mental and physical health, relationships to self and society, and religious meaning.

The legacy of literary theory, narrative theory, cultural anthropology, social suffering, patient and end-of-life studies offers a wealth of information on suffering in the form of cross-cultural case studies, narratives, biographies, and autobiographies. Those who shared experiences of ethnic genocide (such as the Jewish and Ukrainian Holocaust, among many others) bequeathed a wisdom literature on the many dimensions of suffering (Frankl, 1959; Rudnytzsky, 1993; Wiesel, 1961, 1990, to name just a few). One of the richest legators of research into the experience of suffering is found in nursing literature. Although this material primarily addresses suffering within patienthood, nursing research on suffering acknowledges the multidimensionality of the suffering experience as well as the complexity of the *sufferer* (see Duffy, 1992; Heitman, 1992; Kahn & Steeves, 1986, to name just a few).

I acknowledge the inheritance of these theories and also critique them. Several excellent studies have explored the experiential problems of old age, such as decline, fear, illness, loneliness, and grief, and through these experiences, suffering (Kaufman, 1980; Myerhoff, 1979). The infusion of the experience of suffering into daily chores or thoughts, and as narrated by the sufferer in old age, has rarely been addressed as a central focus of study. Research has neglected the intimacy and banality of elders' suffering, and the way in which suffering corrodes or strengthens worldviews, values, and spiritual beliefs. If a theory of suffering is notably absent from research on suffering (Kleinman, Das, & Locke, 1997), perhaps it is because a general theory of suffering cannot hold the depth and breadth of personal suffering. Individual narratives (among other formats such as art, literature, and patient cases) disclose the elusive and ineffable qualities of suffering. Elders eloquently report the significance of subjective meaning in research on suffering through their narratives.

The disciplines of aging studies, narrative studies, and an examination of elders' religious beliefs and spirituality come together as interwoven categories in the study of elders' experiences of suffering. These three rubrics offer a framework in which to loosely place elders' narratives, and are discussed in the following sections.

ISSUES OF AGING STUDIES

One brings a self already fashioned, yet continuing to develop, to the experience of suffering in old age. An individual's question during or after suffering, "Who am I now?" remains based on, "Who was I?" and anticipates, "Who will I become?" (Frank, 1992). Suffering may cause a crisis of self-knowledge and a rupture in identity and worldview. Taken-for-granted meanings about the self, life, and the world are challenged. An awareness of the reflexivity between the past and the present, between subjective experience and the world *out there,* and between *pre-suffering* and *post-suffering* identities is significant in describing the *before and after* and *me and not me* quality of suffering. Because suffering is not a discrete experience with one cause, a linear course and a consistent expression, memories of past suffering influence the present; present suffering may color the past, and an anticipated suffering may shadow both present and past.

Suffering in age challenges the content and integrity of a past, present, and future self. Elders may disclose what qualities, values, and possessions were meaningful in the past, such as family, income, faith, and work, and if the importance of these treasures as well as the treasures themselves obtain over time. Suffering may be the loss of these cherished intangibles and the belief that they cannot be regained (Graneheim, Lindah, & Kihlgren, 1997). The unlikelihood of realizing lifelong dreams during a limited future looms large as the elder takes stock of life. Certainly, older persons may discover an existential meaning to life that is separate from worldly success. Suffering may prompt a personal philosophy that confirms life's sorrows without negating meaning in life. Or, elders may conclude from the same set of circumstances that there is little or no meaning to suffering or to life. In any case, personal meaning systems, or those lenses through which one interprets the world and one's experience, are usually altered with suffering.

Individuals may interpret suffering as alien in light of how they viewed themselves before suffering began. Or, they may consider it a *normal* part of life. Suffering, however defined, usually heralds a need to both re-evaluate the self and find a way to re-integrate the self due to the disruption of suffering. Re-evaluation and re-integration are accomplished by maintaining the roles that give meaning to identity, by assuming a new identity that is inchoate and breathing life into it, and by telling a story about the suffering self in the forum of the interview.

ISSUES OF NARRATIVE

As noted, I explore the personal meaning of suffering to elders; the central activity of personal meaning is interpretation. The fact that the elder has a story to tell is significant; it means that the suffering experience has been processed in some measure. Although a story cannot capture the experience itself, it can recover its context and quality. Through their narratives of suffering individuals embed themselves in a personal and social history, reveal a unique personality, and assign themselves characteristics, roles, and an identity that is usually threaded by a continuing theme (Kaufman, 1980). The individual is also embodied; the body's understanding of suffering as well as bodily memories of well-being, suffering, and resistance to suffering, are relayed in the narrative (Csordas, 1994; Svenaeus, 2000). Despite suffering's "strangeness" to the life lived, the suffering story generally reflects the perceived continuity of the self despite suffering (Kaufman, 1986). The self as the main character in each narrative is "called by name" (Schwartz, 1992, p. 93). That is, if meaning is made of the suffering experience, it is made by the entire and unique self.

The reader will hear two voices here: the respondents', as they narrate their life stories and stories of suffering, and mine, as I interpret their stories. The interdependence of voices is significant to this work. The way that elders relate their accounts of suffering would be different if elders spoke in another setting, such as reminiscing with friends or talking to family members. The relationship between the elder and the interviewer is a unique meeting between intimate strangers. The duration of the interchange is relatively short, but the emotions and self-insight (for both elder and interviewer) that emerge can be deep and long lasting. Because each collaborates (with the other) to make meaning, both are affected by the process (Holstein & Gubrium, 1997).

In the next sections, I examine the roles of narrator and listener. I also explore the use of metaphor and the meaning of paradox in elders' stories of suffering.

The Narrator

The narrator is creator, employer (in the sense of using a tool), evaluator and interpreter of her own story of suffering. She creates the story by deciding what details to include or keep out. She employs the form at hand—the interview—and pours her story into it. The act of telling the story is both an evaluative and interpretive process. The elder both evaluates and interprets the experience of suffering as she slants the story according to her central theme.

The story of suffering does not stand alone; the life story is a frame for the experience of suffering. In a sense, the life story is the preamble to the story of suffering because it introduces significant characters and treasured personal attributes, loved ones, or possessions that are open to attack or loss, and thus to suffering. Similarly, a central theme of the life story usually appears in the suffering story and connects the disruptive experience of suffering to the life lived. For example, in Chapter 8, Metaphors of Suffering, I introduce a man who described his life as "charmed." He did not reject this theme in the midst of suffering, but enriched its meaning by placing his suffering alongside the theme. In his narrative, the short-term oddity of suffering highlighted his theme of a "charmed life."

Narrators who relayed more than one story of suffering often ranked their sufferings. For example, several women in the study said that they had suffered at the hands of abusive husbands. After their marriages ended, however, they learned that "real" suffering was something different from spousal abuse. This realization came through the comparison of several events named suffering and reevaluated with time, distance, and life experience. When I asked the interview question: "Would you describe an event, incident or time period in your life when you were suffering" some respondents added to their response: "I wouldn't have given you the same answer five years ago," or, "My answer might be different five years from now, if I live." The *changing* nature of suffering had to do with personal perception, and the sense that the meaning of an experience is fluid and based on the context of the experience, such as when in life it occurred, an individual's available resources in fighting or finding value in it, and how, retrospectively, one fit the suffering experience into one's life as a whole (Migliore, 2001).

The Listener

As I listened to elders define, interpret, and theorize about suffering, I realized that they were continuing to process their story and discover a meaning they might impute to the experience. For this reason, stories of suffering are compelling, meandering, contradictory, and paradoxical; they are an ongoing act of discursive construction and self-creation. And just as the narrator filled her account of suffering with her meaning; I fill my interpretation of her account with my meaning (Pirandello, 1990). I report elders' narratives not as transcripts, but framed in as broad a context as possible. Recognizing the fluid nature of the "truth" of these accounts and my interpretation of them is an assessment of the research interaction as well as interactions of all kinds.

Both narrator and listener actively join in this creative act. To elicit elders' narratives of suffering may be an hermeneutical and compassionate encounter with the suffering other (Frank, 1992). Perhaps the researcher's moral imperative is to initiate this encounter. If there is a psychological and spiritual imperative for elders to tell a story about personal suffering, then there is a moral imperative for someone to be an audience to such experiences (Schweizer, 1995). The lack of such a listener—and despairing awareness of that lack—is an important element in suffering at any age (Bregman, 1999). In age, suffering may be compounded by the belief that one's story is no longer interesting or that there are few or no persons left to understand the history of the story.

Metaphor in Respondent's Narratives

Metaphors for suffering emerged within elders' narratives in at least three ways, such as: 1) a metaphor of suffering crystallized an overarching theme in the life story, 2) I asked the respondent to imagine a picture or photograph of suffering, and 3) the metaphor was discovered through later analysis of data.

The actual *sounds* of suffering, such as groans, sobs, or silence, are part of a universal language (Bakan, 1968) because there are no cultures without suffering (Kleinmann, Brodwin, Good, & Good, 1992; Parkin, 1985). Yet the meaning of such an intimate yet social experience as suffering relies on shared cultural and historical contexts, definitions, and the perceived value (or lack of value) of the experience (Graneheim et al., 1997). Metaphor is a symbol that represents, stands in for, or suggests something else (Soskice, 1993). But the symbol may be *less* or *more* than words. Gestures, sighs, and facial expressions speak of suffering just as the story of suffering may be the metaphor for the experience. Metaphor provides a way of describing suffering in its private, social, banal, and extreme aspects. It helps elders formulate, dramatize, and elaborate an experience of suffering (Browning, 1966) and to leap beyond the essential privacy of the experience (Fernandez, 1974). If narrative recovers the quality of suffering and struggles against placing suffering in categories, metaphor enriches the quality and paints the struggle with texture and perspective. For example, one respondent defined suffering as "like having an MRI or being in prison." The richness of this metaphor emerged when she explained that she could not complete an MRI test because "they put me in that tunnel and strapped me down." She also related that she believes her brother is suffering because he is "stuck up in a prison." Claustrophobia shaped her answers; for this elder, confinement of any sort, and for anyone, is a metaphor for suffering. I note that in employing a metaphor the sufferer is saying—my experience is not just a metaphor; it is almost indescribable, so I must describe it metaphorically.

Paradox in Elder's Narratives

Paradox abounds in elders' accounts of suffering because the experience of suffering is often confusing, illogical, and uncertain. For example, at the same time that suffering is experienced as all-encompassing, the sufferer may feel diminished by the changes to body, mind, roles, and identity that accompany suffering (Good, 1992). An elder may rationally explain an experience of suffering in order to make sense of the event as well as to contain the emotions that attend the experience. Yet the experience of suffering may be considered so precisely because an individual has little control over the intensity, duration or outcome of the experience. Suffering may open the floodgate to raw and conflicting emotions.

Also paradoxically, suffering may appear unexpected and random, yet one may feel personally targeted. The simple yet profound response to suffering: "Why?" judged by Simone Weil (1951, 1973) as the question all humans ask with innocence, is more than a query—it is a testimony both for the universality and against the naturalness of suffering. In other words, suffering is both inevitable and exotic (Farley, 1992).

Informants' attempts to come to terms with suffering also might be perceived as paradoxical. They experienced suffering as painful and instructional, valuable yet wasteful, and as requiring both a battle and surrender. I note that "surrender" here is not resignation to an external *attack* of suffering. Surrender is an elder's active choice to "wait it out" or "give it up" (give up control of the situation) until he or the circumstances of suffering change.

ISSUES OF RELIGION
AND PERSONAL SPIRITUALITY

There are a multitude of definitions for religion as well as spirituality. The definition of religion that I offer here is: "An impulse to create order and meaning in our world so as to connect with the ultimate order and meaning—the sacred" (Ring, Nash, MacDonald, Glennon, & Glancy, 1997, p. 4). I define spirituality as: a sense of the sacred (Remen, 1999). I use these broad definitions because: they show the connection between religion and spirituality; 2) they show that religion does not necessarily include God-talk (indeed, some elders did not believe in God yet sought to find "order and meaning" in their world); and 3) they illustrate that the impulse to find meaning in one's life and one's world connects sacred and profane enterprises.

Religions may offer guidelines for the meaning of suffering; they may provide one vehicle for discussion of the experience. One of religion's *reasons for being* is the question: Why do sentient beings suffer? Although some religions admit an impenetrable mystery about suffering, most Western religions suggest reasons for suffering that have a range of causality and purpose, such as: suffering results from self-centeredness and suffering is essential to the development of an individual (Bowker, 1970; Hick, 1990). Weber offered another *religious* reason for suffering: Failure to carry one's weight, laziness, and a lack of ambition offend the work ethic morality that is built into American capitalism. *Religious* reasons for suffering derive from Western philosophical thought that proposes autonomy as an individual's central birthright (Rawlinson, 1986).

Personal spirituality is necessarily distinguished from religion and religious adherence in this book. Yet, personal spirituality as a sense of the sacred, the transcendent, the ultimate or God may emerge through traditional religious practice (Remen, 1999). Individuals garner an idiosyncratic spirituality from several sources. Along with adherence to the tenets of a particular religious tradition, at least four other sources of elders' personal spirituality are: 1) popularized versions of traditional religious beliefs that are cultural or ethnic customs; 2) a syncretism of the beliefs of multiple traditions; 3) long held religious beliefs that have been altered, diminished or enhanced by personal experience; and 4) a belief in an other-worldly realm populated by beings that influence and interact with individuals in the earthly realm. I note that some respondents viewed the beliefs, practices, and teachings of their religious denomination as a vehicle of suffering. That is, elders associated particular negative events with their religious tradition, such as: disappointment with a religious authority figure, a sudden or gradual waning of faith, for whatever reason, in the doctrine that one learned and believed earlier in life, and a heartfelt loss of that faith.

Respondents in this study, when asked, named themselves "Jewish, Christian," or as having "no religion." Their stories showed that a syncretism of cultural and religious myths merged into a spirituality of suffering—or a core belief about the non-material value of suffering. This spirituality of suffering was often constructed from the guidelines of religious tenets, life experience, perceived purpose of negative events, and the current cultural and social ethos on how to respond to them. A spirituality of suffering consisted of what is personally believed about suffering and why, and what recompense for suffering is hoped for in this life and the next.

In response to experiences that urge questions about meaning in life, such as life passages, or in this case, suffering, human beings reach toward aids that imbue the event with sacred value (Ring et al., 1997). Humans often participate in rituals to celebrate joyous events, such as marriage or birth, or help "remake the world" during or after a crisis, death, or suffering (Bianchi, 1982; Scarry, 1985). For many respondents finding a spirituality of suffering was important for viewing individual life in a dramatic aspect, and as both diminutive and cosmic. That is, experiencing the self, despite its suffering and its littleness, as a significant and unmatched piece in the universe.

METHODS

Conceptual Framework

The dictionary definition of suffering is to bear, to undergo, to experience or to pass through (Webster, 1972). For me, however, to define or delimit suffering before asking respondents to do so would be to defeat the goal of research. "Suffering" is a word that has personal and communal connotations and elicits sights, sounds, scents, and textures that are culturally and religiously shared, as well as images that are unique and individual. Throughout the original research, I looked to the respondents to provide a definition of what suffering is and whether they have, indeed, suffered.

As will be seen in later chapters, the word *suffering* is used by respondents to describe forms of distress, such as physical pain or illness, or experiences of a negative and extreme type. It is also used to describe subtler forms of torment, such as worry, guilt, shame, or regret. In order to acknowledge the uniqueness of individuals' experience as well as their definitions of suffering, the conceptual framework of the original research was based on a model of the person derived from work in cultural anthropology and gerontology (Rubinstein, 1989, 1992). This model sees the older person as the active constructor, interpreter, and creator of meaning in her own world. This model focuses on the personal meaning systems of older people as part of the larger system of cultural and social meaning. To this I add another orientation of the person—as one who holds a belief in the integrated and unique existence of the self. Both models are especially relevant to the *inwardness* or subjective experience of the person, which in this case is how elderly men and women view themselves and their world in light of suffering.

My approach to this study is culturally phenomenological. That is, I am attempting to describe the experience as well as the meaning of suffering to my respondents (Csordas, 1994). A personal meaning of suffering is created through the web of beliefs, languages, practices, traditions and values that make up meaning systems in a particular culture. Personal meanings are embedded in meaning systems, as well as in the uniqueness of the individual and the suffering experience. The intention in this approach is to explore the phenomena (suffering) as related by the individual and framed by her place in time (Morse & Field, 1995). I am eliciting the "emic" or insider's point of view of suffering (Perakyla, 1997).

Format

I engaged elders' meaning systems through a carefully crafted, open-ended interview schedule (see Appendix, p. 191). I began the interview with a request to hear the "life story." One of the most important functions of the life story question in research is that it provides, for both interviewer and respondents, a framework for retrieving the topical subject, and an interpretive context in which to better situate the questions that follow (Spradley, 1979; Strauss & Corbin, 1990). It is a pool from which to prod respondents' memories and associations, and to draw prompts. After requesting the life story, I asked to "hear about an event, incident, or time in your life when you felt that you were suffering." More detailed questions concern 1) other experiences of suffering; 2) memories of suffering; 3) social suffering; 4) suffering in relation to religion or spirituality; and 5) suffering in relation to old age and dying.

The interview was conversational in nature and interactive. I asked the initial question and obtained a response. I then reframed the response as an additional line of questioning. I probed answers to most questions with tailor-made, follow up questions.

Open-ended interviewing permitted me to construct a mobile framework from which unique data emerged. This methodology of one-on-one, conversational interviewing acknowledges that this type of research occurs in an atmosphere that is both personal and professional and social and private, and contests that reality is not *out there* but is constructed within the interactive environment of the interview (Holstein & Gubrium, 1997).

Procedure

I collected the data for the study from respondents living in Philadelphia and its suburbs in 1999. Private interviews were conducted in the respondents' homes for intimacy and comfort and lasted from 1 to 3 hours in a single sitting. Interviews were tape-recorded with the permission of the respondent. I also took notes during interviews and made notes afterward. Later I transcribed the entire interview. During transcription, I had another chance to immerse myself in the voice and words of the respondents, which added another layer of understanding about their experiences and interpretation to my analysis.

Data Analysis

I used narrative analysis, a specialized form of qualitative analysis, as the method of analyzing data (Mischler, 1986; Polkinghorne, 1988; Reissman, 1993; Sarbin, 1986), and as it follows Bruner's (1990) meaning that protagonists interpret lived experiences, and Polkinghorne's (1988) assertion that in narrative, the past is reconstructed in light of the narrator's present worldview, which in turn is shaped by past experiences (such as suffering).

Narrative analysis was appropriate to the research because it concerns human agency and imagination, and is suited to studies of subjectivity and the self. This method recognizes that "culture speaks itself through a particular actor with a particular story." The narrator's current complexity and context cannot be separated from the story she tells (Gergen & Gergen, 1993; Reissman, 1997). Narrative analysis acknowledges that definitions, descriptions, and interpretations of suffering are personally, culturally, historically, and socially contingent. A lived experience, such as suffering, is precisely such because an individual interpreted a negative event in a particular way at a singular point in place and time (Polkinghorne, 1988; Rosenwald & Ochberg, 1992).

Although internal questions of the research were answered by particular interview queries, analysis focused on the entire transcript in order to gain an understanding of the meaning of suffering to respondents. I looked for themes and patterns inter- and intra-individually; the uniqueness of attributions, definitions, and theories about suffering was apparent early on in analysis.

The Elders

I actively recruited 40 persons, aged 70 and above, and stratified by gender and race, through past rosters of research respondents, as well as through advertising in church, synagogue, and senior center bulletins. I also asked, through flyers, letters or in person, current respondents in other, ongoing projects if they knew of neighbors, friends, and fellow church or synagogue-goers who might be interested in research on suffering. One criterion for eligibility was that a potential informant answered positively the question: "Are you now suffering or have you ever suffered?" One man, who replied by phone to my letter asking him to participate in the study, said, "I'd like to be part of this [project], but I never did that sort of thing [suffer]." My goal in recruiting respondents was diversity of experience (in regard to gender, ethnicity, education, and income, and as much as is possible with 40 individuals) in relation to suffering. No potential informant asked me to define suffering. I explore why this was the case in the conclusion of the book.

In selecting respondents I was sensitive to variation in religious affiliation (all respondents were either Jewish, Christian, or had "no religion), and "good" or "poor" health as subjectively defined (some elders were rejected due to my reluctance to weight the sample with a preponderance of *suffering* due to illness or depression). This variation regarding the above domains was easily accessed at a screening contact.

Ten each African-American men and women and European-American men and women ($N = 40$), 70 years of age and older, were interviewed.

The average age of African-American men was 82 (range 73–90). The average years of education were 12. When asked, "What religion are you?" 5 men in this group answered Baptist, 3 Episcopalian, 1 Presbyterian, and 1 Moravian. When asked, "How would you describe your income status?" 5 answered working class, 2 were middle income, 2 were upper income, and 1 replied, "poor."

The average age of African-American women was 78 (range 73–80). The average years of education were 10. When asked, "What religion are you?" 4 women in this group answered Baptist; 2 Pentecostal; 3 Catholic, and 1 Episcopalian. When asked, "How would you describe your income status?" 4 women answered middle income, 3 were working class, and 3 women said "poor."

The average age of European-American men was 76 (range 70–86). The average years of education were 12. When asked, "What religion are you?" 4 men in this group answered Jewish, 2 Catholic, 2 Protestant, 1 Lutheran, and one man said, "none." When asked, "How would you describe your income status?" 5 men answered working class, 2 said middle income, 2 were poor, and 1 man answered "upper income."

The average age of European-American women was 78 (range 70–91). The average years of education were 12. When asked, "What religion are you?" 2 women in this group answered Jewish, 2 Catholic 2, Lutheran, 2 said "no religion," 1 Baptist, and 1 woman was Mennonite. When asked, "How would you describe your income status?" 4 women answered upper income, 1 was middle income, 2 were working class, and 2 replied, "poor."

Their Shared History

Historical events, such as the First World War, the Depression, and World War II, influenced individual and cohort development for elders who grew up during this period. The catastrophes of the larger public world seeped into the smaller private worlds of respondents to engender a mindset and a morality peculiar to this generation. For example, financial security, elusive during the Depression, became a primary goal for youngsters and adolescents who witnessed and endured family hardship. These elders retrospectively believed that more money would have positively altered their life course. A sense of shared adversity evoked no self-pity; respondents reiterated that "everybody had it hard" during this time. The economic, political, and social circumstances of the period between the First and Second World Wars formed the backdrop for respondents' worldview, such as the prevalence of "Depression mentality" and a strong patriotism (Murphy, 1987). The consequences of large-world events that occurred during elders' developmental stage bind this cohort to the era in which they grew and developed, as it does for cohorts in any era. This binding and bonding is witnessed through a group's identity with a certain kind of music, popular artifacts, sports heroes, movies stars, and shared suffering.

Issues of Class, Gender, and Race

Class is consequential in understanding how an individual defines and interprets a lived experience such as suffering. All persons I interviewed lived in Philadelphia proper and its suburbs and most hailed from the working class. The revival of the American Dream after World War II had a profound effect on this cohort's desire to break through the invisible but impenetrable barriers among classes in American society. The notion of *bettering yourself* is significant to their identity, although men and women achieved this betterment differently. It was more likely for European-American men to move upward both economically and socially through education, and European-American women to do so through marriage. Coming home from the Second World War, men (both African-American and European-American) were offered a college education through the GI Bill. This opportunity was not available to women in this group (unless they had served the war effort); their chance for upward mobility occurred by marrying a man with higher education. The concept of class is placed within at least two categories: financial and social status. If it was difficult or impossible for female respondents to succeed financially, they could self-improve through "learning," "being refined," or cultivating "educated" friends (Black & Rubinstein, 2000). I also note that although elders did not move easily from their class of origin, movement did occur for some members of this cohort through the opportunities that came with education, hard work, and a desire to advance. The immense social barriers placed in front of African-American men and women usually, but not always, precluded *upward mobility,* despite motivation to succeed.

Gender intersected with historical circumstances to form gender-based attitudes and responses in this generation of elderly men and women (Stewart, 1994). Gender roles were put in place after the Industrial Revolution, and produced a morality of family and work values within succeeding generations (Harrison, 1985). For this cohort, rules on how men and women should behave in relation to each other and to rearing children were born from the cultural, economic, and social inheritance of the distant past, the personal *want* of their early years, and the ensuing plenty of the post-World War II boom. Respondents show that just as an experience of suffering is both embodied and inspirited, it is also *gendered* (Black, 2002). Although Chapter 3 is devoted to exploring the gendered difference of suffering, cases used throughout the book illustrate this distinction.

Race, although a social construction, is a component of identity like class and gender that produces certain expectations about life, ensures particular outcomes, and lies at the core of experiences of suffering. For this cohort, the sometimes explicit, sometimes implicit rules about how far an African-American man could climb financially or socially, or what kind of jobs were available to African-American women, produced a normalization of attitudes and behaviors that limited most African-American respondents' ability to move upward (Mussat, 2000). Although African-American men acknowledged that covert or overt rules regarding advancement were firmly in place during youth and adulthood, they believed that they *worked around* these rules to achieve their goals (Allen, 1999). African-American women also *worked around* the tri-dimensional reality of classism, racism, and sexism, and the suffering they produced, to accomplish their dreams (Davis, 1981; Grant, 1989). For all respondents, earlier expectations about life had a role in current perceptions of suffering. Many African-American women interviewed did not expect to be homeowners. Owning a home in old age sometimes mitigated an experience of suffering. For example, a 77-year-old African-American woman defined events of suffering as the murder of one son and the incarceration of another. These experiences of suffering were mitigated by the fact that her deceased son helped her buy the home in which she now lives and her other son will return to when he leaves prison. Although always a symbol of achievement, the home became a symbolic, spiritual place in which one son remains *alive* to her and the other will find freedom.

The Four Groups

For the elderly men, both African-American and European-American whom I interviewed, coming of age during World War II and serving in some branch of the military influenced them in a positive way. Memories of techniques that were learned in the service, such as organizational skills and attention to detail, and characteristics that were forged there, such as self-discipline and leadership, superseded recalling the horrors of war. This modern view of "man" as hero and master of his fate and detached from political and social forces that shape him, is especially appropriate to this cohort (Bellah, Madsen, Sullivan, Swidler, & Tipton, 1985). Personal values that were held dear by this group of men—providing for family, a commitment to work for the benefit of the company and the common good rather than purely for personal gain (Kleinman, 1992), and a conviction that by winning the Second World War their sons would not have to fight in another way—were born by internalizing cultural values and integrating them into an individual and family history.

In general, men spoke proudly about finding and keeping a job during the Depression and their work success throughout life. Men's work, whether professional, skilled, semi-skilled, or unskilled labor, remained significant in their life stories. It is little surprise that a negative change in their working lives, such as losing a job, or for some, retiring—caused suffering. The threat to personal identity caused by a change to men's working roles reveals: 1) how large a part work plays in men's self-view; 2) inability to work, for whatever reason, wounds the social identity of being defined by *what you do;* and 3) The *objective* measure of personal success—financial security and material goods—is strongly internalized; loss of earning ability struck the core of men's identities and engendered suffering (Mowsesian, 1986).

Men discussed their time of active duty in the war as a "time that *might* be called suffering" (Allen, 1999; Spalding, 1999). I note that men were reluctant to call the misery of war *suffering.* Three reasons are offered: 1) the war was part of the distant past and its horrors were blurred by time; 2) the war and its experiences are secret and hallowed in the sense that they can be understood only by those who shared them; or 3) the suffering of war, similar to suffering endured during the Depression, was mitigated because so many others endured it.

For women interviewed, gender shaped expectations about life throughout the life course. Women's choices of jobs or mates and whether they would work after marriage and at what kind of jobs were set in a cultural stone determined by gender and race as well as class status. Despite cultural and social limitations on appropriate and available work for women, however, the jobs women took had an integral role in shaping their identities. During interviews, women's discussion about their work, whether as factory seamstress, laundress, teacher, or waitress, and their perceptions of themselves as "good workers" speaks to the confidence and esteem women of this cohort gained from *outside* work (Mutran, 1987).

Although the difficulties of the Depression were paramount in many women's life stories and in memories of early years, their awareness that "everybody was going through it" diffused memories of suffering during this period. Female respondents suffered through the private conditions of their lives and rarely talked about the *larger* world under such a broad heading. A woman's self-image was fostered, in part, by her social place in the larger world. Unlike men in this cohort, women seldom spoke as having a part in creating historical events. More often she assumed the smaller identities garnered from acceptable roles in society, such as wife, mother, and worker (usually within the caring or service professions). Suffering occurred because of the negative relationships encountered in her smaller world. In other words, the experience and expression of suffering, although uniquely defined by female respondents, was often miniaturized and always expressed relationally.

The African-American men I interviewed were acutely aware of a communal suffering that they included in their personal definitions of suffering. The deprivation of the Depression, experiences of war, difficulties in finding or keeping a job were compounded by their race. African-American men stated that even if they had not personally suffered, they knew the concept of suffering by virtue of being African-American (Allen, 1999). In contrast to European-American men and women, suffering was not miniaturized for African-American men. Rather, it assumed a greater quantity and quality in personal life because communal suffering was added to individual experiences, and because African-American men empathized with the harsh reality that people continue to *suffer* simply because they are black.

The African-American women I interviewed were the least prosperous of the four groups interviewed in terms of income, jobs, status, and mobility. In contrast to African-American men, but similar to European-American women, they talked about suffering within the framework of their personal lives. Many African-American women spoke to a trickle down oppression due to poverty (Black & Rubinstein, 2000). This oppression translated into various types of relational suffering, such as spousal abuse, drug and alcohol addiction by children and grandchildren, and despair over the chances for subsequent generations to succeed.

For some African-American women, suffering due to ill health was related to jobs they held when younger, i.e., working in the only jobs available to black women at this time, such as domestic or laundress. Or, suffering resulted directly from impoverished living conditions. For example, one respondent was forced to walk up and down several flights of stairs every day because of consistently broken elevators in her Section 8 apartment building. This daily trek exacerbated her heart condition.

It must be noted that suffering of this sort is rooted in economic, political, and social conditions that *can be* changed. Personal experiences of suffering are embedded in a society's residual rules and hidden transcripts (Cannon, 1995; Mussat, 2000). In this, "every personal sorrow has a social cause"

(Soelle, 1975), and it is this kind of suffering that is considered "outrageous" (Townes, 1997).

All respondents, African-American and European-American, and men and women, note that even within a limited framework of options structured by class, gender or race inequality in the larger public world, choices are made on the bases of alternatives as personally experienced in their smaller private world (Rubinstein, Kilbride, & Nagy, 1992). In this, an intimate notion of suffering is carved out within the setting that the larger world allows. This miniaturization of suffering shows that respondents generally believed that *they* had created their unique story of suffering through the choices they made throughout their lives.

Certainly, individual lives mesh with a common cohort history in any era. It is for another group of researchers to describe how the events and tragedies that changed and shaped the world at the beginning of the 21st century will inform *our* memories in old age. For present day elders, past events are interpreted as charting a life course. The sense of being molded by the past comes from both the vantage of older age and the uniqueness of this group's moment in history. Although the factors of age, class, gender and race give rise to discrete experiences of *similar* catastrophic events (Charmaz, 1999; Gubrium, 1993; Kaufman, 1980; Lorde, 1980), respondents in this study thought that the shared historical experiences of their cohort group are of a momentousness enough to define individual experiences of suffering as well as those of a generation.

EXPLANATION OF FURTHER CHAPTERS

Chapter 2 introduces cases to illustrate suffering as a form of cultural communication that is spoken through the body, through the identity that is formed through elders' varied social roles, both past and present, and through the language of narrative. Each case study will correspond to, but not be limited to, one of the "voices" of suffering mentioned above, i.e., the body, identity, and narrative.

Chapter 3 explores how gender shapes respondents' experiences of suffering, the way suffering is expressed, and discussion about it in the process of the interview. Individual characteristics influence differences in men's and women's experiences and expressions of suffering. A society's determination of how women should react to pain or anguish, or under what kind of torment men are permitted to succumb, also informs this distinction. Three cases presented in this chapter address these questions: How differently do men and women experience and express suffering? And, Do gender-based expressions of suffering actually create the experience of suffering?

Chapter 4 acknowledges that embodied pain is a significant component in the experience of suffering in later life. The three elders used as cases in this chapter describe suffering as the physical agony they endure or that they witness in others. Their narratives show, however, that despite a generalized view that suffering equals physical pain, the experience of suffering is far more complex. The fact that physical pain interrupts elders' cherished identities as husbands, mothers or workers, thread their stories of suffering.

Chapter 5 explores social suffering. Suffering is both public and private. All private, individual experiences of suffering occur in a public milieu. The three cases used in this chapter investigate how key social constructions of human identity—age, gender, race, and class status—inform the experience of suffering in American society.

Chapter 6 uses cases to examine the uniqueness with which each informant coped with suffering. This coping ability does not spring fully-formed in older age, but like the elder herself, is developed and refined through the many experiences—both joyful and sorrowful—of a lifetime. Elders' ability to cope with their suffering often depends on how they interpret its value either through a practical or spiritual lens.

Chapter 7 discusses, again through three cases, the morality imputed to the experience of suffering. In part, this morality is revealed through the causes respondents attribute to their suffering. This chapter also examines how respondents determine the value of suffering through the story they tell about it. This determination of value is often based on cultural and religious guidelines concerning the meaning of suffering and its *worth* at a particular point in place and time.

Chapter 8 examines three often-used metaphors for suffering. They are: suffering as a threat or attack, suffering as injustice, and suffering as loss. Although these metaphors of suffering are not exhaustive, they are meant to illustrate elders' use of metaphor to stand in for what may not be easily interpreted—a personal experience of suffering. The three cases used in this chapter show both the distinctions and the commonalities of the metaphors that elders use in their stories of suffering.

Chapter 9 talks about the activity of suffering. Through cases, readers will note that one method of coping with suffering is to be active, i.e., to engage in the busywork of grief, to create new roles and identities in the face of impending death, and to "do something" even when the body no longer permits one to be physically active. These activities give compensatory meaning to an elder's life. This chapter suggests that another important activity of suffering is to tell an engaged listener a story about it.

Chapter 10 discusses the major findings of the research on which this book is based. It focuses on the significance of narrative in portraying and recording elders' experiences and expressions of suffering. It also explores the relationship between old age and suffering, and penetrates how suffering affects development and self-concept in later life.

I note here why I placed chapters in their particular order. Suffering must be communicated in some way in order for us to be aware of another's suffering, thus the subject of Chapter 2. Yet suffering is not always communicated through words, but also through utterances, gestures or the anguish that suffering bodies and faces reflect. Whether this communication is verbal or non-verbal, it is filtered through the sufferer's gender, which is the subject of Chapter 3. This leads to the subject of Chapter 4, suffering of the body, which is the first medium through which we encounter the suffering self. The subject of Chapter 5, Social Suffering, shows that personal suffering is often labeled as such through the internalization of cultural, religious, and societal beliefs about the appropriate language of suffering. The cases within Chapters 2 through 5 are, in some ways, inter-changeable, because all are concerned with how suffering is and ought to be communicated.

Chapters 6 through 10 all discuss, in different ways, how elders cope with suffering. Chapter 6 shows that the way in which elders cope resonates to their perceived reasons for suffering. Chapter 7, The Morality of Suffering, reveals the *value* that elders impute to suffering by interpreting its meaning and purpose in their own lives. Chapter 8 views metaphors as a means for elders to translate suffering into a manageable discussion about it, and for researchers to interpret the subjectivity of respondents. Chapter 9, the activity of suffering, took shape as elders revealed the importance of their own brand of *busyness* both in coping with suffering and in staving off suffering. Chapters 6 through 9, then, discuss elders' beliefs about a cultural and social *how to* of suffering. These chapters show what events or incidents offer appropriate reasons to suffer, a fitting way to handle suffering, suitable words to describe suffering, and what activities may help alleviate suffering.

In this book, chapter headings are a researcher's tool. They helped me organize the wealth of data I gathered, and offered a format for classification. I also note the difficulty I had in placing a case in one chapter and not another. This showed me that my material, like the people I interviewed, struggled against being confined under categories or chapter headings.

CHAPTER 2

Voices of Suffering

The definition of suffering is connected to the mores of a society and to a way of communicating within that society (Scheper-Hughes & Lock, 1991). Suffering therefore has a fluid definition; it is defined according to the meaning with which local culture imbues it (Kleinman, 1997) and according to how individuals internalize that meaning from the standpoint of their experience. Definitions of suffering determine its value as well as its lack of value in a particular culture (Graneheim et al., 1997). As a lived experience, suffering is laden with cultural connotations; it is constructed, represented and paraphrased by symbols that are shared throughout the culture (Martin, 1987). Suffering is recognized through related experiences such as pain or grief. Suffering may be named acceptable, unacceptable, a cultural exemplar, a subject for macabre humor, or an "outrage" in a given society (McGoldrick, 1996; Rosen & Weltman, 1996; Townes, 1997; Zborowski, 1969).

As a form of communication, suffering informs others about the suffering individual and about how various aspects and stages of life are perceived in a particular culture. Suffering offers a moral challenge to witnesses. An aged sufferer reveals that life is as much about sickness, loss or tragedy as it is about youth, health, and fulfillment. Suffering discloses the inevitable underside to joy and agency (Connolley, 1996). Suffering also informs others that an individual is not a passive recipient of fate; she singularly defines the suffering experience and formulates the expressions and interactions that attend suffering. An individual interprets suffering in the manner that family, community, culture, and religion deem acceptable, yet does so within the uniqueness of personhood (Zbrowski, 1969).

Facial expressions and bodies usually look different while suffering, and individuals make sounds, such as cries or groans that are part of the experience. A person's daily roles may feel in flux due to a diminishment of activity, and one may *hold oneself together* by maintaining a long-standing identity, or risk *coming apart* (Francis, 1990). Suffering is spoken uniquely by the voices of bodies, identities and roles, and if the elder is asked, through a story about suffering. Although the cultural voices of suffering come through bodies, identities, roles, and narratives, these languages are not neatly delineated. At one time of suffering the voice of the body may echo louder than one's pre-eminent role as a mother or a scientist. At another time, the voice of the story may be one's best-spoken language (Brodwin, 1992).

THE VOICE OF THE BODY

The body is the first means of self-revelation, the medium through which one experiences oneself and the world (Murphy, 1987). When the borders of the body break down through suffering, the body becomes marked through its lack of mobility, distorted configuration, obvious pain, or conspicuous silence. Even when the experience of suffering is kept private, the belief that a suffering body should be hidden is learned through the sufferer's local moral world (Goffman, 1961; Kleinman, Das, & Lock, 1997).

In *The Body Silent,* Robert Murphy (1987) reminds us that a healthy body is "the first assumption in all our enterprises." This first assumption tacitly communicates that good health is a taken-for-granted reality, an entitlement, and a moral imperative (Kleinman, 1988; Scheper-Hughes & Lock, 1987). The oft-used metaphors for the normative body, such as a well-run business, a great city, and an efficient assembly line (Martin, 1987) portray the "marketing orientation" of American culture (Fromm, 1947), and that good health is moral as well as natural. As a primary symbol of a sound society, the not-suffering body offers a representation of what is standard, whole, competent, productive, and good. The suffering body represents non-normativeness, disintegration, inefficiency and something *bad* (Scheper-Hughes & Lock, 1987).

Questions arise when the subject of study is suffering in age: If health and youth are considered culturally normative, is age, and particularly suffering in age, considered abnormal? How does the first assumption of the body as healthy and not suffering inform both narrators' and listeners' perceptions about the old and suffering body? A culture's meaning systems pervade all its members; suffering in age may seem deviant to both the aged and non-aged. In this, suffering disrupts not only "all [elders'] enterprises," but also underscores a cultural belief that elders may never again, in a significant way, engage in any useful or productive enterprise.

Ernest Becker (1972) defined the paradox between the unlimited imagination and the finite nature of the body as one cause of human suffering in Western society. Becker outlined a remedy for humans' fear of finitude: create a legacy that "outlives the self." If human creation is not accomplished in young or middle adulthood, the unfulfilled cultural imperative to create a lasting product may cause or add to suffering in age. The first case introduces an elder who perceives that his lack of accomplishment in youth paved the way for suffering in old age. He communicated his suffering by his demeanor and responses; through them he told me that the borders of his body and his mind have "broken down."

MR. MAY

Mr. May is a 76-year-old European-American man. He and his wife both married for the first time 20 years previously. The couple moved into the home Mrs. May shared with her parents until their deaths 12 years ago. Mrs. May is 10 years younger than her husband.

When I knocked on the Mays' door on the morning of the interview, Mrs. May answered. She told me that she was angry with her husband for two reasons. First, earlier that morning he sat on her glasses and almost broke them and second, he was not yet dressed. Several minutes later, Mr. May shuffled into the living room. He wore a bathrobe over his pajamas. Mrs. May grew more annoyed as she watched him apologize to me. She said that although she would like to "sit in" to make sure that her husband "didn't lie," she had to run errands. Mrs. May did stay for part of the interview and interjected answers when she felt that her husband was less than truthful. For example, when he told me that his health was "reasonably good," she corrected:

> Reasonably good? That's a lie. He has water on the brain and heart problems.
> How could he be reasonably good?

Mr. May seemed grateful for his wife's comments. Although she stood at the front door and sighed, he begged her to stay to help him with responses he "might not remember."

Mr. May's health is a source of concern to his wife. She feels that he is "no help to her" because of his inability to "move faster." He knows that he disappoints her because of his failing memory and increasing slowness in finishing simple chores. When I asked him to tell me the story of his life, Mr. May began with the state of his health. Mrs. May added to his story.

> **Mr. May:** I have hydroencephalitis. That's fluid on the brain. It doesn't affect my getting around, not to any great extent. It's mainly the walking process, and certain mechanical movements.
> **Mrs. May:** He's telling you that but he tells me, "I can't do it. I can't walk." I can't go on any vacations with him because he can't walk and I'd have to schlep. . . . I'd have to pack and unpack. I'm not young either. I have a lot of errands to do, but with all the lies he's telling you. . . .
> **Mr. May:** Basically I have to have my mobility restored in order to assist my wife.
> **Mrs. May:** Ask him what he did before he had that (hydroencephalitis). He never did too much. It was all on me. I'm old now. I can't do it.
> **Mr. May:** My Sheryl can handle things and I can't.

Mr. May nods affirmatively as his wife berates him and he begins to cry. Mrs. May, with a disgusted sigh, does not leave the house to do errands, but walks into the kitchen. Mr. May explains:

> I feel very guilty the way I've treated her over the years. She really deserves a lot more in life. I've made promises to her. Some of them I tried to keep and of course I can't keep them all. At time situations develop that prevent you from doing certain things that you set out to do. (Adds in a whisper) I really love Sheryl. I really do. Very down deeply, I do. (Pause) I can hate her, too.

Mr. May's admission seemed a flash of self-insight. Mrs. May's reluctance to leave the house seemed to mirror her ambivalence about her husband's dependence on her. I guessed that this scene had been re-enacted often during the Mays' marriage. When I asked Mr. May to name the saddest time in his life, he answered:

> When my mother died, and . . . I'm just thinking off the top of my head . . . on my first day of school. With both I was abandoned. With both I felt that I was taken away from my home, you know. I was put into another world.

Mr. May connects sadness with abandonment and admits that he "still feels it acutely." Although he continues to "get help for [his] problems," which consist mainly of depression and anxiety, years of psychotherapy have not eased his angst or cured his procrastination. The roteness of his responses seemed not so much rehearsed as often repeated. When I asked him to describe an event or time period in his life when he felt he was suffering, he answered:

> I think when I was young and my family moved. We moved from a luxury apartment to a lesser one. And it became a very strange feeling for me to adapt to the change.
> **Mrs. May** (calling out from the kitchen): Tell her that you had to sleep in the living room when you lived with them.
> **Mr. May:** That's right. You see, my parents never gave me a bedroom. We lived in a luxury apartment, but it was only a one bedroom, so I always slept in the living room on a Murphy bed.
> **Mrs. May:** See, his mother liked to be with the rich. Only she wasn't rich. So he slept in the living room.
> **Mr. May:** My mother was an organizational woman.
> **Mrs. May:** She was a social climber and a name-dropper.
> **Mr. May:** Sheryl has an astute mind and good perspective.

Mrs. May re-describes her husband's life at home. Mr. May highlights the fact that he lived in a luxury apartment. He relies on his wife to flesh out the embarrassing or negative details that would paint a more realistic picture of his mother and his past.

> **Interviewer:** How was this suffering?
> **Mr. May:** Well, I felt like I was being deprived of the life that I was getting used to. The first apartment was like being in a resort hotel. And then suddenly, it all changed. So I sort of felt that I was being sacrificed, you know, in order to maintain a standard of living.
> **Interviewer:** How old were you at this time?

Mr. May: Oh, I was working, too, and I was paying them board. So I guess I must have been in my thirties.
Interviewer: Tell me again what made this suffering?
Mr. May: I felt that I was coming down in my station in life. I felt that I was being deprived of a life that I was brought into this world to be used to.

Throughout the interview Mr. May recited a litany of "shoulds." He should have gone to college, should have found a better job, should have made more money, and should be "doing more" for Sheryl. Suffering occurred because he did not realize these "shoulds" in the recent and distant past, and the "better" life they would provide in the present. His *event* of suffering begs more questions. For example, when I wondered why he did not find a place of his own to live, or seek a new job, he explained, "I lived with my parents to take care of them," and "I worked for the government; I needed the security." Later on in the interview, when I asked him to define suffering, he answered:

Suffering is enduring something that you're not used to enduring. Something that you cannot control. It's evasive, you know. It's beyond your control.

Suffering is surprising and elusive to Mr. May. He cannot contain, control or explain it. It seems to originate in a place outside of him and his purview. Suffering also is not fully his fault; others, such as parents and employers, blocked his path to the "better life," and so introduced him to suffering. When I asked him what a picture of suffering would show, he replied:

It would go back to childhood. And it would be a house similar to what I remember from the story of Hansel and Gretel. The house was not a home until it was staffed with a family of parents and peers. And suddenly you're without them, and then the house disappears.
Interviewer: So, your picture of suffering is a house?
Mr. May: Yes, an empty house.

Because "staff" implies paid service, I wondered if Mr. May's parents and friends lived in the imaginary house to take care of him. When they failed to live up to his expectations, parents, peers, and house all disappear. His picture of the Hansel and Gretel house evokes the story's unpleasant climax—in the original fairy tale, the house hides an unexpected danger. Mr. May's picture of suffering begs more questions: Does the fairy tale house represent his wish for a home life that never was? Sheryl reminded him earlier in the interview that his home life was not "normal." His parents never owned a home; they rented a one-bedroom apartment. Is his imagined house the luxury apartment that his parents gave up? Did the concept of home disappear when his parents died? He represents suffering as an empty house that eventually disappears. Is the empty house symbolic of Mr. May himself as his body slows and his energy diminishes? He continued with painful memories.

> I was a latch-key child. Then in the night, like in November, when it gets dark. . . . I felt like I was losing them (parents), you know, that they were not going to live. The later it got, I thought at times they died and were not going to come home.

Mr. May retains this picture of himself as a lonely and fearful child; he begs his wife, listening to the interview from the kitchen, not to go out to do errands. She appears in the living room with purse in hand. "When will you be home?" he asks plaintively. She sighs in disgust and goes out the door.

Other pictures of suffering came to Mr. May's mind.

> These older people in the Y group that I belong to—they're like the children that I remember from my past years. They're children in adult bodies. They are now in their 70s, and they have remained about the same in their characteristics, both physically and emotionally.

Are these "children in adult bodies" a reflection of how Mr. May sees himself—as someone who is emotionally and physically stuck in childhood? Do his peers mirror this stagnation as he contrasts himself to someone he believes "made it?"

> My cousin lives in New York City. She's made her way in the world. Her husband is a well-known psychiatrist. In fact, he was honored. He proved he was a big man.
> **Interviewer:** A big man?
> **Mr. May:** I always wish I could have gone farther in life. I wish I could have accomplished things. I can't forgive myself for that. My feeling of unforgiveness for myself is sometimes so consuming that I feel desperate.

Although Mr. May suffers due to his perceived lack of accomplishment, his suffering is not an impetus for change; he is paralyzed by it. For him, suffering is an external object of intense focus and an internal well of regret that he often descends. He remembers incidents from over 40 years ago that show his "cowardice" and replays them.

> I could have helped once in an automobile accident. A car that was behind me was hit head-on by a truck. And I was so overcome with what happened, I was just immobilized. I did not get out of the car. I think about it, about what I could have done differently.
> **Interviewer:** When did the accident occur?
> **Mr. May:** This was in 1954.
> **Interviewer:** That was a long time ago.
> **Mr. May:** Yes, but I think about it. And like when I was asked to do certain things at home by my parents that I promised to do and I didn't do. I felt that I was being somewhat of a coward. When I was engaged to be married to a woman who I later did not like really, I first accepted the role, but then I woke up one morning and began to avoid her.

Mr. May's *bad acts* are very old. He lumps them together as proof of his worthlessness. Mrs. May helps to expose her husband's shame. She reveals to anyone who listens that he is less of a person than he ought to have been, and he seems grateful that she publicly humiliates him. He adapts to his ignominy by standing still. He is stuck on a cycle of inadequacy, shame, and guilt, not so much for having *done wrong* but for *being wrong*. This cycle eventually catapults him into depression. He communicates his suffering through the moral language of suffering, such as "I cannot forgive myself" and an admission that he did not carry out his roles as son, husband and Samaritan adequately.

Although Mr. May wondered if death might be a way out for him, he decided that dying and death are simply other forms of suffering.

> **Mr. May:** There's no freedom from suffering I guess.
> **Interviewer:** What do you mean?
> **Mr. May:** I guess I mean dying. Dying itself is suffering because you're leaving the world that you were a part of. You're going into another type of existence, but who knows what. See, it's the uncertainty of death that causes you to suffer more than anything else.

Mr. May is increasingly unable to leave his internal, empty, fairy tale house or the actual home that he shares with Sheryl. For him, both are familiar prisons where he need not use energy to interact. As much as he calls for Sheryl, he admits he "daydreams" when she responds. He communicates his suffering through his tearfulness, his attenuated actions, his shrunken worldview, and his role as an invalid. His story of suffering is no longer an aspect of his life story; it is the story of his life.

THE VOICE OF IDENTITIES AND ROLES

Roles and identities work in tandem to create a self-concept (Kaufman, 1980). Roles are socially played out; they are created by circumstances and relationships (Francis, 1990), such as being a worker, a retiree, a parent, and a child to a parent. Regarding the integral nature between social roles and identity, Kaufman (1980) describes identity as "the meaning a person attributes to herself in her varied roles through time." An identity is formed by the significance individuals give to their roles, and is maintained through interaction with others who reinforce these roles in familial, interpersonal or social relationships (Charmaz, 1995).

The effect of changes in roles and identities due to suffering are profound and pronounced. Aged sufferers may assume a new or restructured role, such as a "sick person," "housebound elder," "patient," or a "bereaved person" that is framed by current circumstances. For example, one respondent, whose primary identity was as a mother and homemaker, now lives in the home of her daughter. Although she is slowed by arthritis and dementia, her daughter asks her to do light housekeeping tasks, such as dusting and mending. Her new identity is based on present limitations, former roles, and on her lifetime relationship with her now-adult daughter. She maintains self-esteem by keeping her identity intact in light of a restructured role.

Concerning identity, May (1989, 1991) argues that the aged sufferer creates or recreates an identity based on the alteration of roles due to suffering, and convictions about the worth of a suffering individual. A re-created identity may take into account the loss of values once treasured-now mourned, such as good health, strength, beauty, physical prowess, or change of marital or income status or living arrangement. A recreated identity requires the difficult work of acknowledging the altered facts of one's life and measuring losses against what remains (Connolly, 1996). Elders may fight to retain an *old* identity that makes room for suffering, or they may accept a different, limited view of the self. Some elders may forge another—diminished or enhanced—place for the self within the family and society that accommodates suffering. They may slough off certain roles, such as paid worker, and replace them with roles that are easier to manage in light of suffering, such as retiree. Respondents show through their interviews that they rework roles and identities in order to maintain a self-concept that accommodates who they were, are, and want to remain with the *new* facts of old age and suffering. Through this re-work, elders continue to interact with others and carry on in society.

Age in and of itself may not be a legitimate defense against lack of productiveness within a society (Harrison, 1985). Although for elders, age is usually an empty variable (Neugarten, 1977), old age itself may connote suffering because the roles of parent, spouse, worker, and friend collapse under the overarching identity of being old. For most respondents, it is not so much that age caused suffering, as it is internalizing an inability to see oneself in future productive roles. New roles or identities seem closed off because individuals perceive that there is too little time left to pursue them (Charmaz, 1995). A lack of vision in a limited future—because time is viewed as linear and irreversible—is experienced as a consequence of old age and as suffering's capstone.

Although one reaction to the assault of age and suffering is to reconstruct a former identity within the frame of present limitations, it is not the only one. Individuals respond to life circumstances with as many strategies as their unique attitudes and histories offer them. In the following case study, the respondent communicated that his roles have changed very little over the years. Maintaining them is a significant part of his present, non-suffering identity.

MR. WINCHELL

Mr. Winchell is a 90-year-old African-American widower who noted that he is in excellent health. He lives alone in a luxury apartment in a Protestant home for older adults. When I asked him to tell me the story of his life, he began this way:

I was born in Maryland. I don't know what happened to my mother and father; they didn't make it. They broke up. And she (mother) sent me to live with a great aunt in the country on a farm. And I remember when I was about 3 years of age, some relatives were taking me on an electric train to the city. I can remember trying to crawl up the window to get out, believe it or not.

Mr. Winchell introduces the theme of his life in his opening comments. His desire to crawl up the train window when he was three years old foreshadowed his drive throughout life to "get out" of any situation that held him back. Mr. Winchell worked hard on his aunt's farm and although he learned as much as he could in the nearby red brick schoolhouse, he realized that his potential was wasted in a "backwoods" environment. Even as a child he knew that it was up to him to change the course of his life.

There was one teacher (who taught at the schoolhouse) who was especially good in Arithmetic. I attribute my acumen in mathematics to the foundation that she gave me. See, I majored in and taught mathematics. But my aunt didn't mind keeping me away from school to do some farm work which I didn't like. When I was 13 I ran away. In quotes. My mother had married again and I arranged through some relatives to leave the farm and go back to my mother. And that's where I entered the city school system.

Mr. Winchell did not mention his aunt or the farm where he was raised again during the interview. He impressed upon me that he left the farm through his own machinations and did not look back. The story of his early childhood is peopled mainly with a few perspicacious teachers who helped him actualize his abilities.

Have you ever heard of cornfield English? Well, my English was so bad that kids would laugh at me whenever I opened my mouth. And I decided I'm going to have to do something about that. There was an excellent English teacher and on Fridays she'd make a big circle in the floor. She said, "Now you stay within that circle and you talk for two minutes." The first time I did that my knees began to buckle and I began to perspire and I said, I've got to do something about that. So I went on a sort of rampage to improve my English. So when I went to college I took all the English they offered and worked on my pronunciation and so forth. So that's the story of that.

Mr. Winchell took on the task of self-improvement at a young age. Throughout the interview, he reiterated his earlier remark, "I've got to do something about that," as a statement of self-motivation, self-responsibility, and a promise to himself. He believed that he flourished despite his family's ignorance about education. To Mr. Winchell, his family of origin was not significant in his triumphs; they were as indifferent to his potential as he seemed unconcerned about the ongoing struggle of their lives.

Interviewer: The drive to improve yourself is important throughout your story. Was that something your family encouraged?

> **Mr. Winchell:** No. This all came out of me. My mother ended up being a housewife with too many children. I was just self driven. I don't know why. It almost looks providential.
>
> **Interviewer:** So it wasn't expected that you would attend college?
>
> **Mr. Winchell:** No, I wanted it. I developed a hunger and thirst for education. I put myself through school. I'd wait tables, I'd wash pots and pans. I then taught myself to type. I finished college as salutarian of my class in 1931. I was a student instructor of mathematics there. My first job opportunity came in M. (city) where I taught biology, chemistry, and physics. I stayed there for 5 years and I was offered the principalship there. In the meantime I began graduate study. I got my first master's degree in 1957. See, I have a lot of energy. I still have. I don't know what it is to get tired. People say to me, don't you take a nap during the day? I say no. I get 8 hours and I don't see the bed anymore until I go to bed the next night.

Mr. Winchell insists that he has changed very little in regard to habits, values, morality, and worldview in over 70 years. He still possesses the stamina that propelled him to success over seven decades ago. He chronicles his past with stories of his own achievement as well as those of less fortunate others he met along the way.

> As a result of being in the army, I had the GI Bill of rights. I went to S. for another's master's degree. They wanted me to go for the doctorate. And I said no because most of what they make you do for the doctoral program is unnecessary. So, I went into a psychiatric specialty. I did good work. I'll give you an example. There was one woman who finished college and had a nervous breakdown and was hospitalized. She wanted to be a teacher. Well, she was a good rehabilitation prospect. So I took her out of the hospital, told her she should not go into teaching of all places, trained her in book-keeping and typing and that sort of thing. So she got a job with the city; did very well. That's only one example of my work.

Mr. Winchell excelled at each job he held, which led to promotions, contacts with important others, and more prestigious jobs. Although he married early in his career, he did not mention his marriage or the birth of his only daughter in his life story. He introduced his wife by saying, "She did private tutoring." When I asked him how long he had been married, he replied:

> My wife had a master's degree in education. I was very active in the teachers' association when I was principal of a high school and she was assistant to the president of a nearby school. We met through that contact. We were married in 1937, for 54 and a half years. My wife died in June, 1991 and I moved here a year later. We had a beautiful home. Lived there for over 40 years.
>
> **Interviewer:** After having been married for over 54 years, that must have been a terrible time for you.
>
> **Mr. Winchell:** Which?
>
> **Interviewer:** Losing your wife.

Mr. Winchell: No it wasn't. We took many cruises. Our last trip together was to Alaska in '85 and then she went into congestive heart failure. And she was confined to the bedroom for 21 months. I got private people to come in. They would do anything I wanted them to do. Now, I got to the point that I said, 'Lord, how long will my wife have to go through this?' It was just so bad and then you've heard of the caregiver dying before the person. And I thought if my health would break, what in the world would she do? So I was glad to see her get out of that. I was relieved. And I was delighted to leave the house, delighted.

Mr. Winchell paints events in his life that might be construed as sorrowful with a light hand. Throughout the interview, he directed the conversation toward his achievements, full social calendar, and some "well-known" neighbors. After mentioning his wife's death, he picked up a magazine and pointed out articles that were written about him. He was spotlighted in the facility's newsletter as a member of the residents' council and welcoming committee. He is considered an excellent spokesperson for "people coming to see the place—either for themselves or to put family members in here."

Although Mr. Winchell requested to participate in this research, he "could not recall" an experience of suffering in his own life.

Interviewer: This interview concerns times of your life when you were feeling bad.

Mr. Winchell: I don't know when I was feeling bad, that's the problem.

Interviewer: Well, can you tell me one or two of the saddest events or times in your life?

Mr. Winchell: Of course the death of my wife, but then of course that was a relief. I don't know any other really. Did you see this article? (He is mentioned in an article that rates the facility where he lives as A-1.).

Interviewer: Yes. (Pause) Have you ever been depressed?

Mr. Winchell: I don't know what depression is. Remember, I'm trained in psychology. I know what it is from a psychological viewpoint, but not for myself.

Interviewer: Could you in any way define suffering as you know it for others?

Mr. Winchell: I don't know. My mother lived to be 96, so there was nothing to grieve about. I had a great grandmother who lived to be 113. Give me the question again.

Interviewer: [Question repeated].

Mr. Winchell: Well, I see it here. I met a man who since committed suicide. His wife had been dead about 4 years, and he was still grieving about it. And he said, "Are you grieving about *your* wife's death?" I said, "Absolutely not. I did all I possibly could to make her life comfortable. So I have no regrets." But there are people who just cannot get over the fact that they are now alone. Well *I'm* enjoying my freedom. You see, suffering is those people who cannot accept what's happened and who cannot go on with their own life.

Interviewer: What did you feel for him?

Mr. Winchell: I wasn't surprised (that he committed suicide) if that's what you're asking. Because of my observation of him and his manifestations, I thought perhaps he may do something like that.
Interviewer: On a feeling level, what did you feel for him?
Mr. Winchell: (Pause) Well, I felt sorry for the guy. I was sorry he hadn't been able to manage his life in a more wholesome manner. Into everyone's life some rain must fall. God usually sends sunshine shortly after.

Mr. Winchell believes that to grieve means to suffer. He clarifies that unlike his neighbor, the deaths of significant others at advanced ages "were nothing to grieve about." He offers at least two points about suffering: 1) Although he endured a grief similar to his neighbor's, Mr. Winchell "handled" his grief and therefore did not suffer; and 2) pity for his neighbor is not based on the man's suffering and suicide, but rather on the "unwholesome" way he had "mismanaged" his life. His comments hold an indictment against dependence and self-pity. Cultural and religious notions about the propriety of experiencing and expressing grief intertwine in Mr. Winchell's response toward suffering in general and in his attitude toward this particular sufferer.

Interviewer: Do you think suffering is a normal part of growing older?
Mr. Winchell: Perhaps so, but I suspect that some of the people here, even when they were younger, saw more of the hole than they did the doughnut. Also, people don't know how to plan. And see, that (suffering) is a part of the whole life continuum. You're born, you go through life and you die. So you need to plan for all of it. I'm ready to go anytime. I'm trying to prepare my daughter; she calls me every day. When my wife died everything was paid for. So it is with me. When I die all my daughter has to do is call the lawyer. There's no worry because I have order and organization. Things are taken care of. People's suffering has to do with a lack of control.

To Mr. Winchell, suffering is neither surprising nor inevitable. Suffering is ultimately a character flaw that can be avoided by careful planning and a dose of optimism.

Interviewer: Is being older and closer to the end of life a form of suffering?
Mr. Winchell: No, because this time next month I'm flying to Athens; then cruising on the Mediterranean.

For many elders, suffering is linked to the many aspects of loss, and anticipation of loss. Material poverty also saps emotional and physical resources. Mr. Winchell focuses on anticipated pleasures; he is financially comfortable. He has wealth enough to travel and live in a facility with a doctor and nurses on call. Despite a recent "tiredness" that was immediately diagnosed and relieved by a pacemaker, he is in excellent health.

Interviewer: Have you ever suffered because you experienced certain feelings such as guilt or regret over something you did or didn't do?

Mr. Winchell: No, I think I've made some mistakes in life, but I'm not suffering about them. Get up, fall down, get up and keep going.
Interviewer: Have you ever suffered because of not being able to forgive someone?
Mr. Winchell: No.
Interviewer: Are you able to forgive people who hurt you?
Mr. Winchell: I forgot about them to tell you the truth (laughter). And I can't think of any particular situation where I've been terribly hurt by anybody either.

Mr. Winchell lived his life carefully. Subtler forms of suffering, such as guilt or regret, have not touched him, or he chose not to discuss such events with me. He also seems emotionally prudent even in relationships with significant others, such as his daughter. He allows no untoward emotions, such as holding a grudge or disappointment with himself or others, to blur his carefully constructed self-view.

Toward the end of the interview, Mr. Winchell said that, for other people, "there are probably various types of suffering." He witnessed "a type" of suffering when he worked as a psychologist in Family Court.

Well, there's this whole area of delinquency which may cause suffering to the parents. The parents, let's say they have 6 children. And 5 are all right. One child causes them a great deal of suffering because of his determined delinquency. Their other children finish college and do extremely well. It's almost as though some (children) are predestined to be delinquents. (Pause). But life is your own management.

Mr. Winchell handled the discrepancy between believing in "determined delinquency" and "life is your own management," through an interesting use of the words "providential" and "determinist." The fact that he "crawled out" off the farm and into the role of a well-respected educator was providential. Yet, "impersonal determinism" decided that "delinquency" would be another child's fate. Is determinism the shadow side of providence? According to Mr. Winchell, each individual has some input, quite early in age, in choosing his own path through life.

At the end of the interview, I asked Mr. Winchell if he was "ever one to talk about feeling bad." He paused, then replied with a smile, "Not particularly so, not particularly so."

The Voice of Narrative

Just as the body reveals pain, and suffering is shown by rejecting old roles and assuming new identities, telling a story communicates personal suffering. Narrative embeds the story of suffering within the life story, within the pervasive aspects of identity, such as age, class, gender, and race (Kaufman, 1980), and in the multi-layered and "mighty long" vantage of older age.

Elders may offer themes in their narrative that reinforce roles and provide a thread for identity over time. In some ways themes are like metaphors; they employ an image or axiom that "stands in" for what cannot be easily explained (Soskice, 1993). Themes are also like tools that organize the happenstance of life with an overarching phrase or symbolic representation.

The theme that links identities, roles, and self-concept with life circumstances is significant in elders' story of suffering. Stories of suffering re-integrate a self fragmented by suffering (Scarry, 1985). The narrator may use the unifying theme of the life story to connect the "broken" self to an imagined, integrated future, such as "I've always had a charmed life (and will again)," or "I'm always in control (and will be again)." This narrative repair or self-restoration is accomplished by explaining a cause, effect, and probable outcome of personal suffering. Explanations about suffering provide a structure for the story, give the sufferer control over the experience, and often impute personal or transcendent value to suffering that strengthens the self in psychological or spiritual ways (Niebuhr, 1989; Ricoeuer, 1986). Elders often spell out, through themes, the implicit meaning and fit of suffering within their life story (Widdershoven, 1993).

The following case shows the importance to elders of re-integrating the self during or after suffering by linking past roles and identities to present circumstances. This informant's suffering occurred because she was unable to connect her glorious past with her lonely present and dreaded future. It is precisely the sense of fragmentation between past roles and present identity and a lack of coherence between her life story and current circumstances that she named suffering (Haurwas, 1990).

MRS. RICKMAN

Mrs. Rickman is a 91-year-old European-American widow who lives alone in a luxury apartment in Center City. The living room walls are lined with books; the bar is well-stocked, and the grand piano is tuned. Although she described herself as "extremely social," she is housebound due to crippling arthritis. Spending time with other seniors in her apartment building, many of whom are in similar physical condition but do not share her intellectual interests, does not appeal to Mrs. Rickman. Because her only son and his family live out of state, she feels isolated.

Mrs. Rickman is an American success story. Born in a shtetl in Russia, she came to this country with her family when she was eight years old. Although she could not speak English when she arrived at Ellis Island, her grandfather encouraged her to learn "anything and everything." She happily complied.

> When we finally got to New York City, we stayed there five years. But my
> mother had a huge family living in Philadelphia. They had done very well
> for themselves with hard work in businesses. The Koreans are doing it today.
> The Jews did it then. So they sent for my mother. And our fortunes *did*
> change. Little by little she did better and better and I mean *she* did it. My
> father just went along. In my mother, I had a good role model for achievement

and for cleanliness, but not for honesty. I got my honesty from my father and not from her. She was willing to bend the rules to get what she wanted (Mrs. Rickman's emphasis).

Mrs. Rickman revealed that she took the best from each parent—her father's integrity and her mother's ambition to succeed in the new world. Her mother's father, with whom they lived in a tiny apartment in New York City, wanted both of his granddaughters to shine intellectually. Only one granddaughter shared his vision.

> It was very unusual for a woman at that time to be encouraged. And it wasn't that we were a wealthy family. I don't know if it was because there were no boys in the family or whether my grandfather recognized I was astute. My sister never finished high school; she didn't want to. Whereas I was ready material. I wanted to go far. And I graduated into the Depression with no job ahead. And I wanted to teach of course. Because at that time a teaching job, especially in a high school, was prestigious enough. And as I've said I've always been a snob.

Mrs. Rickman reveals both her positive and negative character traits. But beyond an admission that she was ambitious and elitist, even as a youngster, she disclosed little else about her childhood. The focus of her narrative begins when her life "came together" in high school. Because she graduated at the top of her class, she was awarded a scholarship to a nearby state college.

> I had the scholarship to (the state college). But there was little point in offering it to me. I wouldn't take it. Let someone else take it. My mother died without knowing I got that scholarship. I insisted on going to (an ivy league university). Because at that time there was a vast difference between the two and I was a bit of a snob. I wasn't very happy there. But I stayed.

She introduced the fact of her mother's death, when Mrs. Rickman was only 17, as an aside. She did not mention her feelings about this loss at any point in the interview. She refused the state scholarship because she believed it would deny her the status that a "better" university confers. Although she felt unhappy in the ivy-league setting, it served as a means to an end. Early on, she calculated that a "good" education sets the stage for meeting significant others. In fact, she met her first husband, a "brilliant doctoral student" there, and married him during her senior year. Although the Depression delayed some of their career goals, it did not change them.

> I graduated into the Depression with a master's degree in English Literature. In 1929 the city of Philadelphia, like many big cities, developed the dole system. And I was hired to go into homes and establish eligibility for small amounts of cash to pay rent or buy groceries. That was how the welfare system started. My husband went back to school; he got his master's in sociology and his Ph.D. in philosophy at the same time. We worked!

Mrs. Rickman did not describe the Depression the way most elders did; she spoke of it as a "learning experience." She formed theories about the harm of government intervention into "poor people's lives." She did not mention her clients' poverty, but focused on the greed of city and federal instead on her awareness of the grim underside of government politicians.

After the Depression, Mrs. Rickman's first teaching assignment brought her back to the Philadelphia high school where she had been a student.

> That wasn't so good. I was working with my former teachers and I didn't like that. Of course, people who have taught there in its early days or people who have gone to school there—we were a special breed. I could recognize them. There was a liberal attitude. It was a more intellectual group.

Mrs. Rickman clarifies that she was "self-made"; although her parents held dreams for her, she discounts their influence on her development. From an early age, she knew whom she wanted inside her "circle of friends." She found and cultivated "good" relationships, mostly with other teachers who shared her intelligence and social vision. Mrs. Rickman also realized at an early age that faith and reason were demanding task masters; they could not co-exist.

> **Mrs. Rickman:** I think both of my parents had a religious center. I mean they believed in God, but they never followed any ritual. But anyhow they couldn't have encouraged me because I turned against religion very early. Yet I was an avid reader of the Bible, as literature, you know.
> **Interviewer:** Do you practice a religion now?
> **Mrs. Rickman:** No, no, no! I was 9 years old when I became aware of the fact that there was no God. I said to myself stop asking God for anything. He does not exist. Later on I became more thoughtful about it. But I've never had religion.
> **Interviewer:** Do you still believe there is no God?
> **Mrs. Rickman:** Yes. I do not believe in a divinity. I turned against it very early. It didn't bother me. I haven't missed it. I do, of course, have a philosophy of ethics which I follow very closely. It's a way of life.

Disputing the existence of God is hard work for a nine year old. Yet, her decades-old argument fits her self-view as rational and self-reliant. Her self-portrait as a child "not asking God for anything" remains after 80 plus years. There is no need to paint a new picture of a spiritual self. Besides, a powerful deity, randomly throwing fortune or mishap her way, might have blurred her vision of the future.

> Yes, I had everything planned very carefully. I wanted to have a family but I wanted to teach. Nothing could stop me. I was a career woman. Different from society. All my friends were the same, of course. Birds of a feather.

In some ways Mrs. Rickman's *past* world was large—it included a husband, a child, a career, many friends, and knowledge about art, literature, and music. In other ways her world was small, populated only by those who were similar to her in their "differentness." Mrs. Rickman described the period of her life with her first husband as "complex." Although her career flourished—she became head of the school's English Department—her marriage floundered. She explained that there were many reasons for divorcing her husband; the major factor was that she wanted to "save" her son, Tom. After seven years of marriage, the couple divorced. Tom was five years old.

> **Mrs. Rickman:** My husband would not have been good for Tom. He was all right at a distance and very generous. But had they lived together, he would have ruined him. See he couldn't live with a child. He could send a check, he could visit and take him to the zoo, but he couldn't live with him. It was not meanness, it was really ignorance and a hostility to have a child. He didn't really want a child. Tom did not remain close with his father, but friendly.
> **Interviewer:** Was that a primary reason for divorce?
> **Mrs. Rickman:** Actually, no, but the primary result was that I saved Tom. (Pause) About 2 or 3 weeks ago I was with a friend who knew me at the time of the divorce. And we were friends for a long, long time. And she didn't know [first husband]; I had divorced him by that time, but she knew my son of course. We were all a part of a group. All the friends were couples and each had a child or two. I was the only single parent. And she was saying to me you are the most successful parent out of that entire group. They had problems with their children as adults. I had none.

Mrs. Rickman was pleased to have proof—in the form of her friend's affirmation—that she succeeded in raising her son alone. After divorce, she remained busy with "work, friends, and dating—in that order" for over 15 years. She "gradually became attracted" to a fellow schoolteacher and explains that the "misfortune" of his wife's death became her "fortune." After an "appropriate amount of time," she asked her colleague to dinner, disclosed her interest in him, and took the reins of her personal life, which was "somewhat lonely" into her own hands.

> I once said being married to him was like living with the Philadelphia orchestra and a philosopher at the same time. He was very musical; he was very intellectual. When he died, a friend said, "He was a gentleman and a scholar." I was very fortunate in that his wife died, so his misfortune was my fortune. Because in the 12 years that I worked with him in the same school I really admired him above all men. (Pause) That marriage was made in heaven.

She explained why the short period of her second marriage was the happiest in her life.

> I had an active social life, scores of friends, and a husband who was brilliant and devoted. My son was chosen by a prestigious law school. My career just accelerated. Who wouldn't be happy? Then he (husband) died from cancer.

Mrs. Rickman was comfortable with analyzing her thoughts and recalling her past through the vehicle of probing interview questions. With the panorama of old age, she was well able to compare and contrast her sorrows. When I asked her about the saddest periods of life, she replied:

> The saddest times all have to do with losses. I terribly regretted having to divorce my first husband because he was a fine person. Losing him was very sad. The death of my second husband, that was very sad. And my retirement. I taught for 42 years and I had to retire because of my age. My job was as important to me, all my life, as my family. That was a terrible time.

Although most respondents are able to differentiate sadness and suffering, Mrs. Rickman adds an important personal distinction.

> **Mrs. Rickman:** Seven years and he (second husband) died from cancer. In two weeks! It was a shock, although speaking impersonally and objectively, a divorce is worse than a death.
> **Interviewer:** How do you see that?
> **Mrs. Rickman:** That's a personal reaction. A death I felt was not my fault. It wasn't a failure, it was totally outside of me; it was a misfortune. A divorce—I failed. I was filled with guilt and blame and that was worse than just losing a husband through death.

Mrs. Rickman could not control the time and manner of her second husband's sudden death; she divorced her first husband on her own watch and therefore "failed." Perhaps part of her pain is realizing that she could *fail* no matter how well-ordered her life. Vulnerability to death is beyond her purview; susceptibility to her own mistakes engenders "guilt and blame." When asked if she had ever suffered, there was no hesitation in her answer.

> I would say I suffer now. In those other times, I was able to overcome the sadness. In time I turned from the loss of the two men, I turned to other men. It wasn't the same, but it was somebody to turn to. And I had friends. And with the retirement, I was able to turn to other intellectual activities, and so again I was in a structured situation.

Mrs. Rickman's self-knowledge and worldview are built from the same foundation—control, planning, and discipline. Now her internal structure is housed in an unfamiliar body. It is "heavier" and "slower." She describes herself as two people; her past self was assertive, busy and efficient, and contentment resulted from intellectual and social pursuits—mentoring students and entertaining colleagues in her home. This former self contrasts the lonely widow who waits for others to seek her out. When the phone rang during our interview, Mrs. Rickman brightened, and hoped that it might be "an invitation to join one of the neighbors" for dinner, even though she stated earlier that she had "little in common" with them.

> My friends have all died. The friends I have now—we're friends because of our needs. I cannot make new friends because they'd be too young, they wouldn't want me. Traveling is finished. I can't walk to the corner without

pain, even getting into a cab is difficult. That's what causes my present suffering. There's no future.

Mrs. Rickman and her "friends" are drawn to each other by their limitations. She now settles for qualities in friends that would have been unacceptable in the past. Her identity is liminal; it is lost betwixt and between the keenness of her mind and the recalcitrance of her body. Because her identity is based on an external structure that no longer holds, she cannot get beyond, or transcend, her body. Besides, there is no alternative identity to take on; her past self is the only self worth having. She believes that to construct a new identity would be dishonest; it would be to create an illusion. Although she recognizes the "goods" that provide elders with solace—faith and family—she has no practice in cultivating them.

> I have no religion to sustain me as it sustains some old people. But the things that you can't do, you can't do. Like religion—I can't believe—so I dismiss it. I don't wish for it. I miss the comfort of my children (son, daughter-in-law, and grandson). I'd love to see them for dinner, for lunch, a half hour visit. But it's not to be. They live too far away.

Her son and his family are busy pursuing their own goals. His behavior toward his mother mirrors her own actions toward her parents when she reached adulthood. Like Mr. May trapped in his fairy tale house, for Mrs. Rickman there is "no way out" of old age. Mrs. Rickman's prison is her own body.

> I'm not looking for solutions; there are none. I have a friend who thinks tomorrow is going to be better than today. The next person she meets is going to give her life meaning. She takes classes at Community College and thinks that's intellectually stimulating. She lives under an illusion. I have no illusions about anything. People suffer from old age because old age *is* a limitation. Being closer to the end of life *is* a form of suffering (Mrs. Rickman's emphasis).

Mrs. Rickman might have interpreted her friend's optimism as hope rather than illusion. She long ago decided, however, that her goals soared higher than most others'; she will not fall back on dreams that she rejected in youth. Her perceived "specialness" is at the core of her fierce independence, and independence remains the theme that knits her identity. Despite the disintegration of her body, her lack of self-doubt about her convictions remains intact. She will not ask her son to visit; she labels faith a gift to which she has no access and for which she has no need. When asked to describe a picture of suffering, she answered, "Someone's already done it. Picasso's Guernica."

Mrs. Rickman's portrait of suffering, like Mr. May's Hansel and Gretel house and Mr. Winchell's suicidal neighbor, discloses each respondent's take on suffering. In Mrs. Rickman's non-personal picture of suffering, she reveals both her sophistication and her awareness of the ubiquitousness of suffering. Although she remains "above average" in knowledge and advanced education among women of her cohort, she believes that the same cruel fate of needless suffering awaits all. The all-encompassing devastation in Mrs. Rickman's picture reveals her despair.

Mrs. Rickman feels left, at the end of life, with a self that is not growing but declining. She alternates between maintaining the status quo and resigning herself to another, lower level of functioning. Because her morality is based on achievement, she is also left with a self that is *not good enough* to meet her own high standards. Old age and suffering have perpetrated this indignity. To Mrs. Rickman, both old age and suffering have no meaning, order, point, or rules, and therefore no value.

> I cannot plan tomorrow. In a year I will be in worse physical condition. There's no future and the other times I always had a future and now I don't have one.

Three cruel components comprise suffering for Mrs. Rickman: 1) each wonderful memory of the past wounds by its irrevocableness; 2) she is acutely aware of each downward step in her bodily decline and, 3) she holds no belief in a future, either in this life or the next, that will match the glory of her past. For Mrs. Rickman, suffering includes a lack of imagination—she cannot imagine a good end to her story of suffering, or to life. Because death holds no possibility for a successful outcome, the self who dreamed, planned, and achieved is without dignity in suffering. With the certainty of annihilation, death is ignominious.

Suffering Speaks

Suffering is a form of communication that is mediated and understood with several voices—the voice of the body; the voice of past and present roles and identities, and the voice of narrative. At different times during the interview each respondent spoke with all three voices.

Mr. May communicated his suffering by his very presence. He rarely looked at me during the interview. His state of undress revealed that he is unable to leave his home or "get out" of himself. He has assumed the role of invalid both emotionally and physically. His picture of suffering—a deserted fairy tale house—is a symbol of himself as an empty room of regret. Expressions that he used, such as "children in adult bodies" to describe his peers at the Y, conjure up images that are both grotesque and imaginative. They connote that the outer world mirrors his inner world—both contain memories of innocence and wrongdoing, vulnerability and harm, charm and repugnance, and eventual stagnation.

For Mr. Winchell, maintaining the roles that he took on as a younger man is integral to his identity, and his past identity still works. The roles that he currently assumes within the apartment building—educator, representative, goodwill ambassador—are past roles reproduced in the present setting. His strict views on determinism and providence address the mystery of why some people suffer and others, like himself, do not. For answers to the mystery, he looks to human weakness. Suffering is a shortcoming that results from a disorganized mind and lack of planning—qualities that are not consonant with his role as exemplar of *the careful life.*

Mrs. Rickman communicates suffering through her narrative. Her story contrasts the richness of her past with a hopeless present. Her life's theme— to shine intellectually and socially—no longer holds. She admits that the suffering she endures is not a problem of medicine, but of existence (Kliever, 1989). Any chance to escape herself—"looking forward" to the interview or dining with neighbors—is preferable to facing a future she *knows* will be worse than the present. Because suffering for her is rooted in a comparison to a glorious past, old age is experienced as so short on meaning and value that it becomes the symbol of suffering.

The voices of the three respondents—through their bodies and the roles and identities that they assumed in the past and that shape their present, come together through the narrative told in the setting of the interview. Like the voice of art, music, or literature, respondents' stories, replete with characters and methods of plot and development, hold an inherent truth.

THE NEXT CHAPTER

Gender is an aspect of personal and social identity that shapes the direction of and expectations about one's life, especially for men and women who grew up and developed during the Depression and between the World Wars. Chapter 3 explores the gendered differences in respondents' experiences and expressions of suffering.

CHAPTER 3

Suffering:
A Gendered Phenomenon

Reactions to lived experiences, such as suffering, are neither color-blind nor gender-neutral. Just as race is a social construction, gender identity is a cultural artifact. Individuals learn behaviors in regard to being male or female in a particular culture (Stillion, 1995). Masculinity is not a normative referent (Kimmel, 1995), nor is femininity a comparative one (Martin, 1987). Both are problematic social constructs that advocate distinct behaviors for men and women. Individual experiences and expressions of suffering are informed by gender-appropriate reactions that society tacitly and overtly assigns (Mirowsky & Ross, 1995). The cultural impetus for men and women to act in accordance with gender roles is internalized throughout life (Berger, 1967).

Just as attitudes and behaviors toward marriage or work are acquired by modeling and practice, so is the gendered reaction to a lived experience, such as suffering. Male respondents named "taking it on the chin" and maintaining self-control as appropriate responses to grief or pain (Rubinstein, Goodman, & Black, 1993). As defenders and protectors of family and country, men believed that they should be strong, unemotional and for the most part, silent about suffering. Most men in the sample served in the armed forces during the Second World War, yet the horror of combat evoked little negative comment from them. They spoke about losing limbs, losing buddies, and "feeling lucky" when they returned from war simply because they were alive. Matter-of-fact descriptions of war may result from being interviewed by a younger woman who had not shared their history. Or it may reflect their memory of a myth popular during the war years— youth is invincible and young men of this era would, without question, fight wars, obey orders, and ultimately emerge from the trauma unscathed.

Society had a different set of rules for women in this cohort. They were lauded for maintaining *long-suffering* attitudes toward pain and anguish (Ahola, 1992). Feminine characteristics of submission and patience were interwoven with women's major roles as wife, mother, and caretaker (Martin, 1987). These roles

49

often included waiting—waiting to be married, waiting to bear children, or waiting for suffering to cease. If women worked outside the home before the war, their jobs were linked to women's abilities to serve and nurture, such as: nurse, laundress, teacher, waitress, or domestic. Although women were enlisted for "men's" jobs during the war, afterward they lost (like Mrs. Lowell mentioned in Chapter 7) or were expected to resign from jobs they had come to enjoy, such as welder or riveter, and quietly assume former jobs and roles.

Individuals are embodied; men's and women's bodies are integral to their self-concept and their means of communication. Yet, like roles and identities, society suggests different voices for the masculine and feminine body in regard to suffering. The human body, as a text, symbol, and voice, speaks of a "corporeal history" of suffering (Boddy, 1991). Men often regard the body as an asset or liability. The importance of physical strength, pushing oneself to the limit, and remaining stalwart in the face of pain engender a bracketed [an individual separates himself from the experience, or separates suffering from other aspects of his life] reaction to suffering (Charmaz, 1995). Men often view suffering as an external problem to fix or solve, usually privately (Sabo & Gordon, 1995). Because of this, "masculinities" are considered a significant barrier to both men's health and to an acknowledgment that they are suffering (Kimmell, 1995). Women's concern with the façade *and* the utility of the body cause her to view both the causes and manifestations of suffering holistically (Brennan, Moss, & Kim, 1993). During suffering, both men and women in the sample experienced a similar "homelessness" in their bodies (Heidegger, as cited by Svenaeus, 2000). References to "the back, "the leg," or "the head" by both men and women showed the cognitive duality of both "being" oneself and "watching" oneself, and an emotional distancing from the potential stranger-like nature of the body.

Masculine behaviors are rooted in the American concept of the person as a *hero* (Bellah, Madsen, Sullivan, Swidler, & Tipton, 1985; Black, 1995). This model of self-directing independence is linked to moral correctness, social superiority, and control over the circumstances of one's life. I note that the *hero* resonated with both male and female respondents. The notion that "men [and women] should outlive and outshine death and decay" (Becker, 1974, p. 5) is both a cultural construct and a heavy burden to those who are aged and suffer. Unlike societies whose conception of self is rooted in kinship groups, continuity of personhood in American culture is not *built into the system;* it occurs through individual effort (Rubinstein et al., 1993). Suffering in age is a disruption of the ability to self-improve and self-promote. A lack of personal performance becomes a moral failing, a shameful reminder that one did not work hard enough to be successful and healthy (Kleinman, 1992, p. 180), and so adds to the experience of suffering.

This chapter is devoted specifically to exploring the distinctive ways that men and women experience and express suffering. I note class status (income and social) and race, along with gender, form a tri-dimensional social reality that are intertwined in an individual, and must be acknowledged in an examination of suffering.

MR. GORDAN

Mr. Gordan is an African-American widower who lives in a studio apartment in a subsidized senior facility. He looks younger than his 78 years and adds to that impression by a carefree and jovial manner. When I asked him to tell me the story of his life, he replied:

> I was born in R., South Carolina. That's a pretty big city. My great, great grandfather was a full-blooded Indian. The same is put onto my great, great grandmother—she was a full-blooded African. I can remember all this from my grandmother. She was a sharecropper. There was a place where we lived and you didn't have to pay no rent. It was funny back in those days but it worked. Now you can't find a place where you don't have to pay no rent.

The way in which Mr. Gordan began his life story highlights a personal trait that infuses his narrative and I guessed, his life—he focuses on the positive continuum of life's events. He views situations that others might see as unjust or demoralizing, such as working as a sharecropper, with a bright lens, such as not having to pay rent. When I asked him how he remembers growing up as an only child, he recalled:

> Life down there was all right. My mother did domestic work. She actually did washing for the white people. She'd wash clothes and I had to pick them up and take them back. I had a rough time with the young white boys because I was over there in their neighborhood, so they threw rocks at me (laughs). You didn't cross the railroad tracks back then. And then they come to know me.
> **Interviewer:** What do you mean?
> **Mr. Gordan:** Well, I didn't get angry at them for throwing rocks at me. I just say that's their way of life, you know. I'd pick one up and throw it back at them. I let them come to know me. Then after that I used to go across the tracks and we used to play together. I never had no problem after that.

Mr. Gordan described his early introduction to prejudice with a response that he carried through life—"I let them come to know me." His comment shows awareness of the racial lines that divided the neighborhoods on either side of the tracks, and his attempt to erase them. He developed, at an early age, a self-confidence that was stronger than ignorance.

Mr. Gordan has neither memories nor information about his father, and said that he never "craved knowledge" about him. He believed that his father "must have been a disappointment" to his mother, "'cause she never talked to me about him." When he was 8 years old, his mother traveled to Philadelphia with several of her 10 siblings to find "better" work. He stayed behind in South Carolina with his beloved grandmother. Five years later, his mother sent for him. Although his grandmother died shortly after their trek north, he recalled the closeness that his extended family enjoyed.

> Everybody was looking for better things, you know. There was 15 (aunts, uncles, and cousins) of us and we all lived in a little two story house. But we stuck together and everything was smooth. We never wanted for nothing, you know. We had plenty to eat.

Life was good in Philadelphia because the family shared a common goal— to better themselves through hard work. Almost as an afterthought, Mr. Gordan mentioned that his mother remarried a year after he came to Philadelphia so that "her, and me, too, would be taken care of. See, she was sick but she didn't make no noise about that." His stepfather was a man who "needed a wife."

> My mother married one of those nasty [American] Indians. I didn't like him at all because he used to beat me a lot. Sometimes I felt like killing him, but nothing ever happened. I just went ahead and took it. And you know, when he died there was only two people at his wake. One was my oldest cousin Grace and the other was the woman that my mother took in as a friend that was messing around with him.

Mr. Gordan offered a glimpse of his life after his mother remarried. Both he and his mother were abused: he, physically, and his mother through her husband's infidelity and her friend's betrayal. Mr. Gordan witnessed the penalty for such behavior; only two people attended his stepfather's funeral. He hinted at his powerlessness as a youngster to protect himself or his mother from his stepfather's cruelty, and took what he believes was the best route "out of harm's way."

> I wasn't even 18 when I went into the service. I volunteered because, for one thing, I was really getting in with some bad company and then with my stepfather. . . . I said, "I'm going to try to do the best I can to keep from winding up in jail or dead."

Mr. Gordan knew that he "had to get out of the house," yet leaving his mother with an abusive husband added to the grim memory of his teen years. His mother encouraged him "to make a life for [him]self." But one of life's saddest times occurred soon after he joined the service.

> Yeah, I got that telegram (informing him of his mother's death) when I was overseas. So, when my mother died, I wasn't with her. And I would have liked to have been here before she passed away. (Pause) But I didn't cry.

Mr. Gordan's words, "I didn't cry" is a crucial addendum to his comment. It is not clear whether he thinks that it was inappropriate for a man and a soldier to cry, or that no tears came. A proud statement of "not crying" during a time of grief is common in men's narratives. Mr. Gordan literally shrugged off the memory and mentioned that his stint in the service was a "real learning time."

> Oh, I loved it overseas. I saw so much that I would never see, like how other people live in different places and different sceneries. I was fortunate to travel to about 37 of the states. You see, it helps you through life knowing some people are worse off than you and some are better off than you.

Mr. Gordan's early knowledge of abuse, loss, and material poverty paled in comparison to the poverty of civilians he met overseas. His experiences also confirmed that "some people live better lives." He perfected his philosophy of the *Middle Way* because of what he saw during the war. Since then he has walked a tightrope between emotional and material extremes.

After the war, Mr. Gordan found jobs on assembly lines in the textile factories that thrived in North Philadelphia during the 1940s and '50s. Although he "always worked," the type of work he did was not salient in his narrative. He remembers "having so much fun" after work and on weekends that he had no desire to "settle down." Fate intervened one Easter Sunday morning in the early 1960s. He was 45 years old.

> I met my wife on the corner of 8th and L. We were both waiting on the 53 (bus). And I was kind of half-way managing a bar and I was living upstairs on top of it. I told her that I worked there. A couple days later she came past the bar and I was there. She was a Puerto Rican from Brooklyn. A Brooklyn girl.

The petite woman he first sighted at the bus stop was a 28-year-old divorcee with two sons. They married after a courtship of two years. Mr. Gordan said that he always wanted children; he adopted the younger of his wife's sons and continues to have a close relationship with him. The older boy returned to Puerto Rico to live with his father. The new family bought a row home that cost $5,000 in 1965. Mr. Gordan described his happy marriage and its tragic end.

> We were always together. If I went somewhere, she wanted to go. I was true to her and she was true to me. They were the happiest 8 years of my life. That's all it was, 8 years. See, we tried to have children three times. She got sick each time. They told her the first time she'd better quit. So we tried again, like two fools. But anyway, then she got messed up and she had to go to the hospital and they had to give her the hysterectomy. That's what killed her. They must have done something wrong, but who knows what happened.

Mr. Gordan's comments reflect the helplessness he felt when his wife died. The cause of her death remains unresolved in his mind; he is unsure who should be blamed for it. When I asked him if he had ever suffered, he named the period following his wife's death.

> I think maybe I might have suffered a little bit when I lost my wife. I missed
> her so much. It broke up a lot of things that we were doing together and
> stuff like that. You know, it took about two years to actually get over
> that. (Pause) Maybe more. I missed her. I missed her constantly. It changed
> my whole life. But still, I had the feeling that it was meant to be.

Mr. Gordan concedes that his wife's death "changed" him and "broke up" the rhythm of his life. Yet he admits to having suffered only "a little bit." These reserved comments are typical of men's expressions of grief or pain. Men in the sample, when asked if they had suffered, remarked, "I *may* have suffered when . . ." or "You might call it suffering when. . . ." This minimizing of anguish, grief or pain implies at least two things: 1) to label an experience as *suffering* may be to succumb to it; and 2) by toning down an expression of suffering an individual controls the experience, and perhaps lessens the pain.

Like Mr. Gordan, men in the study often defined suffering as a break in the flow of their lives. A 71-year-old European-American man described suffering this way: "to get out of my routine for some reason, not to be able to pay the bills and cook for my wife (who worked outside the home)—that would be suffering!" To describe suffering as in interruption of everyday life highlights the importance of maintaining the status quo. Uncertainty about what follows death or misfortune is suffering. Men's remarks about the unpredictability of tragedy illustrate the assault-like quality of suffering that Mr. Gordan revealed later in his narrative.

Mr. Gordan added that, despite its untimeliness, his wife's death was "meant to be." His conviction that someone should be accountable for her death begs a question: Had he asked himself, if they had taken the doctor's suggestion not to become pregnant, might she still be alive? Perhaps to call her loss "inevitable" releases him from self-blame. When I asked him to define suffering, he replied:

> Suffering is something that gets inside of you. That's the worst thing of
> all. Because you can only come out of it if things change for you. In other
> words, something external would have to change for you to stop suffering.

Mr. Gordan did not link suffering directly with his grief. Suffering is an entity that found its way inside of him. Because suffering has an indeterminate origin and location, he had few inner resources to understand or fight it. He waited for an external power, which is also beyond his control, to stop the internal attack of suffering. The paradoxical nature of this enemy was also part of Mr. Gordan's experience of suffering.

Suffering as an attack (explored more fully in Chapter 8) is an oft-used metaphor in men's descriptions of suffering. Viewed as a physical onslaught, negative experiences are: "external enemies," and "obscene things attacking me" (Moyers, 2000). A sense that suffering is external, mercurial and formless, yet internal, stationary, and concrete emerged when I asked Mr. Gordan if pain, grief, or anguish "can be quick or must last a long time in order to be thought of as suffering."

> I think suffering can happen suddenly, like with me when my wife died. You suffer, and whatever it is hits you bad, and the next thing you know you're not suffering any more. You might feel the after effects because that don't go away right away. But it's not bad like it was.

The coming and going of suffering is as unpredictable as a stranger who attacks quietly but not mortally. Using life experience as a model, Mr. Gordan is convinced that suffering can end as quickly as it strikes. When I asked him what a picture of suffering would show, he considered:

> I imagine you'd see frowns on a person's face, and they'd be all drawn up, like this (he lowers his head and brings his knees up to his chin)
> **Interviewer:** Like someone in a fetal position?
> **Mr. Gordan:** (with certainty) Yes, Ma'am! Like you need protection.

Mr. Gordan's portrait of suffering shows an ultimate state of vulnerability—dependent on another for one's very existence. In a culture that applauds heroic individualism especially for men, dependency itself may be construed as suffering. Although his descriptions of suffering are based on personal experience, they are also based on cultural patterns, for example, that it is a man's responsibility to care for weaker, dependent others. To be the dependent other constitutes suffering. He distinguishes between suffering that results from helplessness and suffering that an individual *should* control.

> A lot of people suffer because they can't get what they want. So, it's up to the person themselves to control your own suffering. See, it's both ways. You cause yourself to suffer, and it's part of what's coming down the line at you.

According to Mr. Gordan, if a person is unreasonable about his expectations in life, he can expect to suffer. He also recognizes the probability that suffering will "come down the line" in old age because of the decline that attends that stage of life. His comments reiterate a theme he mentioned earlier—the wisdom of measuring personal suffering against a universal yardstick—everyone, at some point in life, suffers.

> **Interviewer:** Do you think suffering is a normal part of growing older?
> **Mr. Gordan:** Yes. Because the older you get, the more of them things come down the line.

Mr. Gordan, who enjoys good health and an active social life, is a youthful elder with an optimistic turn of mind. "Them things" are a distant blur in his line of vision. When asked, he clarified with a shake of his head that he spends no time worrying about illness or death.

> You know what? I'm going to tell you the honest to God's truth. I have all kinds of friends—white friends, black friends, Indians, and you know my wife was Puerto Rican. I mean I never go anyplace where I'm not wanted.
> **Interviewer:** What do you mean?
> **Mr. Gordan:** Well, say for instance I go someplace and you look in the faces of people and you can tell people don't want you there. You can tell by their actions and sometimes by their words. You know what I mean? And you just don't go in with those kinds of people, 'cause you're only looking for trouble.

As an African-American male, Mr. Gordan realizes that in some circles he remains on the *wrong side* of the tracks. He crosses only if he is wanted, is aware of tacit or overt rebuffs, and spends no time "worrying about the folks that don't want [him]." He assured me that his "good nature" leads him to serendipitous encounters with all stripes of people.

> I'm not lonely at all. I can always strike up something that will make me feel up, you know. I'm an assistant down in the office here (in the apartment facility). And if I'm not working here, well, I always hit the road. (Pause) You know (with a wink) I'm not gay and I'm not dead. I got lots of women friends.

At the end of the interview, I asked Mr. Gordan if he would like to add anything to out discussion about suffering, or to any subject that he wished we had discussed. After a pause, he replied:

> You know, I was never in jail. Never had no run in with the law or nothing like that. In my younger days, older days. Nothing like that. Everything was good.

In summing up his life, Mr. Gordan measured his success by the fact that he was "never locked up." Although this may be a commentary on Mr. Gordan's personal expectations about life as an African-American male born to a working class family between the two World Wars, it is also a comment on the society that permitted him such narrow expectations. Mr. Gordan's narrative, and particularly his summation, show that the links between class, gender, and race are intricately soldered in an elder's perception of a "good life," in what constitutes suffering or not suffering, and in appropriate expressions of the suffering experience.

MRS. BROWN

Mrs. Brown is an 82-year-old European-American divorcee who lives alone in the home that was bought by her mother. It is an old, eight-room, neatly kept brick house with stained glass windows and elaborate woodwork. Because she suffers from crippling arthritis, and receives only a small social security stipend, the house is now "too big to keep up," yet she cannot afford to move. When I asked her to tell me the story of her life, she replied:

Well, I grew up with five brothers and one sister and we were pretty poor.
At that time my father couldn't get a job and my mother had to work. And
we were pretty happy together. And then, I guess I got married first. And I
had two girls. And well, I didn't have too happy a marriage. The only time
there was happiness was when I had my children. They made me happy.
And I'd visit home quite frequently. And my sister, she got married next,
so I used to visit her. And that was about the extent of my life.

Mrs. Brown began her life story by placing herself in a web of relationships.
She defined her life through closeness with her family of origin and with her
children. The working-class Philadelphia neighborhoods where she lived since
childhood provided the setting. The scarcity of the Great Depression, her father's
inability to find work, and her mother's absence from home drew strict parameters
around her young adulthood. Mrs. Brown's mother worked as a live-in domestic.
She "just about raised" her younger siblings; as the eldest girl in the family
she was expected to stand in for her mother. The historical events of the wider
world and her family's personal circumstances mesh in her narrative. She
described herself as a "home type girl" whose social life was restricted by
responsibilities.

We lived on the same block as two sisters. My sister and I wanted to sit out
on the steps with them. But we couldn't sit out 'til the others (siblings) were
asleep. So, I'd go upstairs and pick the baby (youngest brother) up and
walk around the room with him. And just when I'd try to put him down
he'd open his big blue eyes. I'd hit him on the backside and say, "go to
sleep" (laughter). I was fifteen.

Mrs. Brown left school in the eleventh grade to work in a factory near her
North Philadelphia row house. She worked the early shift in order to hurry
home each afternoon to prepare the family dinner. She followed this routine
for over 10 years. She described herself as a "shy and backward 28-year-old
who hardly ever dated" when a handsome security guard at the factory "picked
her out of the crowd." They married within six months of meeting. Her remark
implied that her husband "chose" her; did she feel that she had no choice in
the decision? She gave birth to her elder daughter one year after marriage;
her younger daughter was born seven years later. She learned early on in the
marriage that her husband was "selfish."

He figured that once you get married you should forget your family. If
I wanted to make a phone call I had to pretend I'm going to the store for
something and make a quick call to see how everybody was at home. That
hurt me a lot. See, it didn't bother him that he didn't see his brothers or
sisters for months. But with me, I worried about all of them.

Mrs. Brown reported that her husband was physically and verbally abusive
to her, "especially when he drank." He was also unfaithful. She admitted, however, that if he had not objected to her visits and calls home the marriage could

have been "different." Despite her husband's cruelty, she wanted the marriage to succeed. Mr. Brown was neither a hard worker nor demonstrative to their children. Mrs. Brown was disappointed with his lack of ambition *and* fatherly love. Emotional and financial insecurity are linked in her memories of marital unhappiness.

> **Mrs. Brown:** In the beginning it was hard because he didn't make that much money and I couldn't work so we really had it tough.
> **Interviewer:** You mean financially?
> **Mrs. Brown:** Financially and the way he acted and treated me.
> **Interviewer:** He didn't treat you well?
> **Mrs. Brown:** No. He wasn't close to the children, like some fathers are, you know, they pick them up and kiss them and I don't ever remember him picking either one of my daughters up or changing their diapers or anything.
> **Interviewer:** So seeing that hurt you?
> **Mrs. Brown:** Oh, definitely, yes, definitely.

Mrs. Brown believes that she was treated badly because her daughters were ignored; she imagined the pain they felt because of their father's lack of affection. Ultimately, it was her husband's unwillingness to perform the role of "family man" that forced her to leave the home that she "scrimped and saved for" because "he just got too bad—with the drinking and what not." She found an apartment not far from the house she left; her children continued at the Catholic school they attended since kindergarten.

> The only thing I worried about was my health, that I'd be able to work and put them through high school, which thank God I did. The three of us got along very good together. Then my oldest daughter got out of high school and she started work and that made things a little bit easier. And then my youngest daughter got out of high school and that made things a lot easier.

While on her own, Mrs. Brown's goal was to make sure that both daughters got the high school education she missed. She said that as her daughters grew, she expected them to "keep up" a relationship with their father. Even after he re-married, she encouraged her daughters to visit him and welcome his visits. She is proud that both girls remained relatively close to him until his death.

> I never talked against him even after I left him. I just thought they were old enough to know what they wanted to do, you know, if they cared about him. And they did to a certain extent. They bought him birthday gifts and Christmas gifts and I never told them not to.

Mrs. Brown's two daughters are now middle-aged women. Both live nearby and maintain a "very close" relationship with each other and with Mrs. Brown. Their mother views them in the way that she sees herself—as defined by family roles.

> My oldest girl is married. She has two sons and they have children. My youngest, she's not married. But she takes in stray cats. She cares for them very much and it makes it like her family.

Although her younger daughter might have proved a disappointment to Mrs. Brown in terms of not marrying and having children, she redefined her daughter's concern for cats as "like her [having a] family." It is not surprising that Mrs. Brown describes suffering as the flip side of closeness with family members—losing them. For her, suffering is witnessing the illnesses and deaths of her mother, brothers, and sister that occurred "out of order."

> Seeing my family go (is the definition of suffering). The first one was my brother and he was only 46 years old. Somebody killed him. He was single, he was an alcoholic, but the way he died. . . . I said why did it have to happen to him?

Mrs. Brown shook her head at the recollection of her brother's random murder almost 30 years ago. Although she noted that he was unmarried, had no children and had tempted fate with "hard living," he did not deserve to be attacked by strangers and left for dead during an alcoholic binge. His violent death disturbed her belief that death has a proper pecking order.

> You know, being as old as I am, you think that the oldest would go first. And then down the line. But it doesn't work that way. My mother lost two (children) before she died. She never got over it. And now, with me, they're all gone. You never know.

In the past 15 years, Mrs. Brown's mother and all of her siblings died from various causes; she nursed most of them through their illnesses. When I asked her to describe a time of life when she felt she was suffering, she named her helplessness as she watched each family member die.

> One was when my mother was sick. I took care of her, but there wasn't anything I could do to help her. I took care of my sister and I felt bad for her because she used to like to get dressed up and go out and she couldn't do that any more. She needed the oxygen tank at all times. And I took care of my oldest brother for a while and my other brother for about a year. And thinking about my brother when he was killed. Did he call for us? So, it's (suffering) when you see somebody suffering and there's nothing you could do to help them. And they were younger than me. And they couldn't see their grandchildren grow up.

Mrs. Brown's suffering is based on the importance of family relationships—and the loss of them—to her self- and world-view. The role of caretaker is the primary fodder for Mrs. Brown's identity. With each family member's death, the role diminished and finally ceased. Her current question is not only: Why did I outlive my younger siblings? But also: Who am I without others to care for?

When I asked her what a picture of suffering would show, Mrs. Brown nodded, as though familiar with it.

> Somebody sick in bed and in pain and somebody watching. One would be trying. . . . Like when my mother had pains in her legs so bad, I tried everything, you know, rubbing things (ointments) on her legs.
> **Interviewer:** In your picture, who is suffering?
> **Mrs. Brown:** Both, in a different way. One is suffering pain and the other is suffering because someone you love is suffering and it makes you suffer, too.

Mrs. Brown's rich moral imagination holds a gallery of pictures. This gallery depicts not only her family's sufferings, but also how each of them would look and what they might be doing if they were alive. A portion of Mrs. Brown's suffering results from her identification with her family. Her story of suffering, like many respondents', is not just about *her* loss, but also what she imagines *her loved ones lost* because of their early deaths. When I asked her whether she thought there were different kinds of suffering, she answered:

> Well when a person is in pain, that's suffering really. And if someone is abusive to you like your spouse, that's suffering in a different way. And loss is real suffering because you think. . . . Even to this day, my mother, I still think of different things, and my sister and brother too.
> **Interviewer:** What do you mean different things?
> **Mrs. Brown:** About the pain, how she suffered toward the end there. And thinking about good times. During the war she made all those cookies. She got names of soldiers that didn't get any letters or packages and sent them cookies. There were cookies all over the kitchen and shoeboxes that she put them in. A lot of work, but she loved it.

Mrs. Brown's memory is a repository for family scenes. In her mind's eye, she sees her mother baking cookies for lonely soldiers, her sister "dressed up" for the holidays, the grandchildren her brothers did not live to see, her murdered brother's rakish smile. These pictures are both positives and negatives; their shadow side is that they cannot be developed further. They are snapshots frozen in a rich, relational past that contrasts with the solitary present.

When asked, Mrs. Brown did not differentiate among sadness, suffering and depression. She did, however, perceive a hierarchy of greater and lesser suffering. *Where* an event exists on the continuum of suffering concerns how she controls the effects of illness or loss. She explained.

> Well, loss is pretty bad because you know you're not going to see them anymore. So that one's the worst. Because pain sometimes is just temporary; it eases up. And abuse, I guess you just don't have to take all the abuse. You take it, thinking he might change. And when you see he doesn't, then *you* have to make a change, which I did (Mrs. Brown's emphasis).

Suffering is neither an interruption in life nor an external enemy to Mrs. Brown, as it was to Mr. Gordon. Suffering shows her that tragedies offer choices, no matter how unappealing each choice might be. *She* must choose to stay or leave a difficult marriage; she must decide whether to treat, ignore, or succumb to physical pain. In regard to her losses, the option offered is how to handle them—long for the past or be grateful for the present. Whatever choice she makes bears a cost that might bring more suffering. When I asked her if she thought suffering has any value, she said:

> Well, I think it (suffering) made me a stronger person and it made me stand up for my rights. Because I was very backward. So, it changed me that I have more nerve than I used to. And when you're younger and you suffer, I guess you grow up fast. And when you get older and you suffer, you're thankful when you feel good. See you wonder when you get to be this age—what day is your last?

For Mrs. Brown, every pleasure has a price tag; every sorrow has a gift. The suffering of spousal abuse was an impetus to change her worldview. She was forced to imagine a future without a husband but *with* self-esteem. The suffering of physical pain offers the relief of "feeling good" when the pain ends. The suffering of finitude makes a reward of each *extra* day of life. When I asked Mrs. Brown if, after a period of suffering, she felt differently about herself or the world, she answered:

> Well, after I left my husband I felt more free. I had a couple chances to get married again but I definitely didn't want to go through that again. Oh, I couldn't be bothered! (Laughter) So I thought I'd be better off, while I had my health and I was able to work, to support myself. (Pause) So that was pretty much the extent of my life.

Throughout the interview, Mrs. Brown ended her responses with: "And this was the extent of my life," or, "that was the limit of my life." Yet, her narrative showed that suffering broadened her life. For example, her husband's possessiveness shrunk her local world. Divorce forced her into a new world of *outside* work, single parenthood, risks, and freedom. It also strengthened her primary role as a caretaker. She spent much of her middle years caring for ill family members. I wondered if and how she maintained this identity after her mother and siblings died.

> **Interviewer:** You spent so much of your life taking care of others. Do you miss doing that?
> **Mrs. Brown:** (Pause) I'm worried about my daughter getting a job 'cause her husband is sickly and can't work, so I pray about that. And I worry about my younger daughter's health. I'd like to see her gain some weight.

Mrs. Brown responded to the question of whether she misses being a caretaker with a list of current worries. Yet her worry seemed neither neurotic nor obsessive. She translated her caretaking role into prayers for one daughter's employment and the other's health. Her concern for their well-being becomes a sort of mental caretaking. When asked how life is for her currently, she answered philosophically.

> You never know from day to day. Well, I know my mother was sick for a while before she died, and so were my two brothers and my sister. But you live one day at a time, I guess. Each day is like your last. You just try to do the best you can and wait until tomorrow and start over again.

Mrs. Brown's referent point for how she continues to live her life is her family. It is little surprise that family members are the lodestar for her thoughts about dying and death. She realizes that she may not be given "sick time" before death as did her mother and siblings. No matter what day is her last, it will be lived in caretaking, mentally and spiritually, the significant others who remain in her life.

MRS. RINK

Mrs. Rink is an 83-year-old African-American divorcee who lives in a high crime neighborhood in North Philadelphia. Her three-room apartment is triple bolted for safety. It is filled with clothes, furniture, boxes, papers, and odds and ends that she accumulated in the 40 years she has lived there. During our interview I sat on a cleared edge of her sofa; she sat on an overstuffed wing chair. When I was seated, Mrs. Rink pointed to a picture of a thin, smiling young man set atop the television and directly across from her chair. She described it as an "old" picture of her only child, a son who died recently. She explained that although she and her son enjoyed a "good" relationship, she did not "miss him so much" because they never lived together. She was not sure about the cause of his death or how old he was when he died. She seldom sees his four daughters because they are "busy with their own lives." When I asked her the story of her life, she answered:

> I'm going by what my mother said. And some I remember. I think I was born in South Carolina, but I was practically raised in North Carolina. Then I went to school and I didn't finish but I wished many days I had.

Mrs. Rink's opening words reveal a theme that threads her narrative: A good education would have changed the course of her life. In fact, during our time together, she worried that she was unable to understand the requirements of the interview because of her lack of education.

Mrs. Rink was the middle child in a family of seven siblings. One of her earliest memories is of her first job. She was nine years old.

> This white lady saw my sister and she say, "Do you know where I can get a little girl to sweep my sidewalk and bring in my coal and wood?" And that's what I did. And then later on she taught me everything about cleaning, cooking and sewing. She would always say: "Stay in school."

(Pause). I can read a little bit and I can count my money. I wish I had listened
to her. Because I'm sorry.

Mrs. Rink can read the newspaper but cannot always understand the point of
the article. She can pay her bills and expect the correct change from shopkeepers.
But she is convinced that limited education kept her from "bettering" herself
in several areas, such as finding a *good* job and marrying a *good* man. She links
the overarching mistake of quitting school at age 12 to "mistakes" she made
throughout life. She was 14 when she became pregnant and 15 when her son
was born. This theme of youthful mistakes connects her past to her present and
her life story to her story of suffering.

> You know how young girls are. Then (after giving birth) I didn't go back
> (to school) because of the mistake. My mother raised my son but I worked
> and helped them out. I always worked.

Mrs. Rink's mother demanded that Mrs. Rink be financially responsible for
her son, even though she was too young to raise him. She traveled from her small
hometown to a large North Carolina city and worked as a live-in domestic.
She sent money home for the baby's care regularly, but seldom visited. A year
after giving birth, she met a young man and married him several months later.
She was 16 years old. The couple found a third-floor room in a North Carolina
rooming house. She did not bring her year-old baby into the new home.

> See, he [husband] wasn't the baby's father, so he didn't care nothing about
> him. He just wanted me to see his family and go to his people. But he went
> out. You know what young men do.

She quickly realized that marriage was "another mistake." Although the couple
was "poor" and she was "lonely for company," her husband did not permit
her to work, go out with friends, or visit family. She describes the eight years
she lived with him as "misery." He was physically and emotionally abusive as
well as unfaithful.

Mrs. Rink's mother, siblings, and son eventually left North Carolina for
"better-paying jobs" in Philadelphia. She said that being "so far" from her
family played a part in her decision to "quit" her husband. One morning, after
he left for work, she hid at a girlfriend's house, then took the bus to Philadelphia
to find her mother. She did not see her husband again. Concerning her decision
to leave him, she said simply:

> I just quick packed up my clothes and came north. When I made up my
> mind, that was it.

Mrs. Rink moved into her sister's small apartment. Both women "made out
pretty good" working as domestics. She remembers having "a good time" her
first year in Philadelphia. She attended the dances, picnics, and parties that
she missed during her teenage years.

> I met the second husband a year or so after I come up here. Then I married
> him, but that was a mistake, too. After we got married he just started running
> around. I can't remember about him too good. But I remember good about
> the first one. I stayed with each one of them eight years apiece. But I didn't
> have too hard a time leaving the second one.

Mrs. Rink's first husband died in 1952. She felt "sad" when she recently
learned of his death, but did not feel real grief because "it (her marriage) was
so long ago." She had trouble remembering her second husband, but thought
that he was "probably dead." She said that life with both husbands seemed
dreamlike. When she thinks of each one of them and herself as a couple, it is as
though she is thinking of "other people."

> It was so long ago it wasn't like it was me. So, I just think about it and
> that's all. I don't feel sad about nothing. In fact I dreamed about my first
> husband last night. I laughed. I tell my girlfriend, we both laughed. See,
> it's like a dream.

Despite the blurred memories of her husbands and her marriages, when I asked
Mrs. Rink to relate an incident, event, or time period in her life when she was
suffering, she answered without hesitation.

> When I got married at 16, that's it. Because you know what young men do.
> So I left him, like I told you. But he was all I thought about. And I just
> wish I hadn't married him. And I got down on my knees and I asked the
> Lord to take him off my mind. I thought that was the only man in the world;
> I loved him so hard. Now that is bad, miserable, suffering.
> **Interviewer:** You wanted to forget him.
> **Mrs. Rink:** (with animation) Oh, yes! Just give him up! Get rid of him in
> my mind and just go on about my business, so I could be happy.

Although Mrs. Rink had physically "quit" her husband, she remained emotionally bound to him. Not even her second marriage could make her forget
her first love. She believed that only "God's power" kept her from "loving him
so hard." When I asked her to define suffering, she answered:

> Can't do what you want to do. Not be free. Tied up in some way.
> **Interviewer:** How were you tied up?
> **Mrs. Rink:** In my mind! I told you I asked the Lord to make me forget him.
> That's being tied up, don't you think?

Mrs. Rink's definition of suffering is an all-consuming hunger for this
young man. Suffering is to be physically "tied up" by her husband's control,
and emotionally by her inability to "get over him." She described herself
during this time as suffering a mental "weakness." She felt powerless to stop
imagining him with other women. Suffering was a bondage from which she felt
unable to escape. When I asked her what a picture of suffering would show,
she described herself:

That young girl there (herself) down on her knees, praying for the Lord to take
him off my mind. Oh, yes, that was suffering.

Mrs. Rink endured the death of her only son, was recently diagnosed with
cancer, is grieving over the deaths of two close friends, and fears that because of
her isolation she will "not be found for days maybe" after she dies. Yet her portrait
of suffering shows herself almost 70 years ago as a woman obsessed with an
unfaithful man and praying to be released from that obsession. The power of her
description is its portrayal of an individual confounded by love and worry, which
according to Mrs. Rink, make up two sides of the same emotion.

Love, Love makes you do that. Because when I was with him, all the time
I was worried, and I was worried because I loved him, and I was suffering
because he wasn't doing right.

Unlike Mrs. Brown, for whom worry became the mental dimension of caretaking, for Mrs. Rink, worry is the negative side of love. When Mrs. Rink was
asked about subtle forms of suffering, such as guilt, regret, or an inability
to forgive or perceive oneself as forgiven, she shook her head in agreement
and restated her sorest regret—a "better" education would have improved her
life in several ways—from marrying well to verbalizing her thoughts during
the interview.

See, that's the same thing I'm talking about. If I had a lot of education maybe
I could tell you all these things I'm thinking. But I can only think them
and I can't say them.

Mrs. Rink thinks that she cannot articulate complex emotions. Her perceived
inability to communicate is a form of being "tied up"; she hesitates to share her
opinions with others. Faltering over words shames her. When I asked her if being
older and closer to the end of life is a form of suffering, Mrs. Rink replied:

I guess it is because you can't do what you could do when you was young.
The best part of your life is your young life. And when you get older you
can't do the things that you did when you was young. And it's no use to try.
So that's suffering, too.

It is interesting that the best part of her life, as well as her most intense
suffering, occurred when she was young. Old age as suffering supports her
image of suffering as being "tied up." She is restrained by mental and physical
limitations; she can no longer "go and do." Sitting on the porch and "watching
all them young peoples running around," is a major activity. She clarified that
she would have it no other way; it is "right" to act one's age and futile to
fight against it. She offered concrete examples of how a person *should* approach
later life.

Since I got older I try to live right and I don't try to do what I did when I
was young—drink, smoke. You're supposed to change when you get older,

> and if you do the Lord is not going to let you suffer. Now I have a girlfriend, she's been in the hospital going on 3 months. She was diabetic, she had heart trouble and she still tried to live the life that a young person was living.

Her comment hearkens both to the Biblical command to "put away childish things" when one reaches adulthood, and a Western cultural injunction to be accountable for one's actions. Like Mr. Gordan, Mrs. Rink views some suffering in old age as inevitable if people fail to change their activities in light of their limitations. Mrs. Rink said that many of her life's "good times" came from dancing, drinking, and enjoying the "night life." She explained:

> See, I haven't drunk nothing since '86.
> **Interviewer:** What happened in 1986?
> **Mrs. Rink:** I lost my hearing aid. And I know that was a warning, wasn't it? Because if I hadn't been drinking, I wouldn't have lost it. The Lord warned me. So I stopped.

Mrs. Rink's picture of God is a stern sentinel who demands a different spiritual etiquette for each stage of life. But God knew she heeded his warning—it was time to step from middle adulthood into old age and act accordingly. Despite regret for her "mistakes," she is now "living right" and God is happy with her. Her proof comes from the fact that because God mandated the Golden Rule, he must live by it.

> The way I look at it, the Lord must be satisfied with me, because I'm still alive. Both my husbands—the way they treated me, and they dead. I try to treat people right. In other words, if you do good unto others, you'll have [good] done to you. See, now I'm up in age and I don't have nothing really to be sad about. When I look at my girlfriend, she laying there, trying to talk and walk, and she can't. Now, they can't help themselves like I can with two legs.

Although Mrs. Rink is "tied up" by the limitations of old age, she knows contemporaries who are more tied up by pain and illness, and compares herself favorably to them. Like many elders, she lowered the ceiling on the level of independence she needs to retain self-esteem. At the end of the interview, when I asked her if she wanted to add anything to our discussion, she posed her own question:

> Now and with age, I forgot some things. Did I do all right (with the interview)?

Mrs. Rink believed she was "not up to" the requirements of the interview. She wondered whether she comprehended my questions, and whether she responded properly. Like most human beings, she questioned whether she was able to understand and be understood, and to communicate and connect. Mrs. Rink believes that more education would make her happier with herself. I doubted that with more education she would have drawn a sharper picture, or told a clearer story of suffering.

GENDER AND SUFFERING

There are many descriptions of gender, such as: an artifact, a category, as contextual, and as distinct from "sex," to name just a few. These descriptions show gender's processual and transformable nature. Likewise, suffering as a phenomenon of lived experience is subject to the vagaries of time and place, and is interpreted as such through an embodied person. If the meanings of both concepts—gender and suffering—are fluid and changeable, can the essence of a gendered experience of suffering ever be captured by narrating it? Words that describe an experience are not the same as the experience. But relating the experience of suffering through the perception of gender allows a glimpse into the experience through its expression.

Experiences and expressions of suffering are often connected to expectations that individuals have about their lives and qualities that are integral to one's identity. Men and women in this study did not speak specifically about how they thought their lives would unfold, except in "large" terms of marriage, parenthood and work. Perhaps not surprisingly, no one in the sample said that when younger, they "expected" to suffer.

The major events of Mr. Gordan's life seemed to occur through happenstance. Entering the service, meeting his wife, and mourning her loss resulted from situations for which he did not plan. Caretaking defined Mrs. Brown's life, the story of her life and her story of suffering. The invisible, emotion work of caretaking is often connected to a lack of validation, lowered self-esteem, and perhaps to suffering. This was not the case with Mrs. Brown. She needed no audience but herself and her family to feel needed, valued, and self-confident in her role as caretaker. It was losing the job of caretaking through death that brought her suffering. Mrs. Rink hinted throughout the interview that it was a woman's lot to be constrained by a man. Not suffering equaled freedom from restraints. It was the memory, perhaps, that this did not have to be a woman's lot that brought her suffering. Looking back at the person she was, tied up by love and worry, was a terrible sight for her.

A feature of suffering in respondents' narratives is that of *time*. Each elder had a personal notion of time in suffering. Suffering interrupted Mr. Gordan's sense of time and the flow of his life. Cessation of suffering signaled the resumption of the flow. Mrs. Brown's experience of suffering as loss is ongoing; she will live out her life missing her family. For Mrs. Rink, suffering is a moment fixed in time. This moment is represented by a picture of a young woman obsessed with unrequited love. Although the picture is as clear to her as her own reflection, the moment itself is so distant that she cannot experience that young woman as herself. Although the memory of suffering is not a part of Mr. Gordan's life in the way that it remains for Mrs. Brown, it is also not as distant and as embodied as it is for Mrs. Rink.

The concept of control emerged differently in Mrs. Brown's and Mrs. Rink's experiences of suffering, yet remained significant to their definitions and stories of suffering. In both cases, their husbands possessed and imposed control over them. Their suffering came not so much from losing control, but from foolishly giving it away. *Not* suffering, ultimately, was regaining control over their lives. Similarly, losing control to fate or to the unknown other who was responsible for his wife's death was significant to Mr. Gordan's notion of suffering.

The word "control" had different connotations for male and female respondents. Men believed they suffered when they lost control over themselves, their bodies through illness, or over the health or well-being of loved ones placed in their care. For women, taking control of their lives in order to change a difficult situation meant an end to suffering.

I note a pattern found across men's and women's narratives of suffering: the relational nature of suffering. Suffering occurs through connection and broken connection, through the relationship that one has with one's self, one's body, with others, with God, with the severing of those relationships, and the attempt to reconnect.

THE NEXT CHAPTER

Chapter 4 focuses on the body in pain. Elders reveal through their narratives that although the body cannot stand outside the experience of suffering, neither can the pained body communicate respondents' entire story of suffering.

CHAPTER 4

Pain and Bodily Suffering

Suffering certainly speaks of the body—the wounded body, the tortured body, the diseased body. But the pain of phantom limbs, of the paralyzed body, and the somatic symptoms of mental illness communicate both that the body "remembers" missing parts and that pain is more than bodily—one suffers as a whole person according to a personal and communal history, a culture that gives meaning to the experience of pain at a particular place in time, and offers a template for appropriate expressions of pain (Kleinman, 1992; Murphy, 1987; Sacks, 1984; Scheper-Hughes & Lock, 1987).

Suffering can shrink the world of the sufferer at the same time that it is experienced as boundless and without end. This *illogical* nature of suffering is reflected in respondents' tacit discussion of the paradox of pain. During pain, the sensation that one is both separate from and tied to one's body is common. One feels both unrelated to one's body and bedeviled by it; the body (or parts of it) seems ruptured from the "I" who both watches and experiences the pain. One both has and is a body that rebels (Black, 2001; Charmaz, 1999; Murphy, 1987; Scarry, 1985).

Suffering as bodily pain shows the contingency of the body; one cannot depend on one's body (Frank, 1995) and its *normal* functioning. Because pain is considered a forerunner of the aging process (Brody, 1987), and the interiority and limitation of pain often mime old age, elders grant a double-lensed view of suffering as pain. For ill elders, there may be little time or stamina to actively work toward healing, and depending on the cause of pain, such as a chronic or terminal ailment, there may be little likelihood of improvement.

For elders, the contingency of the pained body may extend to life itself. Pain usually alters an elder's social life; personal relationships shrink and social roles lose balance. One can no longer depend on life or the self as it was, as will be eloquently stated by respondents in this chapter. Pain also evokes thoughts of mortality; individuals suffer through the anticipation of more or greater pain, through not knowing its genesis, or believing that it signals death. One goal for the person in pain is to find its cause, seek treatment, and eventually be pain-free. If no cause is found, pain becomes purposeless, which is a common description of suffering (Cassell, 1992). To perceive suffering solely as bodily pain fails to address the all-encompassing nature of suffering that elders describe in their narratives. For example, when faced with chronic pain, an elder may imagine that death, not healing, is pain's end. Thoughts of finitude give pain in old age an ominous shape that "threatens the intactness of the person"—which is Cassell's (1982) oft-used definition of suffering. Thoughts of finitude also pose a question: In older age, does the end of pain come as healing or as death?

In the previous chapter we explored suffering as a gendered phenomenon. I expand on this notion in regard to suffering and the body. As mentioned, men attempt to separate pain from other aspect of their lives, such as roles or relationships in order to divorce pain from their identity. Some research shows that older men often compare themselves favorably to others in their age group in regard to "getting around," despite pain (Rubinstein, Kilbride, & Nagy, 1992).

Women's perception that the appearance and usefulness of the body are all of a piece engenders a holistic reaction to both health and illness (Brennan et al., 1993). Female respondents, similar to their male counterparts, spoke of bearing pain quietly. They generally did not bracket it from other parts of their lives, even when they "ignored" it. Certainly, pain affects both men's and women's relationships with others. But women were able to share their "pains" without risk to self-esteem. The ability to verbalize the effect of pain on the self plays a significant part in coping with it.

Both men and women feel individually responsible for keeping the aging body pain-free. Elders often attempt, and sometimes at peril to their well-being, to continue routines that were begun before pain. This attempt forces an impossible task upon elders: To show the world that old age is simply an extension of middle-age. Otherwise, there may be a risk of revealing that one's core, without the props of health or youth, is simply a body whose borders have "broken down" (Murphy, 1987).

Here I present cases of elders who define suffering as the "terrible pain" or "physical agony" that they or close others experienced. Their life stories and stories of suffering offer multidimensional pictures: Past and present experiences of joy and sorrow, roles as family members and workers, and the future that they anticipate or dread, provide complex contexts that both frame and inform their definition of suffering as pain.

MR. INGLUND

Mr. Inglund is a 77-year-old European-American man. He lives in a row home on a narrow street in Northeast Philadelphia with his wife and divorced, middle-aged son. His wife, who also participated in this study and is introduced in a later chapter, suggested that her husband be interviewed. When I asked Mr. Inglund to tell me his life story, he began this way:

I was born and raised in North Philadelphia. That's the badlands today. My parents had two homes. They never bought; always rented. When the war broke out I went into the service, the United States Air Force. I served 4 years in the Army and when I came out I had a little difficulty settling into a job. I believe I had 20 jobs before I finally settled down (chuckles).

Mr. Inglund then listed the jobs he held. By beginning his life story with his work history, he showed that work of any sort remains integral to his identity. The significance of work resides in the type of work he did, and in the fact that he "always worked" even if the job was "just delivering circulars" in order to support his family.

I met my wife at a New Year's Eve party. I was about 18. I married her while I was in the service. She came out to New Mexico and we got married there in the air base. Married a few days and I was shipped out. She was 17. I must have been about 21. Then we had Luke, then Sue, then Mark (children). Luke was born mentally retarded. And we coped with him at home for quite a while and then we finally had to put him in an institution. He became sick there. Something got lodged in his lung. (Pause) I don't really know what happened. And he passed away during the operation.
Interviewer: What a terrible shock.
Mr. Inglund: I guess it was. (Pause) I made all the arrangements. My wife was in the hospital.

Mr. Inglund did not name the ailment that sent his wife to the hospital; I knew about her illness because I interviewed her (Mrs. Inglund, discussed in Chapter 6) previously. He clarified that he arranged for his son's funeral without input from his wife, and his aloneness added to his grief. He named the year following his son's death as the saddest time in his life.

My wife was in the hospital. I was on my own completely, you might as well say because my daughter was married and I can't remember where Mark was. I made arrangements for the burial of Luke, like I said. And I thought that was pretty rough.
Interviewer: I can't imagine the pain of that.
Mr. Inglund: We didn't expect it. You don't expect it. Well, the only thing that made me get through is. . . . I had no plot at the time. And my sister came forward and she had one grave at Sunnydale Memorial Park and she gave it to me. And we buried him. And then it made me realize that things weren't ever going to be the same, and so I purchased graves up there for the family.

Luke's death changed Mr. Inglund's worldview; it gave a before and after quality to the rest of his life. It showed him that despite his best effort, he could not shield his family from illness, sorrow, or death. The fact that his sister "came forward with a plot" was an act of mercy for him; the plot gave him a final chance to fulfill his role as Luke's provider. After his son's death, he performed an important ritual in honor of his *new* worldview—he purchased burial plots for himself and the rest of his family. He became aware of the gravity of his role as breadwinner; he found a factory job where he worked for the next 35 years.

> Yeah, anything can change. And now more than ever, anything can change.
> **Interviewer:** Why now more than ever?
> **Mr. Inglund:** Well, I have a sick wife, so I think everything is uncertain, that's the only way I can put it.

Mr. Inglund became acquainted with suffering because of Luke's death. His wife is now introducing him to anticipatory grief. She is on the waiting list of several nearby Catholic nursing homes, but he "knows" that she will die before she "gets in." He is prepared for her death because she "suffers continuously." He recently lost another close family member.

> My sister died two weeks ago. Cancer. Most of our adult life we were close. We used to go up to their house and have parties—the wife, our kids, their kids. And we used to have cookouts, all that stuff. We used to watch the ball games. I was diagnosed with Parkinson's this year. That's it! It's all gone. It feels like a void in my life.

The loss of his sister represents the end of an era. His degenerating illness poses another loss—a vital younger man now feels old. When I asked Mr. Inglund if he was able to talk to anyone about his worries, he shook his head from side to side. He reached into the distant past to explain why he remains silent.

> When Luke passed away I said something to one of the guys at work. I told him I felt pretty bad. I wanted to talk. But he had problems, too. He had a wife with diabetes and she passed away. So you know what I mean? He wasn't able to talk.

Mr. Inglund worried that to speak of *his* sadness would be disrespectful to the other man—his cup was already full of sorrow. Or, to share *his* grief might seem to minimize his co-worker's loss. Whatever the case, the picture of two men standing next to each other on a factory assembly line, both cowed by grief but remaining silent, is poignant indeed. Their silence speaks to their roles as husbands and fathers in a generation that encouraged men to be quiet in the face of suffering. The rules of communication that he followed so many years ago remain appropriate for him today.

When I asked him to define suffering, Mr. Inglund answered, "Agony. Physical agony." He connects sadness with his son's death, and suffering with physical pain. When I asked him what a picture of suffering would show, he replied:

> It would be people with different types of diseases, such as diabetes and heart disease. That's suffering. People who are suffering, like my own wife.

His wife is the major figure in a portrait populated with suffering others. There is no background scene or color to Mr. Inglund's picture, only the nameless people he sees in doctors' offices and hospitals. When I asked him if he had ever suffered, he answered:

> Well, I didn't know I had an aneurysm and I went in the hospital. The following day they operated. And talk about suffering. I'd say it was worse than the (heart) by-pass. 'Cause I had a by-pass earlier. But, with this (aneurysm) they stapled me up; they use ordinary staples. And they sent me home too early and I started spurting from the guts.

Mr. Inglund's description of suffering is graphic and visceral. He uses words that show the violence of pain, such as being torn "from the guts." The silent efficient body, disregarded prior to pain, became a strange entity that "burst apart" and demanded "stapling up."

Although Mr. Inglund defined suffering as pain, he revealed later in the interview that he had "gone through" other types of suffering. When I asked him to explain, he lowered his voice, pointed to the living room wall, and leaned close to me.

> What's happened with our neighbors (gestures toward the wall). It's very bad, very bad.
> **Interviewer:** What happened?
> **Mr. Inglund:** It all began over the handicap poles. So help me, that's the honest to God truth. I put them up for Millie (wife), you know, with her arthritis. The only thing he (neighbor) said to me was, "If you put up those poles, I'll have to move." Now, that's a simple ass thing to say. Ever since then, they've been archenemies.

The Inglunds and their neighbors had been friendly until handicap poles were legally placed in front of the Inglunds' home. Because his neighbor owns two vehicles and often used part of the Inglunds' parking space on the small street, the poles forced the younger man to park one of his cars a few blocks away. Mr. Inglund explained that when his neighbors realized the poles were not coming down, they began to torment the older couple. They bang on their mutual wall during the night, play loud music, and teach their children to call the Inglunds "dirty names." Mr. Inglund believes that his neighbors' behavior is meant to exacerbate his wife's health problems so they will move.

> They gave her (wife) a heart attack by aggravating her. We had to call the police one day. He (neighbor) says to me, "Come on, put your mitts up." I wanted to punch him in the mouth. Millie screamed. I said, "You're not worth it." I walked in the house. But Millie went out and he kept on badgering her about the poles. He just kept it up. She passed out. When she got in the house we had to call the ambulance. She was having a heart attack.

As Mr. Inglund tells his story, he makes a fist with his right hand and gestures toward the wall. He is disappointed with the fickleness of his neighbors' past affection. He knew that his wife's attempt to explain the situation to them was not only useless but also harmful to her. He is also disappointed with himself. He recognizes that, because of his age, he cannot protect his wife or himself from the younger man's assaults and name-calling. He is again faced with an unpredictable event that challenges his manhood, and feels unable to handle it in a way that would raise rather than lower his self-esteem.

> Things happen at this time of life that didn't happen in the beginning of your life.
> **Interviewer:** Can you give me an example?
> **Mr. Inglund:** Well, things you don't expect, like your wife will have to go into a nursing home and maybe eventually you'll have to go into a nursing home. And with this thing next door. It's unpredictable.

Although Mr. Inglund offered his definition of suffering as physical agony, his narrative complicates that definition. He would like to map his roles as husband and father onto a desired identity as "hero." The tragic events of past and present conspire to challenge his fitness for that identity. In old age, the roles of husband and father remain, but the identity of hero cannot hold in the face of illness, death, and the cruelty of others.

MRS. KEAN

Mrs. Kean is an 80-year-old European-American woman who lives alone in a senior facility in Center City. Perhaps because she saw me looking at the various items that fill her apartment, such as a large screen television, a band radio, and various electronic gadgets, her first comment was that her middle-aged son often gives her presents, such as a VCR, a boom box, and cable television that *he* enjoys when he visits her.

When I asked her to tell me the story of her life, Mrs. Kean chuckled and sighed, then offered a laundry list of her life's events.

> First of all, I was born in Hungary. And secondly I had a stepfather. I never knew my real father. Whatever happened, why I did get into this world, I'll never know, my mother would never tell me. I lived with my grandmother in Hungary, then they [mother and stepfather] brought me here [to America]. I wish they never did.

Mrs. Kean contemplates the mystery of her existence. She explained that her childhood was unhappy—after her beloved grandmother died when she was 14, she was forced to come to America to live with an unloving mother and a distant stepfather. At 19 she married a man "just to get out of the house," and because she hoped that she could "make a home" with him. Unfortunately, her husband was alcoholic, "not a worker," and incapable of providing for his wife and their only child. She left him after three years of marriage. After leaving work one evening her husband accosted her "for money." Because of this incident, she gave up their son for adoption. She explained that she was afraid that her husband "would sell the child for drink."

Despite the tremendous losses that she endured at an early age, especially giving up her son, she spent only five minutes of interview time relating these events. A theme, however, did emerge in her brief life story—that any misfortune was "all [her] fault"—because she had been "so stupid to make so many mistakes at a young age," such as marrying an alcoholic and conceiving a child with him. She admitted one positive quality about herself—she was a hard worker. The number of hours she worked in food services kept worry from overwhelming her.

> I always had a place to go to work and forget about everything and just work. Just work it off. And I never backed off of working.

Work was Mrs. Kean's refuge. Its demands on her time and energy subsumed the interpersonal roles in her life, such as daughter, wife, and mother that "fell apart" through the years. She often worked double shifts for extra money; she visited her son at his adoptive parents' home every other week.

Work provided Mrs. Kean a continuous theme throughout her life. "Work, work, work, that's all I did," she sighed. Because other aspects of life took second place to her role as worker, she hesitated when asked to remember the saddest time in life. After a long pause, she replied:

> Well . . . I used to have an aunt who was like my real home. I used to work at S. Hospital and every night I used to go down [to her aunt's home] because she lived close and she was a good cook. She used to make goulash, if you ever heard of that. I know how to eat it but I don't know how to make it. When she passed away, I really felt bad. Because she was more than an aunt, you know.

Home was not the place she lived with her mother and stepfather, nor the place she shared with her husband. Mrs. Kean strings the words "home" and "aunt" together. Her aunt becomes the memory and myth of how life should be. Her own unattainable goal of "making a home" had been realized to perfection by her aunt. Her aunt's house, filled with food and warmth, was not only home, but also a symbol of real affection in a world filled with the illusions of love and safety.

When I asked Mrs. Kean the question, "Was there a time in your life when you felt that you were suffering?" she did not give likely responses in light of her past, such as poverty, loneliness, divorce, and especially, giving up her child. Instead, Mrs. Kean replied:

> The most I'm suffering is right now. Because I don't seem to get any help really. I go to three different doctors and I get all this medicine. But you know, just like now, I feel like everything that's going on in here [points to head] is woozy. So what is it? It has to be something. Like one of the doctors said, "What do you expect? You're 80." Well, there are people

who are 80 and 85. They get a new heart.
Interviewer: So, he's saying this is what happens when you get older.
Mrs. Kean: Exactly. I know that everything doesn't work as properly when you're older, that I know. But to forever be dizzy and not be able to. . . . In other words I would like to do what I used to do, walk without a cane. Now, there's something that's making me not be able to walk. What is it?

Mrs. Kean's suffering is rooted in her present poor health. Her severe symptoms and their uncertain source seem to obliterate thoughts about her past. She is convinced that there is external proof for what is "going on inside [her]"— if she could just find the concrete "something" that causes her to suffer. Mrs. Kean has looked, without success, to her doctors for help. The fact they do not take her symptoms seriously adds to her misery.

Like one doctor said, "What do you want me to do, take you to the fountain of youth?" I said, "No, I just want to feel better." They just like make fun of you. I guess they think, oh, she's an old woman; she's imagining everything.

Her doctors' paternalism offends Mrs. Kean. A psychiatrist suggested that her "wooziness" resulted from depression, but she carefully differentiated the constructs of depression, sadness and suffering.

If you're depressed, everything just doesn't go the way you want it to go. I'm not depressed. I'm after finding out what in the world is going on inside my head. And I'm not sad! I know what I could do if I could do it. They think I'm depressed. They think I'm sad. I think I'm disgusted.

Mrs. Kean's statement—"I know what I could do if I could do it" testifies to her desire to accomplish realistic goals—to be able to do housework, stop at the market, or simply take a walk. She is aware, like her doctors, that depression and sadness sap energy. But she believes that her physical problems are "hiding" her energy; it will be released as soon as she is cured. Mrs. Kean's use of the word "disgust" to describe her feelings about doctors' unwillingness to "hear" her speaks to her frustration with them. If only they would listen and act! When I asked her to define suffering, Mrs. Kean answered definitively:

Well, I can't go to the bathroom unless I take laxatives. But it has to come out somehow. That's suffering because it hurts all over. And then I have an overactive bladder. I think I have to go and before I get there it's out. Too much the one way, nothing the other.

Each part of Mrs. Kean's body is conspiring against her. She perceives the mechanism of her body as "breaking down," and watches this breakdown with a sort of helpless confusion. Her body is the medium through which she discloses herself not only to others, but also to herself. If she does not understand her body's unfamiliar language, how can she explain it to indifferent doctors?

Mrs. Kean's comments also show the taken-for-granted aspect that her body will perform as expected. While her "healthy" body presupposed all of her prior activities, its gradual obstinacy seems a surprising contingency. As her body closes in on her, the miniaturization of her suffering is as intense as it is reduced. Her body is the place where the unknown meaning of her life, as she endures symptom after symptom, is played out.

Mrs. Kean stresses that she was "never" ill. During childhood, youth, and adulthood, "I never thought about my body," she said proudly. It is only with age that she is aware of its peculiarities. Perhaps the strangeness of her suffering made a few of the interview questions difficult to answer, such as my request for her to imagine what situations make other people suffer. Perhaps because she focuses so intensely on the betrayal of her body, she struggles with empathy. Perhaps because the intricacies of her own mind and body seem beyond her ken, it is difficult for her to envision the mental and physical workings of others.

When I asked Mrs. Kean about her son, she admitted: "he might suffer." She explained that he "never" worked at a paying job, is presently on disability for "mental problems" and described him as a loner. Although she wonders what goes on in his mind, she is reluctant to ask him about this, perhaps because mother and son "never talked about stuff like that." She is not sure what triggered his "problem" because his adoptive parents "never gave a clue that anything was wrong [with him]."

> **Mrs. Kean:** He joined the service when he was 21 and he was doing good. When he came back, he seemed different. Whatever happened, I don't know. And that worries me. What's going to happen to him? They [government] want to stop welfare. He has nobody that he could go to like he can to me [Pause]. See, I think at times my son suffers because he's very handy and he was very interested in electronics and he still is. All this stuff here, here and here [pointing to different gadgets around the room] they're all his. I just wonder. I never ask him whether he would have a chance to try to work somewhere. I think he never fulfilled himself. Like he started at community college, but then. . . . In other words, he starts things and he doesn't want to finish it. So he left college and didn't go further.
> **Interviewer:** How do you think this is suffering?
> **Mrs. Kean:** Well, I don't know what his real feelings are, I can't get myself imagining myself in his mind or body, but I always felt that when you start something you ought to keep on doing it, sticking to it. So, yeah, I think that he's suffering.

An image of suffering for Mrs. Kean is that of her son—a middle aged man who has never worked and cannot finish what he starts. The way he spends his time—visiting his mother to watch television and listen to music—is not, in her opinion, fulfilling. In fact, his life is unimaginable to someone for whom work *was* life. Although she worries about her son's future, especially after her

death, she stands as a sad observer of his life. She feels shy in asking him about
the past, the events that "changed" him, or what currently motivates him.

When I asked her what a picture of suffering would show, Mrs. Kean answered,
"I'm not good at drawing." When gently pressed to visualize what would be in
the picture, she chuckled.

> **Mrs. Kean:** Me, I guess.
> **Interviewer:** What would you look like?
> **Mrs. Kean:** Another thing—my hair is falling out. I can't even hardly comb
> it. So, it would be me, with no hair [chuckle].
> **Interviewer:** What would you be doing in the picture?
> **Mrs. Kean:** [Serious] Okay, the picture would be me and I'd be wishing I
> could find out myself just what's going on inside of me and do something
> about it.

Mrs. Kean poignantly portrays herself as both subject and object of a body
that has become "foreign territory." While its borders have "broken down" to
suffering, they are not razed sufficiently for her to see inside herself. She would
like to stand outside, witness her suffering objectively and somehow prove the
reality of it to anyone who asks, especially her doctors.

Mrs. Kean's picture of suffering shows her without hair. Hair loss symbolizes
age and illness, as well as the identity crises that occur in later life. Who are
we and who have we become to others when we look old and unfamiliar to
ourselves? Mrs. Kean readily admits that she focuses "too much" on herself,
but rationalizes her self-scrutiny.

> I would like to see what's going on in here [points to head]. I mean I'd like
> to get away from myself. I guess people think that's all she thinks of is
> herself. But I'm really not. I don't want to think of myself all the time but
> it's always with me. You can't get away from yourself!

Mrs. Kean's profound statement testifies to the all-encompassing nature of
suffering. She both watches and experiences her pain; she imagines "getting
away," but knows she cannot escape herself. She poignantly shows that the crises
of her body are also crises of self-knowledge and spirit.

> It feels like my eyes are full of liquid or something. And then sometimes
> I just fall. Something inside of me just gives out. I just go down. Everytime
> I go down I wind up on the back of my head. My head must be full
> of something, full of bumps. My feet feel like they don't have any life
> in them, like a piece of brick is in there. And right here underneath my
> tongue, it bothers me, it hurts, it feels like there's too much of something
> in there.

Mrs. Kean is full of her own body. Her bowels, bladder, and tongue have
expanded beyond her capacity to see what is wrong with them, because her
eyes are also "full." Her lack of control extends to her legs. Since she "just goes

down," her head is now also "full of bumps." Some parts of her are too "full," while other parts are "weak" or "have no life in them." Her depiction of falling apart speaks of the body's destruction; its impact on her is cognitive, emotional, and spiritual. At the end of the interview, when I asked her if she would like to add anything to our discussion on suffering, she considered, then laughed.

> **Mrs. Kean:** Yeah, try and get a magician to go like this (waves hand).
> **Interviewer:** To wave it all away. I wish I could.

Mrs. Kean sees the resolution to her suffering as existing in the realm of fantasy. She suffers because she cannot "get to the bottom" of the inexplicable workings of her own body. She believes that her doctors are unwilling to help her because of her age. The mystery of her existence has been reduced to the mystery of her suffering and expanded to encompass her entire world.

MRS. McDOWD

Mrs. McDowd is an 82-year-old African-American widow who lives in a subsidized housing facility. She called "come in" when I knocked at her unlocked apartment. She sat in a wheelchair in the middle of her living room. Her left arm was connected to a machine that I later learned "drains [her] lymph nodes because after surgery [she] doesn't perspire anymore." Before I turned on the tape recorder, she remarked that her extra weight exacerbated her "many [physical] problems." When I asked her to tell me the story of her life, she answered:

> I had a happy childhood. I had a wonderful mother and father. And I had one sister. And we was all close.

Mrs. McDowd said nothing more after these few sentences. Each prompt I offered elicited one word or one sentence answers. She was born in South Carolina and came to Philadelphia with her parents and sister when she was 25 years old. She met her husband "at one of the jobs [she] found here." She described herself as a "quick breeder" who had five children in quick succession. When I noticed a myriad of family pictures on her tables and walls, I asked whether her children live nearby.

> I *had* five. Three living. Two deceased. [Mrs. McDowd's emphasis]
> **Interviewer:** Is there anything you'd like to tell me about your life?
> **Mrs. McDowd:** Well I don't really have nothing. The onliest good thing is that I had a happy childhood but it seemed like after I got grown and got married things start changing. While I lived on K. Street I had a cancer in my right breast. And before that I had a hysterectomy. And then I got down with high blood pressure. And since I've lived here I've had a cancer in the left breast.

Mrs. McDowd had difficulty beginning her narrative, perhaps because she believed a life story should balance joy and sorrow—unlike the way she viewed her own life, which seemed weighted with tragedy. Or perhaps because she knew that this interview concerned experiences of suffering, she focused on what she thought I wanted to hear about—her illnesses. When I asked her about the saddest time in her life, she answered:

> The saddest time of my life was when my son got killed. I mean I was sad when my husband died, and when my mother and my father and my sister died. And when my oldest son died with the kidney trouble. But the saddest. . . . I almost had a nervous breakdown when the man stabbed my younger son. Oh, that was horrible.
> **Interviewer:** When did this happen?
> **Mrs. McDowd:** I can't tell you right now because I have pushed that so far back in my conscious so I don't even remember the person. I don't even let myself think about that. Not no more. I almost had a nervous breakdown.

Like many respondents, Mrs. McDowd ranked her sorrows. The greater the sorrow, such as the murder of her son, the less she allowed that memory to surface. But she stands on the brink of recalling her son's murder on a certain date each year.

> But every Fourth of July. . . . See, that's his birthday and we were going to have a party and it [the murder] happened at the end of June. So that holiday kind of stirs me up. Because, see, this thing was heavy. The onliest thing that got me through was work. Oh, I loved my work.

For many respondents, both male and female, hard work was an analgesic for the pain of losing a loved one. Mrs. McDowd operated a steam machine in the laundry room of a large food company for over 30 years. She described the work as strenuous but important and remembered her superiors and co-workers as "people who loved me." She retired from this job reluctantly. She was in her mid-60s when her mother suffered a stroke.

> She was supposed to stay with me for three months, but I took care of her for seven years [chuckle]. And it was kind of rough because I had to do most of the lifting and bathing and everything. And my sister wasn't too much help. She had her own family.

During this time, Mrs. McDowd received little physical or financial support from any source "especially when [she] could have used it." When I asked if her husband was supportive while she cared for her mother, she said that they had separated by that time. She shook her head as she remembered those years of caregiving. She recalled the routine of her life as occurring in a "kind of a haze—I was just doing what I had to do, day by day, night by night." She describes her mother's death as a "relief for both of us." Shortly after her mother died, Mrs. McDowd fell sick with cancer. When asked to name a period in her life when she suffered, she recalled:

When I had that cancer. I really felt that I was suffering then.
Interviewer: What made that suffering for you?
Mrs. McDowd: Ummm. The pains. I had terrible pains and the burns from the radiation. My breasts were just raw.

For Mrs. McDowd, suffering is the physical pain that resulted not only from breast cancer but also from the cure of radiation. When she first learned of her illness she urged her family to "keep it quiet" because of the shame she attached to it. Her embarrassment about cancer and ignorance about its cause and prevalence became a dimension of the disease that added to her suffering.

Down south I never heard of cancer or things like that. And when I heard that I had cancer I told my children, don't tell nobody. I was ashamed. But I'm not anymore. As I went along to the radiation place and seen all those other people that have it and talk with them, I see. I understand about cancer now. Anybody can get it.

Mrs. McDowd's misperception about cancer was that only certain types of people—those who are different from her and "her people"—get particular diseases. Her worldview [and view of cancer] was re-produced by communication; talking with cancer survivors showed her that the disease was color-blind and affected all income and social statuses. Cancer and its painful remedies became normalized in her mind when she realized "anybody can get it." When asked what a picture of suffering would show, Mrs. McDowd considered:

Well, I would have some of that crying in there that I did from the pains I had. Then I would want the Lord to be in that picture. Because he would take away the suffering. See, suffering has nothing to do with the Lord. That's the work of Satan.

This picture speaks to Mrs. McDowd's assumptive world. Her portrait of suffering shows a cosmic duel between good and evil. Suffering represents evil and the Lord represents the power that overcomes this evil. Although this picture might seem simplistic, the duality between good and evil is offset by her nuanced distinction among the constructs of sadness, depression, and suffering. Sadness followed the murder of her son. Suffering was the pain she felt undergoing radiation therapy. When I asked her to define depression, she considered:

I think depression is worse than suffering because after my son died, I started having anxiety attacks. And if you never had them, when they come on, you think you're dying. So I think depression's worse than the other two. When you're suffering and when you're sad, you don't feel like you're dying. But with this other, you feel like you're leaving here.

Depression was highest on Mrs. McDowd's hierarchy of negative experiences because depression augers the possibility of death. Depression heralds mortality; mortality hints at annihilation. Depression is therefore worse than physical pain.

When I asked her if she had experienced subtle dimensions of suffering, such as guilt, regret, or an inability to forgive someone, she hesitated.

> At first when I found out he [husband] was running around, that was kind of bad. But I tell you the truth, I had lost all love for him by then. But as the years went on, I didn't hate him anymore. And before he died he asked my forgiveness. And I told him yes. After I forgave him, I just didn't go along each day and think my husband laid with that woman. To forgive—that should be the end of it. And that's what I did. I even went to his funeral. So I don't have no trouble with forgiving.

Mrs. McDowd revealed that her husband was consistently unfaithful throughout their married life. Shortly after their marriage she became aware of his infidelities. After their separation, she believed it would be "wrong in the eyes of the Lord" to marry again. When I asked her if she had experienced any positive relationships with men after her divorce, she pulled a face, shook her head vigorously, and laughed, "No, no, no!" She admitted that she had no interest in marrying or "being with a man" again. She was adamant, however, that she "held nothing over him [husband]," and "forgave him completely."

Mrs. McDowd was able to forgive her husband because she stopped expecting anything from him. She became invulnerable to his betrayal when she "lost interest" in him. Still, forgiving him was active; she deliberately "forgot" his misdeeds. When I commented on the rarity of real forgiveness, she smiled.

> Well, I'm going to tell you a story. I generally don't hold anything against anyone. But after the cancer, I seemed to lose all of my joy. I used to be always in good humor. Then I was sad because I had the cancer. But then I started praying. I asked the Lord to give me my joy back. And I couldn't hear the Lord's voice. I couldn't hear it. But something dropped in my spirits, see. "What about the man that killed your son?" I suddenly heard. See, I never forgive that man for killing my son. And I begin to cry. I said to the Lord, "If I ever see the man again, I will tell him I forgive him for killing my son." And I don't hold anything against anybody [with a smile].
> **Interviewer:** Did you get your joy back?
> **Mrs. McDowd:** Oh, yes! [with animation] People call on the phone and say, "What? Oh, you sound so good." I say, 'I feel good!' See, if we don't forgive people, God ain't going to forgive us. So I don't hold anything against anybody.

Mrs. McDowd's story shows the intricate connection she makes among cancer, a loss of joy, and a lack of forgiveness. In return for her prayer, the Lord questions her obliquely about *her* role in her loss of joy. She understood the Lord's cryptic query and offered him the intention of forgiving her son's killer even if she "never sees him" again. Her joy returned because the intention to forgive was as efficacious as the deed. She perceives physical, emotional, and spiritual health as linked, and concludes that, along with the Lord, she is responsible for her own well-being. Just as she views the management of her own health a duty, it is also a spiritual imperative for her to find joy through action. To Mrs. McDowd, forgiveness is labor intensive. In addition, because she forgave the man who killed her son, she was blessed with a vision of her son in the afterlife.

> One night he [son] came to me in my room. By looking up on the window, I saw him. He looked good. He was all whole, and he was resting there. And he says to me, "A man walked by and said, 'How you doing?'" He [son] told him, "I'm doing pretty good." And so the man started off and my son followed him and the man led him to the Lord. So I always talk to that one [son] because I had more time with the one with the kidney trouble. Besides, he was already saved.

Mrs. McDowd's vision eased several of her worries. First, her son had a conversation with her—something they had not done for several years before his death because she "hated" his drug use. Second, he told her [through the "man"] that he "felt good." He was not riddled with knife wounds, perhaps as she imagined him to be. Seeing him "looking good" guaranteed that he would not be in bodily pain for all eternity. Third, he followed the man [whom Mrs. McDowd believed to be an angel] who led him to the Lord, which assured her that he was intact spiritually as well as bodily. The sum of Mrs. McDowd's vision shows that her son is "saved" and "whole" and that she may continue, through dream-like conversations, to share his progress in the afterlife.

When asked, Mrs. McDowd said that she presently was "not suffering" because she has "a lot to look forward to." This sense of hope, that is, of anticipating pleasures both in this world and the next, was an antidote to suffering in many respondents' narratives. Whether respondents' hope was in a joyous afterlife, that an ill or cognitively impaired spouse would "die first" and so not be left alone, or, as in Mrs. McDowd's case, that her children would be "saved," this hope sometimes involved a bargaining with suffering itself. For example, respondents sometimes said: "my suffering is worthwhile or bearable . . . if my wife dies before me so she doesn't have to go in a nursing home," or, ". . . if I know I'll meet my (son, daughter, wife, husband) in the afterlife." Mrs. McDowd believes in a balance between suffering in this life and rewards in the next.

> I'm looking forward when my time is up to see my mother again. Every soul that goes to heaven, you'll see them again. When you die and go to heaven, you'll know your mother, your father, you'll know all your family and friends.

Mrs. McDowd has two major goals that give the latter stage of her life meaning and purpose. The first is to be well enough to "go home," that is, back to South Carolina, where she "still has plenty of family." She was unable to make this annual visit for the past three years because of being "crippled up" with the debilitating effects of her double mastectomy. The second goal is more important to Mrs. McDowd.

> My daughter's not saved but she's working on it. And then my baby son,
> he said he's saved.

She hopes that before she dies, she will witness her daughter being "led away from her loose lifestyle" that includes using drugs and alcohol. Because her "baby son" is already saved, she does not name him on her list of "hopes." She believes that prayer activates God's power to shape her hopes into reality.

Mrs. McDowd's daily life consists of sitting in her wheelchair, waiting for visits from her remaining children, grandchildren, and homecare nurses. Her hope transcends this small space into an imagined future—where she will return South to see family members "one last time," and her daughter tells her that she has "returned to the Lord."

EMBODIED SUFFERING

The three respondents discussed in this chapter defined suffering as physical pain. But the suffering body is more than a body in pain. Respondents' own bodies or bodies of significant others made up their portraits of suffering and also revealed a unique component that either added to or ameliorated their pain. Despite Mr. Inglund's illnesses, it is his wife and ill others who are major characters in his portrait. Mrs. Kean drew her self-portrait with no hair, and Mrs. McDowd's portrait of herself includes the Lord. In other words, respondents' portraits hint at the complexity of suffering and show its multi-dimensional nature.

For Mr. Inglund, suffering is the pain he experienced after surgery, and the pain his wife endures due to many illnesses. The background to his "portrait of suffering" is his certainty, because of the "terminal" label attached to his wife's diagnoses that her pain will end only with death. Although he defines suffering as physical pain, his narrative of suffering includes his shame. The importance of protecting his family is salient in Mr. Inglund's narrative. His events of suffering are rooted in personal and social expectations that men should be able to solve their family's problems. Proof of this failure—inability to provide a resting place for his son and a nursing home for his wife—makes him a disappointment to himself. The image of the silent defender of his family remains his benchmark of masculinity, even as his neighbors further threaten its reality.

Mrs. Kean describes suffering as the painful physical problems she "is going through now." Her suffering includes not knowing the cause of her illnesses. Mrs. Kean continues to view her body as a tool for work and an instrument to understand herself and the world around her. She sees the world through the lens of her full bladder, full bowels, full eyes, and feet that "have no life." Despite confusion about her illnesses, she questions society's assumption that to be old *is* to be ill. She challenges her doctors' diagnoses and is convinced that "something"—a provable illness is "at the bottom" of her suffering. She waits to learn the cause of her "wooziness" and a prognosis for its end. This waiting is itself suffering.

Like Mr. Inglund, Mrs. Kean adds another definition to suffering as physical pain—her son's inability to finish what he starts. Because her major and best-fitting role was "hard worker," she finds it difficult to imagine that her son's productive years have not yet begun. She is convinced that an individual who is unproductive has little personal or social value. She therefore interprets the experience of suffering in old age, because it removes any hope of productivity, as having no meaning to life as a whole.

For Mrs. McDowd, suffering is pain, yet she does not believe pain is a harbinger of death. She is unlike Mr. Inglund who believes that his wife's pain foretells her imminent passing. She is also dissimilar to Mrs. Kean, who yearned to know the cause of her pain. Mrs. McDowd defines pain as evil, as the work of Satan, and as the opposite of good. For her, suffering can be cured or modified by medicine or time, according to the will of the Lord. Because she knows the cause of her pain, she feels a sense of control over it. Because suffering is not the final answer, it is her attitude toward suffering that determines the intensity of her pain, her self-esteem in this life, and her existence in the afterlife. Her reactions to suffering reveal her belief in a karmic-like ontology about the nature of suffering. Suffering has spiritual causes, such as a lack of forgiveness, as well as ramifications, such as a loss of joy. Unlike Mrs. Kean, Mrs. McDowd comprehends her fairly tidy world both because of and despite suffering. The physical and spiritual laws of this world are predictable to her. Like Mrs. Rink mentioned in Chapter 3, God's ways are not so mysterious; she believes that because God created the Golden Rule, he must follow it.

Mr. Inglund and Mrs. Kean dwell in a liminal state highlighted by a lack of control over their pained bodies. Mr. Inglund waits for his wife's death because he believes her body's breakdown is irreversible. Mrs. Kean and Mrs. McDowd feel that bodily breakdown is reversible. If Mrs. Kean could "just get to the bottom" of her body's mysterious workings, she would tell her doctors, who would then find a cure. For Mrs. McDowd, patience, prayer, and following medical advice from both doctors and informed others will probably heal her. Mr. Inglund is pessimistic about suffering's end. Thus far, he feels he has been woefully inadequate in protecting his family against the many faces of suffering.

Although all three respondents described suffering as physical pain, their stories, like their portraits, revealed multiple dimensions of suffering. Mrs. Kean spoke of the frustration of being unemployed as an aspect of suffering. Mr. Inglund's frustration with himself appears in his narrative as authentic suffering. For Mrs. McDowd, suffering is not the end of the story. Depression is "worse" than suffering because it speaks to the annihilation of her very self.

THE NEXT CHAPTER

Chapter 5 concerns Social Suffering. The cases used in Chapter 5 investigate how the components of human identity—age, gender, race, and class status—inform the experience of suffering for elders in American society. This chapter also explores how internalized social rules about the propriety of suffering affect elders' experiences and expressions of suffering.

CHAPTER 5

Social Suffering

The ethos of the *larger* social reality sometimes stridently, sometimes quietly bears on the *smaller* event of individual suffering. For example, male respondents said that, for the most part, silence was their preferred response to suffering. This response was mitigated, however, by the event that caused suffering. To cry because of pain may connote weakness; to cry because of a son's or daughter's death is acceptable. In other words, cultural and social dictates for silence while suffering are moderated by the personal and social tragedy of losing a child.

For African-American men interviewed, experiences of segregation, discrimination, and the economic, political, and social validation of prejudice was an underlying cause for many events of suffering throughout their lives. Similarly, when female elders were young, tacit and overt societal approval of male dominance in all forms, from spousal abuse to economic disparity in the workplace constructed a social reality that few women overcame, and so informed various types of suffering. For some respondents earlier incidents of abuse or discrimination *continued to be felt* as suffering in later life. In other words, present suffering could be rooted in the memory of suffering, in the recollection of conditions created by oppression, poverty or racism, or in subtle sufferings that emerged from a regretted or unfulfilled past.

In the experience of communal, group or social suffering, memory can be both dangerous and liberating (Metz, as cited in Chopp, 1985). Collective wounds bind a community, as does their chronicle of oppression. Hidden in the memory of common suffering is common solace. In the case of oppressed groups, memory poses a particular danger to those who hold power, because it exposes the harm of long-standing cultural, religious, and social traditions that the powerful have created. Memory liberates because it discloses the mores of a given time and reveals them not only as society's artifacts, but also as its weapons. In regard to elders' life stories and stories of suffering, individual narratives divulge society's covert and overt laws, residual rules, and the limitations that agreed upon conventions placed on individual lives (Langer, 1997).

I mentioned in Chapter 2 that the language with which an individual communicates suffering can be transmitted through the voice of the body, the voice of identity and roles, and the voice of narrative. These voices appropriately and effectively relate the experience of individual suffering to the larger social world. Yet, voices are often silent in suffering; suffering can render an individual mute. Can an experience be called suffering if it is not communicated to another, or if no one listens to an individual's account of suffering? Some elders are inwardly, mutely, and torturously focused on their suffering. Soelle (1976) saw suffering as a progression whose first stage is muteness. Lamentation follows muteness and progresses toward transformation. For Soelle, the second stage of suffering as lamentation resonated to the haunting cries of the psalms. As the benchmark of mourning over individual and communal exile, the psalms show suffering's social origin. Here, I suggest that telling a story about suffering is a form of social lament, and one of suffering's primary activities.

The topic of this chapter—Social Suffering—is inextricably linked to all other chapters. Certainly, older persons' notions about gender-based expressions of suffering (Chapter 3) the perceived morality of suffering (Chapter 7), or the acceptable ways to cope with suffering (Chapter 6) reflect the unique characteristics of an individual—personal history and the cultural template into which they were born. The cases that follow show the directness and subtlety of the social roots of suffering. Two of the cases convey that suffering is often rooted in one group's disregard or disrespect for another group. The other case illustrates a social morality of suffering. As respondents poignantly illustrate, however, the genesis of their suffering is complex. They believed that suffering would continue to be an aspect of life even if social equality transformed our world.

MR. CALLEN

Mr. Callen is an 81-year-old African-American widower who invited his brother to live with him after his own serious illness. Although he reported that he and his brother were "never close," the arrangement suited both men because neither wanted to live alone. They share expenses and look out for each other. Mr. Callen is a lawyer who continues to work a few days each week. When I asked him to tell me the story of his life, he looked at me questioningly.

> The story of my life, you mean what it was like for me? Well, it was very good, all the time. I come from 13th and F. I was born there. My mother was born here in Philadelphia; my grandfather was born here. We lived a very comfortable life. Even in the Depression we were very fortunate. My father had a job. He fed us, took care of us. Life's been very pleasant for me, very, very pleasant.

Mr. Callen believes that his "pleasant" life resulted from the legacy of his father and grandfather; both men taught him to be ambitious and self-confident.

> My father was a waiter at different hotels. He was also a sexton and super-intendent at our Church. So my father in my eyes was a big man. And I used

to . . . , I wouldn't speak to people if I felt they were beneath me. I always felt that I was better than other people. I have friends right now that tell me that they think I run the world. See, I always ran with the movers and shakers. I knew S.L. when he was the mayor. I knew J.K. (a Philadelphia judge) when she was a kid.

Mr. Callen realized as a child that he wanted to be a lawyer. He emulated his father, who associated with the city's African-American elite. The self-confidence of Philadelphia's "finest black minds" was catching. A friend of his father's, a leading criminal lawyer, left a deep impression on Mr. Callen. His parents supported his decision to attend law school.

When I graduated I was the only stud in my class. It wasn't too hard because when I went to C. [high school] there weren't that many blacks in the class and we lived in a mixed neighborhood. That didn't bother me. I told you, I always thought I was better than everybody.

When I asked him about the saddest times in his life, Mr. Callen gave a chronological list of loss.

When my grandfather died. When my mother died, and I was told about her death and I couldn't get back here because I was in the Army. Then of course the next thing was when my wife died. And then Joan [daughter] died and I was in the hospital and I couldn't do anything about it. But I didn't let the grief get to me.
Interviewer: What do you mean?
Mr. Callen: Well, I've seen people who are so grief stricken that they felt like they wanted to climb in the grave with them. For me, it comes every once in a while and I think about it and it even causes a tear to drop but nothing to cause me to sit down and suck my thumb.

Mr. Callen's wife and daughter died from cancer within three years of each other. He admitted that he was "a little devastated" after the death of his daughter. The sorrow he felt after his wife died was not for her death, which he described as a "blessing," but because she "got only about 20, 21 years of good living out of marriage." When I asked him to explain this cryptic remark, he offered a list of painful health problems that spanned 20 years of his life, but denied he had ever suffered. When I asked him why he agreed to be a part of a study on suffering he explained that, as an African-American, he understood the "concept of suffering," but learned to remove himself, emotionally and physically, from its grip.

I try not to get into a pity bag that will bring about suffering. But I have to have a concept of suffering because I'm black. We as a group of people have come through many trials and snares with amazing grace. So I have a concept of suffering because it's part of my culture and part of my having been brought up. But see, I don't worry about the white folks, about the oppressor.

To Mr. Callen, suffering is an entity that is incarnated by the oppressor who sets "trials and snares" for the oppressed. Suffering is represented by those who "worry" about the oppressor, care about what the oppressor thinks of them, or leave their emotions open to attack. Mr. Callen believes that inner strength and worldly possessions shield him from the suffering that most African-Americans endure. He admits to having knowledge of suffering as a concept rather than through personal experience; he controls negative experiences through the strength of his will. To Mr. Callen, people suffer when they empower the person or emotion that threatens to overwhelm them. He uses his own history of grief to illustrate that a certain amount of emotional distance, even from loved ones, protects him from suffering.

> I think people suffer when they have a, let me use a word, a hurtness. It could be physical, mental, spiritual. Poor little old me, why did it happen to me? Why did I have to lose my wife, my daughter? Why couldn't it have been someone else's wife; why did it have to be my daughter? See, with my daughter it was a little devastating. But I was not so involved that I was so grief stricken that I felt that the world had come to an end. So I never let myself get to a point where I was at bottom.

Mr. Callen controls how close he gets to anyone, even loved ones; his boundaries shield him from "hurtness." To him, real grief would be to focus so intensely on your loss that you touch "bottom"—a murky area where you lose sight and control of yourself. But it is not only self-control that protects him from despair. His belief that he sits a "step above" most people in talent and intelligence keeps him from sinking "down that low."

As the interview progressed, Mr. Callen disclosed that he "knew" suffering more intimately than he first admitted. He revealed that he came close to "getting down low" during his drinking days. As a recovering alcoholic, he concludes that alcoholism causes a unique form of suffering. Although he "belonged to the never club," i.e., he "never missed work, never went to the hospital, never hit [his] wife," he discovered that "hitting bottom," for him, was to enter the fantasy world he created through drunkenness. Suffering was to become lost in this artificial place that robbed him of self-awareness, identity, relationships with others, and thus a sense of control.

> Alcohol does things to your body, your mind, your soul. You live in a world of make-believe. You become an actor in a play which you are the producer, and the author and everything else. You have your own little world.

Mr. Callen climbed out of this imaginary world 20 years ago but continues to look back. He admits that his "good times" ended when he stopped drinking, but he feels contemptuous of those who stayed in that make-believe land. He repeated a remark he made earlier—although he and his wife had been married for over 45 years, he gave her only "20 or 21 years of good living—[his] sober years." The morning he felt "so sick he prayed for God to spare [his] life" he stopped drinking and gave up his closest friends. He rejected coworkers and neighbors who continued to "live life like it was one big party." He described himself during his drinking days as:

> Nasty, just plain nasty. I insulted everyone—men and women, the wives of my friends—and thought it was the greatest joke.

Because he has heard people ask, why me, in the midst of "suffering from drink," he is adamant that he will never ask this question. Why me? poses a question to others only he can answer. To blame anyone for his drunkenness would deny the insight and self-reliance that 1) allowed him to recognize his descent into alcoholism, and 2) courageously arise.

> That's when I found out what suffering was—by looking at what was happening to the other drunks, and when they asked, Why me? But I knew. It's more than your liver; it destroys your soul. And then you have suffering because as you crawl on the bottom, "poor little old me" comes out. Yeah, that's when they ask, why me?

Mr. Callen's perpetrator of suffering, "poor little old me," is an actual entity; it represents self-pity and loss of control. It is Mr. Callen's nemesis as a man and African-American; it is the symbol of purposelessness that, according to him, all African-Americans should battle.

Further into the interview, Mr. Callen offered another description of suffering. He confessed that physical pain is his ever-present companion.

> I would say suffering can be awful like some of the things I go through now with this stomach of mine. But you know, there's always some suffering before some great change. And you may have value that way.

Mr. Callen conceded that there is a form of suffering—physical pain—over which he has little control, and that the pain he experiences "may be suffering." In this, he admits to pain without succumbing to the personal weakness that he views as the root of suffering. His comment shows that if suffering, as pain, strikes despite his efforts to resist it, he will control the outcome. Suffering then becomes a vehicle that portends "great change."

As the interview progressed and Mr. Callen shared more about himself, his definitions of suffering grew increasingly interpretive, poignant, and profound. Witness his depiction of suffering as an abiding lack of self-knowledge.

> Then suffering can be imaginary. Thinking that you are something that you are not and when you find out that you are not what you think you are, then you really—commit suicide, crawl into the grave. How great am I! And that's to suffer spiritually and oh, that is something I can't even describe to you.

This form of suffering—thinking you are something you are not and thus becoming "lost" to yourself—seems a fundamental description of suffering. The "punishment" for self-absorption is alienation, isolation, and self-delusion.

Mr. Callen's depiction of suffering speaks to his vigilance against "losing" himself through drink, self-doubt, and self-hatred. Despite the fact that he enjoyed "great success in the world," he knows that the *real* battle occurs within; he remains on guard against either the "other" or "poor little old me" defining him.

> There's a very famous illustration of a man who was a black multi-millionaire, spoke ten languages, married a beautiful woman and had every thing he could think of. And he asked a white man, so what do you think of me? The white guy said, "Yeah, you're a good n____." [Pause] See, regardless of what you have, regardless of where you go, you're not just a good man, you're a good n____.

Despite his sense of purposeful struggle and tales of triumph, the effect of long-standing racism has reached and wounded the core of Mr. Callen. His troubling anecdote allows the reader a window into his internalized racism and offers another portrait of suffering. In the illustration, the black man asks the question, what do you think of me? Throughout the interview, however, Mr. Callen emphasized that he "never worried about what the white man thought of [him]." In fact, he distinguished himself from most members of his own race.

> **Mr. Callen:** I'm 81 years of age and the Negro, Black African or African-American, whatever you want to call him that you have in the city of Philadelphia right now are different from the ones I grew up with. And the group of Negroes that we have in the world today, black folks, they haven't the slightest idea of what happened so they could be free to go and sit up in a movie, sit up at some counter, order what they want to order and do what they want to do. Then, the war came along, they came up here in the army or to work and they settled in the city of Philadelphia and they brought with them their own concept, their own prejudices and their own culture. They never had anything and don't know how to appreciate anything. So that makes people like me more prejudiced against blacks than any white person could possibly be. I have more fear of black folks than I have of white folks. The white folks are on the other side of the street and I'm on this side. I got more money than they got. I got everything, I've got a big house, I've got two degrees. I'm different from them. They're just scums. And the same way with them black folks. [Pause] Now let me ask you something—What degree do you have?
> **Interviewer:** Ph.D.
> **Mr. Callen:** Let me tell you, one of the things I learned in law school about a Ph.D. A Ph.D. is an expert on one corner of a fly's wing, and they don't know a doggone thing about the rest of the fly. And I think the same thing about people who get their Ph.D. They're an expert in their own little world.

As the interview progressed, Mr. Callen's many demons came to light: Alcoholism, the white oppressor, the youthful blacks who had not borne his cohort's struggle against racism, and the researcher who attempts to understand the suffering of others.

In deference to Mr. Callen, his narrative is *not* his life (Ricoeur, 1986), and it presents only a portion of the personal attributes, family background and historical events that he both shapes and that shape him. Mr. Callen's life *and* his story, as is true of all respondents, are more complex than his case could ever show. Likewise, his experience of suffering is more complicated than tracing its genesis to racism or alcohol.

It is to the contradictory and paradoxical nature of social suffering that Mr. Callen's story is focused. Although he measures himself as superior to his external demons, he cannot dismiss them. Fighting against them through the years have not only magnified and made them more loathsome, he has internalized them into "poor little old me"—the demon most dangerous because of its potential to "become" him. The ferocity of this demon, and his struggle against it, continue.

At the end of the interview, Mr. Callen offered a final picture of suffering which is perhaps his most comprehensive and reflective. It starkly shows the penalty exacted for "never getting too close."

> The first time I saw a picture of the monkey, the one they cloned, it clung to the other party, as though he had nothing else to hold onto. That's suffering. When I saw that picture it reminded me of something I read a million years ago. Here is a creature who has no pride in ancestry, no hope of posterity. In other words, you're just a plain bastard.

In this picture, the second monkey, as the clone, is actually clinging to himself. Distance from family, neighbors and former drinking partners, and disdain for most whites and young blacks sketch a terrible outline of having only oneself to hold. Throughout the interview, Mr. Callen described several pictures of suffering. They show, variously, how he views others and keeps guard against his nemesis—"poor little old me"—from appearing in his gallery. The most poignant picture of suffering, however, is Mr. Callen's portrait of himself throughout his life, as the lone and lonely judge and jury over himself, others, and the increasingly diminished world that he inhabits.

MR. WICKERS

Mr. Wickers is an 84-year-old African-American man who lives with his second wife in a senior facility. He is now housebound because of sudden vision loss. On fine days Mr. Wickers and his wife sit outside on the park benches provided by the apartment building and talk with neighbors. In winter the couple feels especially isolated. Until a week prior to our interview Mr. Wickers was volunteering at a local hospital.

> I woke up one morning and I started to shave and I thought, I can't see. So this thing happens, but I look around and from volunteering at the hospital I see so many people laying there worse off than I ever hope to be. I'll settle for this.

Mr. Wickers prefers to think that he has a choice in how he suffers. He therefore chooses to accept the losses that come with blindness—loss of mobility, loss of independence, and loss of the routine that he enjoyed when he volunteered. Like many elders, he has lowered the ceiling on what personal limitations are tolerable. His comment shows the importance of choice and control in perceiving an experience as "suffering" or "not suffering." When asked to tell the story of his life, Mr. Wickers replied:

> I was five years old when my oldest brother took his own life. There was all this confusion with his funeral. I remember my family going to the cemetery. It was raining. And they made me stay in the car because it was raining. I saw a lot of people taking his casket over to the gravesite. I never knew my oldest brother; I only remember seeing him on two occasions. My mother and father were upset. He was young. There was a whole lot of neighborhood gossip. You know, a story don't lose no heat in its travels.

Mr. Wickers gives this narrative in staccato, and it is noteworthy for all that is not said. His brother's death became a neighborhood mystery. Like his account of it, the suicide was shrouded in sadness, confusion, and a lack of resolution, and shows his youthful acquaintance with loss. Beginning his narrative with this story shows its salience in his life.

Mr. Wickers said that he remembers little else of his childhood and adolescence. After his father died in 1932, when Mr. Wickers was 15 years old, he quit school "to help my mother along." He condensed his narrative by listing the various jobs he held and how much money he made. His intuitive sense of both comparison to others and compassion for them is evident throughout his narrative.

> I was a regular letter carrier at Ninth and M. My route was what they called skid row, where all the drunks and bums are. They weren't bad people, they just had something in their life that set them back.

After a stint as a postman, Mr. Wickers became an agent with an African-American owned insurance company. This job offered him a chance to use his ambition, common sense, and friendly persuasion to sell insurance.

> I had enough of those initiative-robbing jobs. Like at the post office. All you had to do is stand there and put the letter to John Smith on Fourth Street in a bin. Nothing challenging about that. So I got the job with the insurance company because I was going from place to place and meeting people from all walks of life that broadened my idea of living.

Mr. Wickers learned as much as he could about insurance and about life while working at the insurance company. His observation that "money attracts more money and power attracts more power" convinced him that his employer was doomed. He explained why.

> Big insurance companies went into the Negro market and skimmed the top off. They took the physicians and the lawyers and the people who were

economically well off. That left all these truck drivers and laborers down here. Some one had to insure them. So that's where the smaller companies got their start. The bigger companies, they took the best. I couldn't insure a doctor. A doctor would tell me point blank, look, Chuck, I wouldn't mind going to your company, but with this bigger company I can get the same thing for x number of dollars cheaper.

After the insurance company's inevitable collapse, Mr. Wickers took a job as a clerk with the school district. He defined his work as "another initiative-robbing job," but a sure means to support his wife and three children. He described this period of his life as:

Like most people—we struggled. We had ups and downs, ins and outs like any other marriage. And then she got sick and passed away and I was on my own for a while. And then Sal [points to wife sitting on sofa] and I, we knew each other from way way back. So we got married.

Mr. Wickers quietly slips the tragedy of his first wife's death from cancer into his narrative. Although he admits that losing her caused him "sadness," it was the series of events that preceded and came after her death that caused him to suffer.

Mr. Wickers: I think I was suffering when my first wife got hooked up with this here religious group. Those people travel around in pairs and go to homes. I let them in there one day. So she hooked up with it and she followed it pretty closely. They're the ones that advocate no medicine. So when she got sick, I took her over to the hospital and she told the doctor she didn't want any tests or nothing like that. Let the Lord take care of the whole thing.

Interviewer: Do you think her religious beliefs got in the way of the help she might have received?

Mr. Wickers: Yeah, I do. People have children that have illnesses and they refuse to have the medical profession do anything. To me, it's not fair to the person who is ill. Then she got to a point where she was more or less helpless and couldn't do too much about it one way or another.

Interviewer: What made this experience suffering?

Mr. Wickers: Well, losing my wife, that was a big sadness. But then you had the children who knew just what her condition was and they were all in their teens and they saw the whole thing. I felt that the children were being robbed of having a mother over the years until they grow up and really get out into the world. So, it was kind of rough, you know, but you still look for a dawn.

Mr. Wickers' intricate description of suffering is difficult to unpack. It contains several notions of suffering—he endured a relational suffering as he watched his wife die and his children become motherless. Suffering also resulted from anger with the religious group that condemned medical care. As his story continues, he elaborates his experience of suffering.

Before she got sick, we bought a house. Then one of the kids got sick and then I lost my job. I got behind in my payments. I went to the people who

> held the mortgage to see if I couldn't pay the interest on the loan until I get myself squared away. And they refused it, so I lost my home. We got an apartment up this way and we stayed there and that's when she got into this serious illness. That's the way it was.

Grief for his wife and home are intertwined in Mr. Wicker's narrative. Each loss represents his physical and emotional diminishment. He could not protect his wife from illness, shield his children from witnessing her suffering and death, or keep his family from being put out of their home. Because an important source of esteem for Mr. Wickers came from his role as protector and provider, the loss of his wife and home threatened his roles as husband and father. He became powerless in the very roles that are, especially for men of Mr. Wickers' generation, based on male authority. When he realized that he could not control the financial or physical well-being of his family, he was bowed both by God and by those who "held the money." Social and spiritual suffering are linked in Mr. Wickers' narrative.

> The thing that annoys me now is you turn this thing [television] on and they tell you how easy it is to combine your debts, and what it amounts to is a second mortgage. I didn't get it. So I lost a home. Those people that held the mortgage, they could have done something about it. Friends of mine, and family, they didn't have any money to help me 'cause they were scratching around themselves. And now, I mean you can have 55 credit cards and someone would be glad to give them to you.

For Mr. Wickers, the mortgage company represented his impotence in the face of structural power without compassion. Despite doing the *right* things in life, such as working hard to provide for his family, he was powerless to keep tragedy from his doorstep or elude the inevitability of suffering.

> **Mr. Wickers:** You go on and one day you realize how little control you have over things.
> **Interviewer:** When does that awareness come, that you have little control?
> **Mr. Wickers:** It comes at different times in the course of things. Sometimes you feel there's some hope and all that. And other times you just feel this is the way it's going to be.

Perhaps Mr. Wickers "stopped looking for a dawn" when he lost his wife and home. His comment also speaks to the realization that suffering resulted from having no control over the unfolding of his life. Powerful others, such as the mortgage company, decided his family's fate. When asked to define suffering, he replied:

> Suffering is a condition whereby you are at a point where you don't have anywhere to go. I need money to pay this mortgage off. And there's no place to go. And you can go out and play lottery numbers, thinking you might get lucky and get enough money to lift this burden from you. That's the way I feel about it.

Mr. Wickers remembered that during this period of suffering he felt he had "nowhere to turn." The prison-like nature of suffering resonates to other respondents' belief that they "didn't know which way to go" while suffering. The sense of being held captive by circumstances, perceiving no way out of them, and feeling powerless to create or find an exit, is a core experience of suffering.

> My only problem was that I didn't have any money. And I tried. I went to see if I couldn't salvage this thing. That's the thing that hurt me.

Although more money probably would not have saved his wife's life or spared his children from seeing their mother die, Mr. Wickers translated his experiences of suffering into social symbols of power and loss. His interpretation of suffering is tied to a cultural mandate to "be and do your best" and a social injunction to assume his proper gender role as head of the family. Yet he was unable to perform this role because of larger social structures, such as the health and housing industry that left him impoverished.

The individual and private, yet communal and public nature of suffering emerged when Mr. Wickers responded to the question: "What would a picture of suffering look like?

> Not so much a picture of someone in ragged clothes, but a picture of a normal person who comes to the realization that this is the end. At that point you don't see any avenues. You're there alone. That's the pathetic part about it. Especially when you know there are people who have millions of dollars. Why don't I have something to help me? That's the way I feel about it.

A poignant mixture of hopelessness, loneliness, and inequity are drawn into Mr. Wickers' self-portrait. Despite the social roots of suffering, one ultimately suffers alone. Still, he continued to work hard and persevered despite his losses. He believed that he must control the areas of life that remained open to his control; taking the reins of your own moral and spiritual sphere is divinely mandated.

> I think you're going to be judged on what you do about it (suffering of self and others). Sure, there's a superior being, but you have to utilize everything that's available as far as you are concerned since you don't have any real control over life and death.

Mr. Wickers strongly identifies with the suffering children of the world, perhaps because he experienced the helplessness of being dependent upon, but not receiving, the kindness of strangers. He considers these children the most deserving of his sympathy.

> You can turn this thing [points to television] on to the news and you see where so many people are killed in different parts of the country. And my heartfelt feeling always goes out to the innocent kids that didn't have a darn thing to do with it. So much, as far as I'm concerned, is based upon money. Greed. Money is the root of all evil, whether it's a franc or a yen or a dollar.

Lack of money remains Mr. Wickers' most compelling symbol of suffering. Those who "hold the money" also hold the ability to cause or relieve suffering. Despite his conviction that powerful people are generally greedy and cold-hearted, he recognizes the futility of wishing his life had been different. He believes that useless hope leads to a dangerous passivity.

> If, if, if. If I hadn't lost my home I'd still be living there now. If my first wife hadn't been sick. . . . Or my mother and father would still be around. Or my brother at least. I mean we all have these expressions, you know. If, if, if. Well I say they're all dreams. It's raining out and the roof leaks. What do you do, buy an umbrella or fix the roof?

Mr. Wickers reviews his life with pride; he knows that he consistently tried to "fix the roof." His ability to both self-reflect and focus outward allow him to discern those who are "worse off" than he. Although he was stung by misfortune that changed the course of his life, he judges only himself.

> **Mr. Wickers:** When I was at the hospital, sometimes you see a close friend and you know he's not going to walk out; he's going to be carried out. If you see a black station wagon drive up there and park, you know if you stand there long enough they're going to come out with a gurney on it and put a body in there. And what it does—you say to yourself, I'm here. I don't know what took him (my friend) away from here, but I'm going to sure get my backyard cleaned up before I leave the same way.
> **Interviewer:** What do you mean?
> **Mr. Wickers:** Well, be sure I'm on the right track, that's the first thing. The way I see it, 50 years ago it was my world and I could do anything I want. Now, today, you think, wait a minute. You've got more time to sit back and control your activity, then just be forced into it. When I see a guy running down the street, you used to say, I think I'll run down there, too, see what's going on. Now you say, I don't see why you're running.

Wisdom comes from knowing that life holds the cards; Mr. Wickers believes that he must choose whether to gamble with life or not. For him, suffering mimes age, but each gives rewards. Both age and suffering offer choices and lessons; both force him to take stock of his talents and ask what he has learned from past mistakes. Although he has fewer choices in age, as in suffering, he believes that at least two remain—he can act or he can do nothing and wait. If he acts, he may still control some aspects of his life. The lesson he learned with age, however, is that "to wait" *may be* the wiser choice.

> Time is on your side. The river that flows will continue to flow. In this, patience is truly a virtue. Just wait it out.

As Mr. Wickers loses control over the mechanism of his body (he cannot digest certain foods and has trouble sleeping) and the large issues of life (blindness, illness, and the approach of death), he has redefined loss of control as patience. "Waiting it out" may fit into Mr. Wickers' belief that loss of any kind is reimbursed by an immanent justice. When I asked him to name people who suffered as a group, he considered.

> Well, let's see. The only people here were Indians. No one is going to tell me that the Indians were lined up on the east coast saying, "Come on over." And then you have this idea of slavery, people being brought over here, especially those from Africa. They were killed and exploited. Somewhere along the line, some one has to pay for that. And then the Japanese literally crucified the people in Nanking. Well they're going to pay for that. Everything carries a price. You're not going to get away from this world scot-free. I knew one case where there was a policeman at 40th and W. He had a reputation for hitting people with his club, wham, wham, wham. He got kicked off the force and he used to sit outside the liquor store begging for money. Men would go by there and spit on him. They spit on him because when he was in his prime all he knew was to hurt people. You're going to pay for it. That's all there is to it.

For Mr. Wickers an ultimate sense of fair play must exist somewhere because the notion that life *remains* unfair is unbearable. Immanent justice takes many shapes. Like a form of karma, your may be punished "down the road" by your own harmful actions, harmed by those you hurt in the past, or judged by those who witnessed your life.

> Death is the last chapter in life and those who survive you will figure out just what kind of life you lived. If you were selfish and exploited people—well. Or were you faithful to those who you professed to love? And how much good you did over and against the bad part of your existence. If you had a life where you helped people and haven't been any liability to those around you, why all well and good. If not, well . . .

Mr. Wickers believes that winning or losing at life will ultimately be decided by his survivors. They will testify as to whether good acts or bad intentions held greater weight in his life. Those who are left will tell the sum and meaning—the story—of his life.

MRS. KOHN

Mrs. Kohn is an 82-year-old European-American widow who lives in a luxury apartment filled with pictures of great-nieces and nephews. When I commented on the elegance of her apartment she smiled and said that even after seven years of widowhood she misses her husband greatly. The emotional emptiness of her apartment detracts from its beauty, yet she is adamant about not marrying again.

> I know what I had. I don't know what I'd get. Being alone isn't easy. But I'm coping.

Mrs. Kohn admitted that "coping" was a word she used often. A central theme in her narrative was the ability to deal rationally with life's sorrows and to come through adversity "in one piece." When I asked her to tell me the story of her life, she began:

> Let's see. I'm a Depression child. That left a very deep impression on me as far as finances are concerned. But I think I had a good childhood. The year before I graduated high school the Normal School closed and of course there was no money for me to go to college. So that was it. I went to a business college. After a month or so they approached me and my parents about whether I would be willing to teach a class in English. And I did that [teach] for my tuition.

Mrs. Kohn's parents hoped that both of their children would graduate from college, but had resources enough for only one to attend. The opportunity was given to her younger brother, whom she described as brilliant, and who eventually graduated with an engineering degree. Mrs. Kohn remembers her growing up years in North Philadelphia as "pleasant and just normal." Her parents, especially her mother, carefully monitored her social activities during her teen years.

> Where we lived there was only one other Jewish family on the block. But I had girlfriends who were not Jewish. And this one friend was having a party for her 16th birthday. I wasn't allowed to go because my mother learned that there were going to be boys there—gentile boys. I said, "I'm not going to marry the boys." And my mother said, "You're not going to have the chance. You can't tell your heart what to do. It does what it wants." I still remember that.

Mrs. Kohn was 19 years old, working as a secretary and living at home when she met her husband. He was the "Breadman" who delivered bread and rolls to her parents' home at the same time she left for work. The couple married after a year of dating, and she became pregnant soon after. Both she and her husband "loved children" and wanted a large family.

> For a while we lived with my parents and my first baby was born there. He cried constantly. And it was too rough for everybody, so we rented a room a mile or so away. We stayed there about a year after he died. Then we found an apartment. From there we went house hunting. This was after my second child died.
> **Interviewer:** So the loss of your children occurred early in the marriage?
> **Mrs. Kohn:** Right away. Then that was it.
> **Interviewer:** You mean you didn't try to have more children.
> **Mrs. Kohn:** That was it.

Mrs. Kohn mentioned this shocking loss almost as an afterthought. There was no preamble or follow up to her statement that both of her sons died from a congenital disease before they were a year old. She offered a short addendum to her feelings about this loss.

> I was very uneasy when I went visiting people in the family where there were other children. I was unhappy about it. It took me a long time. Even today, I find myself saying, will I be in the conversation if there is talk about children? I don't want to go through that. It never leaves you, never leaves you. But you learn to get over it. You learn to cope. That is a favorite word of mine—cope.

Mrs. Kohn's remarks seemed to be more a practical concern about fitting in at family gatherings than about grief. This is not to suggest that she did not grieve, but that it was easier for her to focus on the social effects of her loss rather than feelings. Also, she believes that it is futile to have angst over, or perhaps even talk about, the past.

In the early 1980s, Mr. Kohn fell ill. A doctor advised him to give up the stressful lifestyle that came with managing a bar-restaurant, which was his occupation for over 25 years. The couple sold their suburban home and moved to the luxury apartment Mrs. Kohn occupies presently.

> He had a by-pass shortly before we moved here in 1983. But he was sick for most of the time.

Despite her husband's long illness, she was not prepared for his death. She described their relationship as "extremely close." Although his death was neither sudden nor unexpected, it shook her view of herself and her world.

> After he died I felt differently about myself. I felt that I had to become even more independent than I was. I had to take care of myself, there was nobody else.

Mrs. Kohn's salient personal traits, such as independence and reserve, became more integral to her self-concept after her husband's death. "I did everything on my own," she said proudly, and "never burdened" family or friends. When I asked her about the saddest times in her life, she answered without hesitation.

> There were five of them. My parents, my children and my husband.
> **Interviewer:** So, the loss of your family. How did you get through those times?
> **Mrs. Kohn:** I think I'm strong-minded enough to understand that what's gone is gone. That does not mean to say that I don't grieve. I do. You learn. Nobody can do for me. I have to do for myself.

Mrs. Kohn reiterates that aloneness and strong-mindedness are related, just as being realistic is connected to grieving privately and moving on. There is little sentiment and no self-pity in her revelations; there is a pragmatic assessment that she is her own best friend and keeper. Her individualistic mindset reflects a cultural belief that is considered positive for both men and women in our society—strong inner resources help individuals face life's sorrows. When I asked her to tell me about an event, incident or time period in her life that caused her suffering, she answered:

> When my brother came back the way he did from the war as a bi-lateral
> amputee. His left arm and his right leg. That was hard because I was 24 years
> old, and to see how my mother and dad reacted, that was. . . . I never saw
> my father cry. And he did then.

Mrs. Kohn's event of suffering is similar to Mrs. Brown's (mentioned in Chapter 3). Mrs. Brown suffered because she witnessed the deaths of her mother and siblings after a lifetime of caretaking and kept images of her family *alive* in her mind. Mrs. Kohn's suffering was also represented by a memory that continued to color her present life—it pictured her brother returning physically disabled from the war, and the family that was devastated by *his* disablement. Although Mrs. Kohn admired her brother's independence, she believed it placed a barrier around him.

> He came home from the war on a Thursday. The next night was the beginning
> of the Sabbath. And my mother was observant and made a nice dinner.
> This was before I got married. So I set the table and took the water pitcher
> out of the refrigerator and I started filling the glasses. My brother came in
> from the living room and he said, "Not mine." I just looked at him. He
> said, "Just put the pitcher there." I couldn't fill his glass. He had to do it
> for himself.

The worse her brother's disability, the more independence he craved. His behavior after the war reminded me of Mrs. Kohn's earlier comment—that her aloneness after her husband's death reinforced *her* independence. Her brother distanced himself from his family and increased the pathos of his situation.

> He was that way [independent] before [the war], but he was three times as
> much afterwards. You couldn't do a thing for him. And he bought a car right
> away, and he had no extra gadgets to help make it easier to drive.

Mrs. Kohn repeated that she loved her brother dearly. She described him as the childhood ally who became her closest confidant in adulthood. But his latest illness tested their relationship with each other as well as their faith.

> In 1998 he suffered a stroke that left him with no tactile ability. He now has
> an aide that stays with him 24 hours because he is unable to bathe or dress
> himself. Mentally he is not affected, yet he cannot accept it. His suffering,
> it's not pain, or anything like that, it's the inability to do for himself. I know
> that's what bothers me more than anything else.

Mrs. Kohn defines her brother's suffering as dependence and frustration. In discussing his reaction to the stroke, she traded the pronoun "him" for "me." Her strong identification with his personality traits, such as independence, intelligence and self-awareness, causes her to suffer both for him and with him. He has become, through his inability to do for himself, her benchmark for suffering. She compares her own independence with his lack of it.

I don't have to rely on anybody. If I want to go someplace I pick myself up, get into the car and I go. I'll do anything I can for anybody else but I find it very hard, like my brother, to accept help.

For Mrs. Kohn and her brother, independence is doubly valued because it is perceived as the morally correct way to be. The fact that she is not permitted to help him is part of her pain, yet she understands his response and would, in the same situation, act similarly. I again recalled Mrs. Brown from Chapter 3, who had the *pleasure* of caring for her ill family. Mrs. Kohn, however, is forced to stand by and witness her brother's despair.

It's worse for him and it's worse for me. It's hard to explain. I mean we had great discussions. His speech was affected, but his mind wasn't. But if he didn't know what was going on, I wouldn't be able to see him suffer the way he does now.

Just as no one in the family discussed her brother's physical condition after the war, neither sibling discussed the effects of his stroke. Mrs. Kohn was recently diagnosed with hypertension; she believes that this illness was a physical effect of their silence with each other. Hypertension, which she described as a "silent killer," became her metaphor for standing close to her brother and knowing he would refuse her extended hand. When I asked her to define suffering, she considered:

Suffering means not being able to pick up pieces and go on with your life. And I was always able. It took a while. It didn't happen overnight. But I was able to learn to do that. When you suffer you are unable to go on to pick up the pieces.

Her comments imply that an individual goes to pieces or comes apart during suffering. She learned to be flexible through tragedy and to "move on" rather than "break." She acknowledges the brittleness of her brother's pain. If he "comes apart," will he allow her to "pick up the pieces" for him? She ponders the mystery of her brother's life and the injustice of suffering.

I wonder why my brother had a stroke after all the things he went through. Fifty years of doing and trying to overcome being a bi-lateral amputee and then to have the stroke and make him to where he says, "Why am I a nothing?" He's sad now. He doesn't laugh much.

Because the stroke robbed her brother of independence, it also took away his self-esteem, a sense of accomplishment, and communication between siblings. Mrs. Kohn cannot answer her brother's troubling questions. When I asked her to differentiate among the concepts of sadness, suffering, and depression, she replied:

> Depression is a medical term I think. And I can be sad but I can still go on
> with my life with the things that I have to do. When you suffer, you are
> unable to cope.

She defined depression literally and distantly; sadness seemed inevitable but manageable. Suffering, however, usurped an ability to cope, which was an important theme in Mrs. Kohn's life story. When I asked her what a picture of suffering would show, she shook her head and shrugged.

> A picture of suffering? That would be very difficult. To my way of thinking,
> it's someone that can't make up his or her mind about things, can't do for
> himself. Someone unable to do.

Respondents' pictures of suffering showed similarities. They often portrayed a disheveled person who seemed mired in indecision, confused and fearful in their surroundings, but unable to escape. Respondents described this individual as having "nowhere to turn," or "no way out." Mrs. Kohn described her *suffering person* as someone who "can't make up his or her mind about things." This description puts the onus on the individual to take a stand, make a decision, and eventually "get out of himself" through strength of will.

At the end of the interview I asked Mrs. Kohn if she would like to add anything to our discussion. She paused, then admitted she was perplexed as to why anyone would want to research the subject of suffering. When I asked her if she thought this subject was an inappropriate area for research, she shrugged.

> The fact that I feel unhappy, sad, depressed or suffer—well there is nothing
> you can do about it. So why talk about it? I try to work things out for myself.
> My life has always been a black and white thing, no gray. And I know that's
> hard for people to accept. So I try not to burden them with *my* feelings. I live
> by *my* code. And it's pretty clear cut [Mrs. Kohn's emphasis].

There is no irony in Mrs. Kohn's reply. She does not see that it was her brother's reluctance to share his pain or ask for help that adds to both of their loneliness and causes them to suffer. Yet she articulates well our society's preference to act rather than converse, to do rather than be, to progress rather than be still, and to demand action of oneself in order to escape suffering.

SOCIAL SUFFERING AS PARADOX

Despite the fact that suffering is often a lonely and private matter, society determines not only how to behave while suffering, but also whose suffering is more *real* and more noteworthy. For example, a culture determines whether old age is revered or ignored. The political and social climate at a given point in time decides that suffering in old age demands attention and care, or is to be expected and therefore dismissed (Amato, 1990).

Does suffering in age earn a story in the annals of a cohort history? The elders discussed in this chapter generally rejected the right to name their own anguish or grief as suffering. Rather than accepting the "right to suffer" because of their age or circumstance, they struggled to maintain the characteristics developed in youth, such as agency, independence, privacy, self-control, and stoicism in the face of suffering. Although society may have rescinded the demand for these characteristics in older age, it was too late for elders to adopt another way of relating to themselves and the world.

Mr. Callen linked the data about himself—his ego, race, and alcoholic past with the conviction that he never gave up the reins of his life, and therefore never suffered. He retained control over his suffering by defining it as "not suffering." Because he confronted and overcame attacks of racism, illness and loss, his personal interpretation of suffering as a lack of control (to which he never succumbed) kept his personal integrity and social value intact. He acknowledged the tremendous amount of worldly suffering within the context of African-American history, which for him is the standard of suffering. Mr. Callen's suffering is social—it was born in his early awareness of racism, and has expanded through the years to include other personal and social demons. The demons that continue to haunt him, despite a belief in his own superiority, add to his suffering through a profound loneliness.

The death of Mr. Wickers's wife and the loss of his home are intricately intertwined to create a unique experience of suffering. A healthy, secure family and a piece of the American Dream—a home—were symbols of his achievement. His losses were also symbols of his impotence—a word loaded with cultural and moral value—to shield his wife from cancer and his children from witnessing their mother's suffering and death. Mr. Wickers' suffering resulted from the cultural notion that material goods equal success, as well as from the social barriers that placed these goods beyond his reach. Mr. Wickers' realization that "there is no dawn" diminished his area of control, but forced him to exert a greater watchfulness over the state of his soul. He is comforted by the thought that social justice occurs sometime and somewhere, even if it does not occur in this life.

Mrs. Kohn witnessed her brother's return from the war with helplessness; after his stoke, she watched the decline of his body with a sorrow that is tinged with wonderment. Why did these events befall him? Mrs. Kohn was always able to "pick up the pieces" of her life even after the tragedies of losing two children and her beloved husband. But watching her brother lose the ability to do for himself is too much for both of them to bear. The theme of independence helped Mrs. Kohn maintain a consistent and continuous identity throughout life. She acknowledged that suffering comes from both holding independence as one's greatest treasure, as well as from its loss.

The paradox of social suffering is poignantly and tacitly stated by the elders discussed in this chapter. Society's injunctions to work hard, maintain a private

dignity and be self-sufficient during crises resulted in a suffering that was mani-
fested by intense loneliness.

THE NEXT CHAPTER

Chapter 6 explores the unique ways in which elders cope with suffering. The
cases used as examples in Chapter 6 explore how elders accept, handle, manage
or refute their experiences of suffering. Elders' methods of coping with suffering
also depend on their perception of suffering's cause.

CHAPTER 6

Coping with Suffering

Respondents define and express suffering uniquely as well as with commonalities that span the sample. Uniqueness speaks to persons and circumstances that cannot be replicated. Commonalities speak to our common humanity filtered through cultural responses to experiences considered negative. The individuality and similarity that respondents show in reacting to negative events extend to how they cope with them. If suffering is viewed as a normal part of life, respondents may assimilate the experience to a long-standing view of the self (Becker, 1997; Belsky, 1997). If suffering so disrupts an elder's self-view and model of how the world operates, the elder may re-build a cognitive schema that accommodates new information about suffering. Most respondents considered themselves unchanged by the experience. They struggled to remain intact by preserving basic personal characteristics and core values despite suffering.

The way in which older persons cope with suffering also depends on its perceived cause. When suffering results from pain or illness, respondents may use the expertise of medical professionals or alternative therapies to discover the root of illness, to alleviate or manage pain, or to find healing. When suffering results from loss, elders may use social means to deal with grief, such as seeking the comfort of an existing social network, cultivating a new reference group that has experienced a comparable loss, or, as we have seen in the cases of Mr. Callen and Mrs. Kohn in Chapter 5, relying on inner strength to privately work through suffering. When thoughts about dying or death evoke an existential suffering, elders might turn to the religion of their childhood, rework prior beliefs into current appropriateness, seek out others who are on a similar quest, or practice or cultivate a personal relationship with God (Smith, 1996), to avoid the existential vacuum shaped by thoughts of finitude.

An aspect of coping with suffering is comparing one's suffering with the suffering of age peers or with suffering that occurred earlier in life. Many elders reported that they believe "everybody, by the time they reach old age, has suffered." Belief in the ubiquity of suffering removes the feeling that one was specifically targeted by illness or loss, affirms that tragedy strikes all people at some point in life, and shows that one way of coping with the aloneness of suffering is to generalize the experience (Harper, 1990). There is a cultural aspect in comparing one's suffering with others'. In a competitive society, to outlive one's contemporaries or to suffer and survive is to triumph.

An essential method of coping is to form a plausible answer to the why of suffering. To ask this fundamental question is not to know the precise root of suffering, although this might be the case, as much as it is an attempt to understand the place of suffering in one's life. Is suffering seen as a lesson or a punishment? Is it deserved or unfair? An elder may create an answer to the why of suffering with the same tools that she employs to classify other tragic or incomprehensible life events. Some elders use a long-standing or newly generated theodicy to answer the why of suffering and thus to have some control over it.

Suffering that results from causes such as guilt, regret, shame, or an inability to forgive someone or perceive oneself as forgiven is especially painful because elders may see no point to this suffering. Poor choices made decades earlier seem irrevocable in older age; their tragic ramifications seem immutable because of "no second chances." Paths not taken, shame over actions or forgiveness not given or received may cause a subtle dimension of suffering (Alexander et al., 1992) that profoundly disturbs an elder's sense of wholeness.

The obvious question of this chapter might be: How did elderly individuals interviewed for this study cope with their suffering? Are answers to the why of suffering gleaned from elders' existing world views? Or, must respondents because of suffering, construct a new schema of the world? I offer three cases that illustrate how these questions might be answered.

MR. DANDERS

Mr. Danders is an 83-year-old African-American widower who lives with the youngest of his four sons in their West Philadelphia home. I interviewed Mr. Danders seven years previously for a project that explored men's experiences of fatherhood.

When he arrived at my office for our interview he seemed unchanged— he walked as straight, spoke as deliberately, and acted as gentlemanly as I remembered him. He revealed that despite appearing the same, he felt "much different" because he was "still grief stricken" over the death of his wife and "kindred spirit" four years previously. When I asked him to tell me the story of his life, he replied:

> I was born in South Philadelphia in what could be characterized as a poor neighborhood, and ethnically diverse. There were persons of Afro-American extraction, Jewish extraction, Italian extraction and a few Irish-Americans. As far as I can recall there was never any racial strife; we all played together. And it wasn't up until 8 or 10 years of age. . . . Children don't put a lot of

stock in the color of your skin. So, you get a case where you start out at the epitome of innocence and then your soul becomes contaminated by external forces.

Mr. Danders' opening comments set the tone for the interview and provided at least one theme for his life story—he places himself in the context of the smaller and larger, private and public world of his childhood. He is acutely aware that his personal history is embedded in a communal history as well as within the ethos of a larger world. This ethos accepted the "contamination" of a people's spirit through prejudice. He learned early in life that individuals and communities are affected by racial hatred at the core of their existence—their soul.

But the neighborhood didn't stay the same. There was an exodus. The commercial enterprises in the neighborhood were mom and pop stores. And the Jewish entrepreneurs—their families lived on the premises. They had a great drive for education for their kids. As soon as they got on their feet, they relocated. And the Italian Americans, they had a great family structure. If one family had a father who was a stonemason, and another had a father who was a carpenter and another a plumber, they helped each other do better and get out. So you had that loss of ethnic groups. And it was not an upheaval; it was a gradual thing. They all disappeared. I wondered about my own people, but it didn't hold true.

Mr. Danders has the aura of a philosopher. He takes pride in using the word that best conveys his meaning and ponders the cause and effect behind social events, such as the "exodus" of various ethnic groups from his neighborhood. Family and community members, such as pastors, teachers, uncles, and especially his mother, were the benefactors of his character and skills.

The greatest influence upon me was my mother. She was the kindest, most loving and the most. . . . [Pause] It's very rare when I become lost for words. The most . . . patient. Yes, that was the quality I associated with my mother because she was not quick to anger. And if you're not quick to anger, you think first. And she epitomized that. And that is the greatest legacy that she left me. Patience.

Despite doing well in the South Philadelphia schools he attended, he had little desire to attend college. His parents could not afford, and did not encourage higher education for any one of their three children. He admitted to having a "wandering spirit" as a youth. With a laugh, he told me that he loved the "sights and sounds" of the boxing gyms above the neighborhood storefronts. A boxing scout spotted his talent, took him on as a protégé, and promoted his career.

Yes, I aspired to be a pugilist. But I discovered that if I could get my opponent rattled I could beat him. It was a case of mind overcoming brawn I guess.

Another theme in Mr. Dander's narrative is the fact that his intelligence was his greatest asset in and out of the boxing ring. He laughingly recalled that his boxing "career" lasted for "all of 26 fights." He eventually joined the Marines at the start of World War II.

> I was in the Seventh Separate [Marine Corps]. See at that time there were two Marine Corps, the white Marine Corps, which according to them was the bona fide Marine Corps and the black Marine Corps which was vehemently opposed in some quarters. Oh, segregation was alive and well. I rose from a private to the exalted status of Buck Sergeant. Three stripes now and I'm running the outfit [chuckle].

Mr. Danders ascended the ranks of the Seventh Separate because of his ambition and attention to detail. He described himself as "lucky" because the only time he saw combat was in his own camp. The black Marines opposed their "separate and unequal" treatment and started a riot in quarters. This incident was neither the first nor the last time that he felt the sting of segregation, discrimination, and the rage they engender.

> We were housed in a hut. The sides were literally made up of pressed paper, and I could hear the bullets coming in, whoo, whoo, whoo. And of course I was on the floor, flatter than last week's beer!

Mr. Danders shakes his head, and remembers that although he did not oppose the reasons for the riot—the lesser quality of housing, rations, tools and armaments that the black Marines received in contrast to their white counterparts—he believed that there were more productive ways to fight the system. His account of the incident also shows his use of humor to defuse the effects of painful memories.

> Because I've seen a whole lot of stuff it's a wonder that I'm not a bitter man.
> **Interviewer:** Why do you think you're not?
> **Mr. Danders:** It would be extremely counter productive to become a rabble-rouser and all that sort of thing when I can use this (points to head) to achieve a positive result.

Despite the discrimination he experienced, Mr. Danders described his time in the service positively. He learned a great deal about people and acquired concrete skills that made him marketable in a boom economy after the war.

Mr. Danders left the Marines in 1950; at 36 years of age he was married with two children. He worked as a metallurgist for the city during the day and earned a college degree at night. He hoped to use his intelligence and engineering skills to fulfill his potential, to provide for his family, to offer a role model to his sons, and to "change the world." Although these were difficult goals for an African-American man to achieve in the 1950s, Mr. Danders felt prepared to meet any opposition. His desire to succeed emerged as another theme in his life story and story of suffering.

> My work afforded me a great deal of personal satisfaction. I traveled extensively. And when I would show up on assignment invariably I was looked

at askance due to my high visibility. And right away I was subject to veiled quizzes. And I could see what they were up to.

Mr. Danders laughingly recalled an incident that typified the daily scrutiny under which his colleagues as well as his superiors placed him.

> Every Friday we had a progress meeting with management. They wanted my opinion on something and I know they were trying to trip me up. So I recited a whole bunch of gobbledygook, and the Lord was with me because He's the only one would, could put words in my head and bring them out of my mouth. When I finished the room erupted in uncontrolled laughter. When order was finally restored I said, "Gentlemen, what I have just passed on to you is not my opinion, but your opinion. You wrote it in your guidebook." Silence.

Throughout his career, Mr. Danders anticipated hostility from his co-workers and higher-ups. Being "one step ahead of the pack" was his weapon. He clarified that the silent partner in his life was God. By himself, he could adequately play the game with his co-workers and win. But his dependence on God's help kept him from any hubris that occurs through besting others. He believed that God *must* be a co-conspirator in his conflicts or he would fail.

During the 1950s Mr. Danders was busy raising four children. He enjoyed consistent promotions at his job. This period also brought one of the saddest events of his life—the death of his mother.

> It was 1957. But I didn't brood about it. I was engaged in raising a family and that was therapeutic in itself.

With this brief comment, Mr. Danders relays both his strategy for coping and a reaction to loss frequently made by men in the sample. First, he did not allow grief for his mother to become suffering. Raising children demanded focus and commitment. Investing himself in his children's development honored the memory of his mother and helped him cope with the loss of her.

Second, his comment concerning her death: "I didn't brood about it," reminded me of the words of Mr. Gordan discussed in Chapter 3—"But I didn't cry"— after the death of his wife. It was not that both men felt no grief, but it seemed essential to them that they did not succumb to it. For Mr. Gordan, showing the emotion of sadness was to give in to it; for Mr. Danders, time was better spent in generative action than in mourning his mother. When I asked him if there was an event, incident or time period in his life when he suffered, he replied:

> In 1971 I was invited to Ohio to present a paper for a convention of engineers. I took my wife along because she had never flown before. We flew first class. When we checked in they issued the badge. On mine, I had a big blue circle that identified me as the guest speaker. Anyhow, that first night we go into the Rathskellar for a nightcap and here are some other conventioneers. As we walked in I think I spoke. But they totally ignored my wife and myself.

The next day I was to present my paper. They called my name and I got up, approached the podium and it was just like somebody said hush! Because it was just like I told you before, my high visibility, there was a whole lot of quizzical looks on people's faces. What's this guy going to do? And so I went on to present my paper and I was received with quite a great reception. And I knew that those same ruffians who had even ignored my wife, were not even civil, were in the audience. [Pause] But retribution is sweet.
Interviewer: That was suffering.
Mr. Danders: (With a wave of his hand) Oh, I dismissed that as churlish behavior. I don't allow myself to suffer. Why am I going to suffer for Joe Blow's transgressions? I won't allow myself to do that.

Mr. Danders clarified that suffering is a choice. Like most respondents, he stated that "suffering is in your perception" of tragedy. He might have sffered through this incident had he allowed ignorance to defeat him. *He* chose how to react to the pointed and random cruelties that he experienced throughout life.

But I think I'm an eternal optimist. Listen, I've been refused a cup of coffee and a doughnut by the Red Cross. So what am I worried about? Ever since then, when I came out of the service one of my favorite charities is the Salvation Army because they were good to me. So I support them.
Interviewer: Did you tell your children these stories?
Mr. Danders: Occasionally. But they don't encounter what I did because they're not doing what I did. The oldest boy, he's a stockbroker; the second boy works for the gas company, the third works for S. University, and the fourth boy is an entrepreneur. A whole lot of us were on the cutting edge. That's why you have Dr. Martin Luther King.

Mr. Danders fought on the frontier of social change. His comments about the "next" generation reminded me of Mr. Callen's remarks, mentioned in Chapter 5. Both men stated that younger African-Americans enjoy open doors because their cohort paved the way for equal opportunities and social justice. Mr. Danders believes there is one sure route toward social equality.

The keystone to improvement is education. I had the most trouble out of those who had the least education. Because the easiest thing in the world to do is to denigrate. It doesn't take any intelligence to do that. But if you're going to make a contribution, you've got to be prepared, See? Mentally, physically, morally. You will always have confusion when you're dealing with people of limited intelligence. They just aren't ready.

After this comment, Mr. Danders used the word suffering to describe a period in his life that he seldom permits himself to remember, and almost never discusses.

When I was working at the arsenal, I had a fine engineering background and I just couldn't achieve a breakthrough. That really got to me. As a result I got ulcers. I really suffered there. Mentally and physically.
Interviewer: How did you come through that?

Mr. Danders: I had to have surgery for the ulcers. And I did get advancement so that was some sort of balm.

Interviewer: How did the advancement occur?

Mr. Danders: By instituting an Equal Opportunity suit against the powers that be and going all the way to Washington. And when Washington made their decision they sent it back to the arsenal, and they told them that this man had to be placed in the position commensurate with his qualifications. And that was that.

Interviewer: How did that make you feel?

Mr. Danders: Vindicated, of course.

Interviewer: How was it working there after that?

Mr. Danders: Well, I was almost feared. I had devious tricks that I used. See, I was in the unenviable position of having a boss who didn't know what I was talking about. So, in a case like that, I would never talk down to him, no. I would talk on the same plane that I learned, and if the listener didn't understand it, too bad! I'll tell you, it was something else. And they would leave the area, quickly.

Interviewer: It must have been very hard.

Mr. Danders: Well, a lot of my co-workers, some of them came to me and said, you know, I don't know how you could stand it. I said well, somebody had to do it. So it had to be me.

Mr. Danders fought this injustice for his own sake as well as for those who came after him. After all, he explained, he followed a long list of heroes who had stood on the frontline of social change.

Interviewer: How long did that go on?

Mr. Danders: About a year.

Interviewer: After that period, did you feel or think differently about yourself, about the world, about God, or about anything?

Mr. Danders: No, I felt the same about myself, because I was focused. I felt the same about the good Lord because I depended on Him. Sometimes the fact that you go through suffering, either voluntary or involuntary makes you redouble your efforts to do something. If you're sitting here suffering the pangs of hunger, the only intelligent thing to do is to go out and earn the money to get a square meal.

Interviewer: But it didn't embitter you?

Mr. Danders: No, no, I always wanted to change things. I was able to change a whole lot of things as far as segregation.

Mr. Danders interpreted this event—one that might bow many people—as an opportunity. A concrete experience of suffering demands a well-planned response. He differentiated the experience of suffering from incidents of depression and sadness.

Sadness is an emotion and depression is a melancholia that you can overcome. With suffering, there's no way out. You're up against a stone wall. What do I do? Suffering is where your spirits are at a very low point, it might be the nadir. That's suffering. But see, if you have a religion, there's always a way out.

Mr. Danders, along with many respondents, spoke of the prison-like nature of suffering. That is, suffering permits "no way out" of a negative situation. His religious beliefs, however, construct an exit from suffering. Faith replaces suffering with hope.

Mr. Danders' cared for his wife at home after a disabling stroke, and felt "great sadness" after her death.

> One morning she came downstairs and I made a visual assessment of her condition. I decided attention was needed, so I dialed 911 and she was transported to the hospital. That was it. She was not laid up there. She was taken on an emergency basis and x number of hours later she passed away. [Pause] Upon the death of my wife, that was quite a different story. Because I was retired and I was looking forward to a fine retirement for the two of us. Her death had quite a negative effect on me. But I was able to overcome my melancholia. I gravitated into volunteer work and that type of thing. Church was a great influence, so I was able to overcome the trauma, but not completely.

Mr. Danders' use of words might seem to distance him from his feelings. He spoke of the period before and after her death almost clinically, but admitted that most of his dreams died with his wife. When I asked him what a picture of suffering would show, he answered:

> Well, it would be a man with a very haggard face and obviously disheveled and perhaps if you took another photograph that included hands, for example, his hands would be clasped tightly together, indicating anxiety.
> **Interviewer:** Why disheveled?
> **Mr. Danders:** Because when a man reaches that point the last thing he thinks about is his personal appearance.
> **Interviewer:** Is there anyone else in the photograph?
> **Mr. Danders:** No, he's alone. See, that's the epitome of suffering—you're alone.

Mr. Danders' suffering "man" endures a silent lack—of peace, of others, of fullness—a variation on Augustine's view of evil, or suffering, as privation of the good. His portrait shows an uneasy familiarity with the power of loneliness to diminish self-esteem. Although God is absent in his portrait of suffering, Mr. Danders reveals that after his wife died and before he "re-found" his faith, he was the man in the picture. In reviewing his life through the interview process, Mr. Danders retrospectively sees value in his suffering.

> Sometimes in speaking to an audience that you know, I have used the expression so and so has been tried in the crucible of suffering. It makes you stronger, it makes you a better person. You take for example when I was

blatantly discriminated against. I, well, suffered as a result of that racial discrimination and all like that. But it made me a better person because it made me see I could do something to change that.

Interviewer: Do you think that suffering is a normal part of life?

Mr. Danders: Yes. There's nobody that's laughed their way through life, believe me.

Mr. Danders recognizes that there are various kinds of suffering, such as disappointment, frustration, and an inability to use one's talents. To him, the worst form of suffering is that which people bring on themselves.

Sometimes suffering can be self-imposed. You might as well expect to suffer economically and otherwise if you have nothing to offer society like skills or education. Because one thing is certain, the world doesn't owe you a living. Complaining about life being unfair is spinning your wheels. Talking about it when you ought to be getting an education doing something about it.

Mr. Danders' themes—that he took part in changing the larger world, that he recognized his talent and used it as a weapon against potential foes, and that he suffered for the cause of social justice, binds together both the various stages of his life and his life story. His message to others: "Don't tell me life is unfair; I know all about it," is the premise upon which these themes hold. At 83, Mr. Danders is involved with college scholarship programs for neighborhood youngsters. He also volunteers with a Marine veteran group and his Baptist church to distribute food and clothing to those in need. Through his life and his narrative, he shows that the job of improving the world continues to be *his* job, and that activity done for the common good is an effective method of coping with suffering.

MR. O'HANLON

Mr. O'Hanlon is a 77-year-old European-American man who lives with his second wife in a small apartment in a subsidized housing facility for retired policemen and firemen. He began his life story this way:

Well I was born in 1922. I was raised in Fishtown during the Depression. I'm the 7th son of nine children. There's two younger, my sister and my brother. All the other siblings have passed away. Things were tough. I worked at a young age, quitting school at 16 and I worked at bricklaying. When I was 19 years old I married my first wife. We were married in 1941.

Mr. O'Hanlon spent little time on his childhood. Like many men, he began his life story with facts about his early years and quickly arrived at the time in life when he made his own decisions, such as in his choice of work and marriage. As devout Catholics, he and his first wife hoped for a large family. Their inability to conceive was a great disappointment in their married life.

> It was rough. We done everything [to try to have children]. So finally we
> adopted. Maureen was 23 days old when we adopted her [1957]. Lenny
> was nine days old [1960].

After 16 years of childlessness, Mr. O'Hanlon reported that adopting the
two children were the happiest events of his life. For the O'Hanlons, because the
"kids were doing good . . . life was great."

A major part of Mr. O'Hanlon's life story focused on military service and
the jobs he found after he was discharged.

> I got out of the service in 1945 and I went back to work at bricklaying. In
> 1950 I took the exam for the police department and I fared very well on it.
> And I was appointed in November of 1950. Then I was assigned to the
> 6th police district and spent time there. I was made an acting detective in
> October of '51. In 1952 I was transferred to the homicide unit and worked
> there 'til 1961. In that capacity, I had all kind of murders, a lot of mob
> murders and so forth that I worked on.

Mr. O'Hanlon's formal, chronological way of relating his life story, especially
his work experience, is reminiscent of stereotyped police talk. Because he worked
at many levels of law enforcement, he met "all types of people—the good guys
and the bad guys." He admits that he internalized the lessons that he learned
from both groups—"how I wanted to be and what I didn't want to touch—like
drugs." His experience as a homicide detective introduced him to the dark side
of human nature. His belief that all people share this darkness caused him
neither to judge others nor to think of himself as too different from those on the
"opposite" side of the law. He learned early in life that a thin line separates moral
from immoral behavior, self-control from rage, impoverishment from plenty,
and despair from hope.

> An old-timer taught me that. I was a young detective. Talking one night,
> I guess I was being critical, you know judgmental about one of the prisoners.
> And he said to me, "Well, son," he says, "Put yourself in his shoes and see
> how you think." And I did. And I thought, well, I'm a very level headed
> person, what would I do if the same situation arose?

Throughout his narrative, Mr. O'Hanlon posed this question to himself. His
answer: "Nine times out of ten you would have done the same damn thing."
This response, as a pervasive theme throughout his life and narrative, becomes:
1) the reason he believes he was not "corrupted" by police work like many
of his fellow officers and, 2) a statement of connection to other human beings.
When his knowledge about mob crimes and abortion rings promoted him
"inside—to a desk job," his work "lost something."

> I was assigned by the commissioner on different special investigations. I
> worked there until 1973 when I retired. I went in one day and the job didn't

have it no more and I just retired. I had no plans on retirement; it was a spur of the moment thing. Just walked out. That's it, I've had it.

Mr. O'Hanlon's need "to be moving" and "on the street" was a major reason for leaving police work. His wife's disability also factored into the decision. By age 50, the first Mrs. O'Hanlon was crippled with arthritis. Her constant worry about her husband's safety exacerbated her physical problems.

> She hated to see me strap on a gun and go to work every day. She was petrified. I'd get a phone call at two o'clock in the morning and get up and have to go real quick. And I never talked police work at home. She'd read it maybe in the newspaper, but I never discussed it with her. When I retired I come home this day and I said I retired today. Her condition improved. I didn't do much for the next couple years because of tending to her. She had her feet rebuilt; her hands rebuilt; they were all like this here (gnarled) and they straightened them out. And we were raising the kids, the kids were doing good. 1980 she died. Then I got work as a private investigator.

Mr. O'Hanlon describes his first marriage as "good, oh, the best." By today's standards, we might wonder if the couple's lack of verbal communication exemplifies a "good" marriage. Perhaps they agreed to skirt discussion about the danger of police work. Or, as the breadwinner, perhaps Mr. O'Hanlon felt that the date of his retirement was his decision alone. For members of this cohort, subjects for decision-making often fell under strict categories of men's or women's domains.

After his first wife's death, Mr. O'Hanlon felt "lost for a while," but was determined to stay busy. "I was going nuts sitting here," he said. He earned a license as a private investigator and at the same time, a new opportunity presented itself.

> I went to visit my sister at the soup kitchen. She worked there. This place [soup kitchen] just opened up the year before. I had to see her about something and that happened to be in the afternoon, so I stayed and helped them serve dinner. Then I started going back on my days off.

Mr. O'Hanlon could not stay away from the shelter. He felt "transformed" by the people he encountered. The seed of compassion, always within him, was germinated by his experiences there.

> Finally I decided to leave the job [private investigator], and I volunteered at the shelter full time. I worked there 7 days a week. Then I met Rose, my present wife there. They call her Mother Superior. She still goes every day. And we've been married over 15 years.

Mrs. O'Hanlon has morning duty at the shelter. She makes breakfast for the hundreds of homeless that visit the shelter daily. Time spent there is both work and pleasure for Mr. O'Hanlon. He clarified that he receives more than he gives, and delights in the joy that he witnesses and shares.

> There's a lot more laughter down there than there is in this building (where
> he lives). Sounds funny, but that's the only thing that keeps them going, I
> think, that they can laugh.

Throughout the interview, Mr. O'Hanlon contrasted his "cranky" neighbors
with the people he serves at the shelter. He reasoned that because the latter possess
so few worldly goods, they also have less to lose. They seem far removed from
the worries his neighbors struggle with—fear of losing their children's attention,
their security, their health, and their lives. He credits the priests who run the
kitchen with feeding "spirits" as well as "mouths."

> With the priests, it's because of their outlook. They take the vow of poverty
> and they live it. When they talk about turning the other cheek, they do it all
> the time. They practice it. And being around them, you have to be influenced.
> If you're not . . .

Mr. O'Hanlon's worldview holds various perspectives about life—that of the
city poor who receive their daily bread at the shelter, the priests who run it, and
his neighbors—the former policemen, their wives and widows who were tainted
by the harshness of police work.

> See, policemen are very prejudiced, and not just the whites. They become
> that way in their job. Prejudiced against a lot of things, even against each
> other. It's because what they see everyday. Their outlook on life is a little
> different than the average person. They resent the drug addicts, the robbers
> and the murderers. They can't help it. I say to them [neighbors], if I was in
> the street I'd be no different from them; I'd be a bad ass, because I'd be
> out there for survival. So I always look at the other guy and I figure what
> would I have done? Most of the time you'd do the same damn thing yourself.

Mr. O'Hanlon is able to imagine himself in either of life's opposing roles, such
as prisoner or policeman, or resident at the shelter rather than volunteer. He
admitted, however, his abhorrence for drug users and his reluctance to take
even over-the-counter medications because of his negative experiences with
"junkies on the street."

> I never even take an aspirin. I just don't like drugs. I like to be in control. I
> don't ever want to be out of control. I seen so much of it with drugs, with
> people out of control, and what they do to themselves and their families—
> their kids, their wives, their mothers and fathers.

Mr. O'Hanlon's "need for control" negatively affects his health. Because he
refuses to take any drug, he "lives in constant pain" from angina, arthritis, and
skin cancer. He emphasized that he does not equate physical pain with suffering,
but that he *has been* suffering for ten years, since the loss of his son, Lenny, in a
head-on car collision. He describes this suffering as different from pain. To him,
it is an ever-present entity, a constant companion, and a demanding teacher. His

suffering teaches him that where life's major issues are concerned, such as life and death, he holds "no control."

> Lenny died on New Year's Eve; he was working as a private investigator. And no alcohol involved. Since then, I take life one day at a time. Nothing bothers me; whatever comes, comes, I have no control over it. I control what I can control and accept what I can't control. But even to this day it don't feel real. It's a pain you can't take anything for. Every waking moment is filled with it. I mean you could take a punch in the mouth and it wouldn't bother you, or a broken leg, or whatever. I had a lot of pain in my time but nothing could compare with it. Even now, it don't seem real. It gets easier but not better.

Mr. O'Hanlon's statements are dense and intriguing. To say, "it don't seem real" resonates to the shock he feels ten years after the loss. His comment that his suffering "gets easier but not better" implies acceptance of his son's death without feeling less grief. To remark that he could "take a punch in the mouth" is men's talk—his body could and *would* ward off any kind of physical punishment. The death of his son, however, is outside an acceptable hierarchy of pain—it is beyond the emotional and physical limit that any person should endure.

Mr. O'Hanlon said that he was "never the same" after Lenny's death. He admitted that "part of him died" with Lenny, yet an integral aspect of his identity remains tied to his son's. Past and future meet in current sorrow. Lenny's death reminds him that his own hopes mingled with Lenny's—father and son were planning to work together as private detectives. The future is filled with events, such as the births of grandchildren, vacations and holidays, that will never come to pass. Mr. O'Hanlon's suffering is connected not only to the loss of his son, but to the loss of being father to the son.

> He was on the list to become a policeman in Philly. He was working as a private investigator. So if he didn't get in the police department. . . . See, I was retired at the time—we were going to work together on my license as private detectives. But it never come about. And you know, Lenny died on New Year's Eve and we had planned to go to Canada for a fishing trip in May. We always wanted to. I had taken it several times, that trip, then I was going to take him, but it never came about.

Mr. O'Hanlon's enduring grief attunes him to both subtle and gross dimensions of suffering. He generalizes suffering by believing that all persons, at some point in their lives, suffer. He personalizes suffering by putting a face on each type of anguish he encountered, such as unemployment, feeling inadequate or not using your talent.

> Loss is suffering and I don't know, but a person unemployed I imagine it's a mental suffering, you know, not feeling adequate. And not being able to do what you want to do, that frustration I think can be suffering.

Mr. O'Hanlon's permeable boundaries were formed early in life. They allow him the ability to empathize with the suffering of others as well as the right to judge how elderly people, like him, *should* react to the ubiquitousness of suffering.

> Suffering is a normal part of life. But I think by the time people get to be say 60 plus, I think you should have a little more maturity to go beyond suffering—really to go beyond a lot of things.

This thick statement may speak to Mr. O'Hanlon's religious beliefs. When I asked him to imagine what a picture of suffering would show, he replied without hesitation, "Christ on the cross. That says it all." If one sees the crucifixion as a model of suffering, suffering takes on a meaning that is inherently valuable. No matter how profound the loss or bleak the future, suffering is never the end of the story. For Mr. O'Hanlon, God's role in suffering is to nudge people beyond their own pain in order to witness the suffering of others. God "offered" Mr. O'Hanlon work at the shelter, which eventually became a remedy for suffering that must be "taken" daily.

Mr. O'Hanlon said that he "tried but failed" to "move beyond" suffering. He named "being in control" as a significant personal characteristic, but said that he relinquished control over the big issues of life, such as life, death, and suffering "ten years ago." Although he is still reeling from the "punch in the mouth," that life dealt him through his son's death, he does so while working to alleviate the suffering of others. When I asked him if he ever asks the question of *why* about suffering, he shook his head affirmatively.

> Of course, all the time. But you don't get an answer. This lady at the shelter, we're going back maybe 15 years, she had 11 children. She had three home but the other 8 were adopted out. One of the daughters, the oldest, was real pretty. And her and her sister were adopted out. And the kid done good; she was going to college. And then last year she was killed in a car crash. And that's the thought I have about her. She had the good life for several years. What happened? Why? There's no answer, there's just the question.

Mr. O'Hanlon embodies a paradox in suffering. He handles *his* suffering by serving suffering others. Although he believes there is no answer to the why of suffering, he continues not only to ask, but also to *live* the question.

MRS. INGLUND

Mrs. Inglund is a 75-year-old European-American woman. She lives with her husband and middle-aged son in a row home in the Northeast section of the city. She suffers from arthritis, emphysema, heart failure, and ulcerative colitis. For our interview, she sat on the hospital bed that replaced a dinette set in their small dining room. When I arrived, her husband offered me coffee and donuts, which Mrs. Inglund, although diabetic, also took. Her husband remained upstairs for the remainder of the interview.

Mr. Inglund also suffers from heart disease and can no longer drive. The couple depends on their middle-aged son who is unemployed due to "nervous problems" to cook, clean, and run errands for his parents. The Inglunds also have a married daughter, aged 55, who suffers from various physical and psychological problems. Although Mrs. Inglund's daughter calls everyday, they see each other infrequently.

The foremost way that Mrs. Inglund suffers is relationally. She worries about her daughter, whose troubles she attributes to a "bad marriage," and about her son who was "never right" after a breakdown 10 years previously. Mrs. Inglund's relational suffering reached a zenith when she lost her older son, over 35 years ago, through a bizarre accident. This loss altered the course of her life and charted a path toward extreme suffering.

> Luke was retarded. He got pneumonia. We took him down to F. Hospital because his lungs had collapsed. They inflated them, they collapsed again. And they took x-rays and they found out he had an obstruction in the lung. He must have swallowed something and he didn't tell us and we didn't know it. And during the operation his heart gave away. He was 17.

Luke's "sweet" disposition and the fact that he "needed" her more than her other two children bonded her to her middle child in a special way. Ten days before her son's death, her mother died. This forced her to question one of her mother's favorite adages: "God never gives us more than we can bear."

> But it *was* all too much for me. I went into shock. And they put me in the hospital. When I got home my husband had all the funeral arrangements made for Luke. There was a [Roman Catholic] Mass and a undertaker and everything was taken care of. We had the expense of the funeral but I had to go to a psychiatrist for one year. I could accept the death of one or the other but not both [Mrs. Inglund's emphasis].

Mrs. Inglund clarifies that she never expected to escape suffering. The loss of either her mother or son would be pain enough. The death of both within 10 days was unbearable. The expense of the psychiatrist along with her son's funeral added another worry. As a semi-skilled laborer, Mr. Inglund "never made much" and the couple struggled financially throughout their married life.

> He had 20 jobs in one year. Can you imagine? He'd walk out of one job, just quit it. But then he'd walk right into another one.

Mrs. Inglund admits that she was "never the same" after her son's death. She lived in a world of her own and found a perverse comfort in focusing on her ailing body. She now realizes that her all-consuming grief for Luke and her many illnesses affected her relationships with her other children.

> I said some terrible things to them. And I wasn't there for them. All I did was cry all day, cry all the time for no reason, drop a pin and I cry. I shook,

I was afraid all the time. I would stay in my room. It was a horrible, horrible feeling. Then I started with colitis, and from then on I got all the other sicknesses.

When asked if her husband was supportive during the illnesses that came in the wake of Luke's death, Mrs. Inglund shrugged.

Not exactly. He took it all in stride. And he said he wasn't able to figure it out, so he didn't want to talk about it.

Mr. Inglund was a committed husband and father. His actions toward his wife after their son's death reflect *acceptable* behavior for men in this cohort about openly grieving. Mrs. Inglund also echoed the appropriate responses for her gender and generation. She accepted her husband's inability to give her emotional support as long as he provided financially for his family.

We talked about it [the death] just once. One night, a couple months after Luke died—we lived in a three story house on Sixth Street. Luke's room was on the third floor. My husband was out in the hallway and he said, "Come on down Luke, you can come down." And he was already dead. I felt so bad. I guess it was in his sleep. I don't know if he was asleep or awake. I said to him, "Come back to bed. Luke's not here." He said, "Oh, I forgot."

This poignant exchange highlights the gender-based reactions of the couple to each other and to their son's death. Although both parents grieved for their son, Mrs. Inglund "fell apart" while Mr. Inglund carried on, worked even harder to provide financially for his family, and kept feelings about Luke to himself. After Luke's death, he found a job where he worked for the next 35 years and from which he retired.

As a devout Roman Catholic, Mrs. Inglund is convinced of the power of prayer. She worries, retrospectively, that her devotion may have played a part in her son's death. The fact that prayer both "holds her up" and causes her guilt speaks to the popular practice of Catholicism, especially when Mrs. Inglund was a youngster and adolescent.

You know, I always prayed that he'd be taken care of if something happened to me. I prayed awfully hard. Then I thought to myself, maybe I prayed too hard. Because then he died and I didn't have to worry about who was going to take care of him.

Mrs. Inglund's physical pain is extreme. Although she "lives on pain pills," the duration and intensity of her pain has made her immune to the pills' analgesic effects. Although she does not know the remedy for her pain, she knows its cause.

All my pain comes from doing men's work. After Luke died, I wasn't satisfied with the kitchen the way it was. I'd knock a window out, put in another window. I put in two layers of bricks in the floor. I put blocks in the ceiling by myself. I paneled the kitchen. I did all kinds of work. I did everything. It pulled my insides out. They just dropped out of me. That's why I'm suffering now. I did men's work.

Mrs. Inglund's statement about doing men's work may have many meanings. Do rage and grief come together as a heightened, but false sense of strength? Because her husband was unable to talk about their son's death, did she also do *his* grief work for him? After Luke died, did nothing satisfy her? Her graphic description of her "insides being pulled out" show the violation and wrenching pain of suffering.

Contrary to many respondents who differentiated sadness, suffering and depression, and even ranked them, Mrs. Inglund offered no such distinction. To her, these concepts merge on a continuum of sorrow. Loss leads to depression, which leads to periods of mania, which leads to physical pain, which leads to suffering. Witness Mrs. Inglund's all-inclusive definition of suffering:

> Suffering is a hurt. A pain that never goes away. Like with my son, or with my arthritis. Sometimes you wish you were dead when you have that pain.

Mrs. Inglund said that her doctors described her condition as "terminal." For many respondents, this label might lead to relinquishment of personal control. Mrs. Inglund retained control over herself and her life by altering her identity to fit her suffering. Because of doctors' prognosis, she changed her identity from a sick person to a dying one. This new identity assumes several aspects. It has a practical role—she organized her funeral and settled mundane affairs. She told her husband and children what she wants to wear for her "laying out," and how her gravestone should be marked. It has a spiritual role—she is embarking on a pilgrimage of self-review and making peace with her past. It even has a humorous aspect. She planned a "mock funeral" for herself and greatly anticipates how her friends will eulogize her.

Mrs. Inglund's sudden animation during the interview showed that the assumption of this new (dying) identity uplifts her.

> Tell me something, when do you think the soul leaves the body? I've been trying to figure that out. Now if you die during the night, in your sleep, the family wakes up next morning and finds you dead. They send for the priest and the priest gives you the healing sacrament. But you're already dead! When did the soul go? Some people say right away. And some say 24 hours, I don't know. I'm very curious.

Mrs. Inglund translated her lifelong curiosity about various subjects, such as history and current events, to issues of death and the afterlife. She currently feels she is in a kind of vestibule, waiting to be called to the next life, because she is confused about her existence in this one.

> As I grow older my friends are dying off. A few have died and they weren't sick; and I'm sicker than they are and they're gone and I'm still here. And I wonder why I'm here. I know I must be here for a reason, what I don't know.

Despite being housebound, Mrs. Inglund keeps in close touch with several friends who also have severe health problems. These women anticipate their death with a fervor that could be considered comedic, morbid or realistic. One of her friends had a mock funeral. Mrs. Inglund described this gala as "so much fun," and said that it gave her the idea of throwing one for herself.

> We had a good time. She fixed up her sofa like a casket. She laid on it and then got up and said, "Make sure you say good things about me. I can still hear you." Oh, we all laughed. Then we all talked about stuff, you know, experiences like what death is like and what not. I've heard some people say that when somebody died, they can feel them pass through the room. What do you think?

Just as Mrs. Inglund delights in a lively discussion about death with her friends, she seemed to enjoy our interaction, and tried to make it more conversational by asking my opinion, especially on other-worldly matters. Unlike some respondents who had difficulty "drawing" or "taking a photograph" of suffering, she relished this imaginative aspect of the interview. When I asked her what a picture or photograph of suffering would look like, Mrs. Inglund answered after a deliberate pause:

> It would be plain, not any trees, not any flowers, things that don't look right. Somebody with a deformed body. People hunched over, some people not walking right. You know they're suffering.
> Interviewer: Are you in that picture?
> Mrs. Inglund: Yes, at times. But there's other people in it too, lots. People from the senior center, and my friends who are sick or dying. We're all together.

Mrs. Inglund does not feel isolated in her suffering. She and her friends have created a new reference group of ill others in which the norm is sickness and imminent death (Murphy 1987). Perhaps because of this, and contrary to most respondents' portraits of suffering, hers is well populated.

Likewise, many respondents did not speak as easily as Mrs. Inglund about suffering and dying. Her religious beliefs, which are similar to Mr. O'Hanlon's, convince her that there is value to suffering, that her body will be resurrected, and that existence after death will be more joyful and less painful than existence in this life. She added a personal take to the Catholic doctrine of the afterlife.

> In the next world there's no suffering; all the sick will be healed. I won't have arthritis in the next world. I won't have aches and pains. And we'll all be back together like we were when we were young. Some woman I know was born hunchback, all hunched over. She suffered all her life; she was born that way. Her father and mother didn't want her; nobody wanted her. In the next life, she'll be all straightened up. And Luke won't be retarded.

Mrs. Inglund's description of suffering, crowded with pain-filled and heart-broken others, includes the "end" of suffering in the next world. Mrs. Inglund constructed a relational bridge to others' suffering through her empathy. She travels this route daily and at a time when many elders might feel closed off by their pain.

Mrs. Inglund chose how to present herself in the face of suffering. She maintains, with effort, the roles that have identified her through the years, such as wife, mother, friend, and practicing Catholic. In the wake of information that her illnesses are terminal, she created a new role for herself as a dying person. By defining herself as someone who still has family, friends, a sense of humor, and faith, Mrs. Inglund does not experience suffering as a descent into despair, but as an upward struggle toward self-knowledge, an understanding of others, and a movement toward God.

TOOLS OF COPING

Respondents used qualities and strengths that they acquired throughout life to control, manage, understand or cope with suffering. These internal tools, such as curiosity, empathy, faith, intelligence, self-esteem, and a will to survive and thrive, all were part of elders' arsenal in warding off the enervating effects of suffering.

For example, Mr. Danders' method of coping with suffering was to use internal resources, learned from his mother and acquired throughout life, to handle suffering. When confronted with incidents that "could be called suffering," he used words instead of fists, appealed to the judicial system instead of allowing ulcers to destroy his body, and prayed instead of succumbing to despair. Coping with suffering was not a private affair. Suffering fueled him to battle social injustice for those who follow him, with weapons such as education and hard work. Mr. Danders "won" his bouts in the boxing ring and in life by using his most potent weapon—his brain.

Mr. O'Hanlon asked the ageless question of "Why?" after his son's death. While awaiting the answer, he turned outward in service to the homeless and acknowledged the ubiquitousness of suffering. He broadened the question of "Why me?" concerning the loss of his son to "Why anybody?" Although he will "never get over" his son's death, his grief gave him first hand knowledge that not only does the mourner's bench "grow ever longer," but also that the "eternal pity never rests" (Neuhaus, 2000).

Mrs. Inglund's experience of suffering was developed, interpreted and refined through the events of a lifetime. She related how a series of incidents, such as the loss of her son, worry about her living children, her own physical ailments, and the bitter memory of "doing men's work," resulted in a "life such as this" (Picard 1991).

I note that I considered Mrs. Inglund a paradigmatic case study because: 1) she narrated a range of types of suffering, such as emotional, physical, psychological and spiritual; 2) her willingness to share her life story and story of suffering with me is both poignant and illustrative of elders' desire to tell their story; and 3) her story of suffering compelled by its uniqueness and its commonalities with other elders' stories, especially women.

Respondents took strength from their religious beliefs to fuel them toward purposeful work that re-filled inner places that had been emptied by suffering. Both Mr. Danders and Mr. O'Hanlon volunteered for church-related organizations that reimburse them with emotional and spiritual goods. Mrs. Inglund challenged her suffering by imbuing it with religious meaning. She believed that the tragedies of this life will heighten her joy in the next. Each respondent's personal theodicy kept the integrity of the self and Divine intact, absorbed the power of individual (smaller) suffering, and acknowledged the tremendous amount of earthly (larger) suffering.

All three respondents talked openly about suffering and set their experiences within a framework of cultural meanings, religious traditions, personal belief systems and social roles. They were not mute in the face of suffering, but schematized and organized it through dense and complex narratives. Their common method of coping with suffering was to work—cognitively, physically, and spiritually, and all three worked with a diligence that buffered them against suffering's meaninglessness. While suffering may have caused (in Mrs. Inglund's words) "their insides to drop out" it did not leave them empty; a self persisted. For all three respondents "life," in whatever degree of fullness, was the preferred choice.

THE NEXT CHAPTER

Chapter 7 explores the Morality of Suffering. There are no morally neutral experiences; individuals evaluate incidents, events, or times of life as good, bad, worthwhile, worthless, useful or meaningless, according to personal and social frameworks of meaning. As an extreme in life experience, suffering evokes the use of morally charged words. Chapter 7 examines how three elders judge their experiences of suffering.

CHAPTER 7

The Morality of Suffering

The morality of suffering lies in the perception of its value (or lack of value) to the life lived. Cultural and religious beliefs and traditions guide the elder in an examination of suffering's meaning and worth. Yet people use, alter or reject these guidelines based on individual experience. Respondents' stories of suffering, similar to their life stories, are filled with morally dynamic words, such as "injustice," "righteousness," "shame," being wrong or feeling justified. These words convey a judgment about the experience of suffering based on a personal sense of right, wrong, and justice. Amato (1990) says that morally evaluating the experience of suffering is an ancient art because "all [people] are experts on suffering."

Despite "all being experts," and despite several definitions of suffering offered earlier, there is no standard for what suffering is. The definition of the word is culture bound; the connotation of the word reflects the ethos of the society and historical period in which it is used. The meaning of suffering is shaped by the perceptions of the individual who experiences it. To paraphrase most respondents regarding their experience of suffering: suffering is bad, yet inevitable. Living this moral paradox requires a response that is both culturally appropriate, yet communicates the unique subjectivity of the sufferer.

A culture suggests suitable reactions to suffering, as well as whose suffering counts in a society (Amato, 1990; Das, 2000; Kleinman, 1997). For most respondents, fighting against suffering and surviving it are perceived as appropriate responses that carry a moral message. Strength is an important characteristic in American society; to survive suffering from any cause is to prove strength through endurance. Another culture-based reaction to suffering is to minimize its effects. At interviews, respondents often chose to understate suffering. One reason might be to "appease the gods." To call one incident or event suffering might expose one to worse suffering. The perception of the sufferer about where an experience falls on an imagined continuum of suffering is significant in judging the experience.

A wealth of literature explores suffering as a status of patienthood, or as an experience of illness, especially in older age. Patienthood is a distinct category for elders who are hospitalized or housed in a long-term care facility. An individual assumes an identity within the institution; her connection to the community is delimited through her status as patient or resident. Once inside the facility, elders' suffering may be considered a transitional state that will be alleviated. Decline or illness in elders' bodies and minds that cause suffering are, as much as possible, controlled. Medicine, as a science of healing, attempts to rid elders of physical and psychic pain through appropriate therapy. Even in the context of hospitalization or long-term care, however, suffering is understood to be different from, and more encompassing than pain.

There is no specific status for the community-dwelling elder who suffers. Suffering outside of patienthood is confusing and uncertain to sufferers as well as to those who witness their suffering. Despite a threat to identity through suffering, community dwelling elders usually continue, as much as possible, in the roles that shaped their life with a binding identity (Kaufman, 1980). Yet, one of the central tasks of any sufferer, whether hospitalized, institutionalized or remaining in the community, is to find a meaning for the why of suffering (Frankl, 1959). How do older persons glean meaning from suffering when they are not patients, that is, when their status is ambiguous, and the emotional work of aging is, in itself, a daunting and lonely task? One method may be to give an account of suffering.

By recounting stories of suffering, elders assume a moral status; they take on the role of hero or heroine of their stories. By re-organizing their life retrospectively, they reveal a moral perspective. They show an outsider, as well as themselves, how they reap meaning for suffering from their understanding of the world and from their thoughts about suffering's value in relation to their entire lives.

It is within stories of suffering that powerful cultural myths and concrete individual experiences sometimes clash and sometimes merge. Elders may disclose the morality of suffering as they reveal both how they have internalized their culture's definition of suffering and how they describe the singular meaning that suffering holds for them (Reich, 1989).

The unique personal history of the informant I introduce as the first case informs her morality of suffering. The steady, long-term erosion of self-esteem due to relationships she was both born into and chose resulted in suffering and challenged her to find dignity and meaning within the experience.

MRS. JANSON

Mrs. Janson is a 79-year-old divorced European-American woman. She lives on the first floor of a duplex apartment in the Northwest section of the city. Her living room is large and bright, with white walls, light furniture, and pastel-colored upholstery. Pictures of her son and daughter and their families are hung on walls and set on end tables. A parade of small plush bears lines the television set. Mrs. Janson mentioned at the outset of the interview that the medicine she takes for "nervous problems" makes her hands shake and her voice quiver.

Mrs. Janson learned about our research from a church bulletin; she knew that the subject of the interview was a discussion of personal experiences of suffering. She held in her hand a tablet with answers to questions that she thought I would ask her and therefore "not waste time". Written responses also aided her forgetfulness, which she named a "problem that was growing worse." When I turned on the tape recorder and asked her to tell me the story of her life, she seemed surprised.

> **Mrs. Janson:** I can tell you about my husband and his drinking. Do you want that?
> **Interviewer:** Whatever you want to tell me.
> **Mrs. Janson:** I have three things I wanted to tell you. Okay, I wanted to tell you about this one time when my husband used to stop at the corner tap and you would never know whether he was going to be drunk or what. One time he said, "Why don't you come with me?" This was when my daughter was about five years old. And I finally went with him. I was very unhappy in that place and all of a sudden a man came in and said, "There's a little girl out here and she wants to know where her mommy is." I jumped over that barstool and went to my daughter and took her home and I never went in that place again.

Although Mrs. Janson's description of "jumping over the barstool" is emotionally graphic, her answers had a rote, inventory-like delivery. She revealed that she had been in counseling for over 40 years and feels comfortable scrutinizing painful events in her life and relating this information to intimate strangers. But the event she recalled was so painful she began to cry.

> The memory of that. . . . It is terrible if I dote on it. It's very sad. [Pause]. But I had to tell you.

Mrs. Janson believed that a brutal honesty must be part of the interview process; she saw our dialogue as something akin to both therapy and penance. To hold back might affect the purging and atonement inherent in confessing to either a therapist or a priest. She checked the paper in her hand and slowly related the second incident on her list.

> Another time he [husband] stopped at a bar and came home loaded. It was after dinner and I said my son could go out to play first and then do his homework. My husband was so angry [that I said that] he took the plate of spaghetti and threw it so hard that it made holes in the wall. The reason I was concerned about that was that the next day my son was having a scout meeting and I needed something to cover up those holes because I didn't want anybody to know what he was doing.

For Mrs. Janson, suffering is a record of her husband's abuse of alcohol *and* his family. Pride and shame motivated her to "cover up" his actions from acquaintances and neighbors. She reported that she became expert in hiding her husband's behavior from her family; by "that time" the couple "had no friends." She revealed that she could endure her husband's abuse more than she could accept that outsiders would "see the holes in the wall" *and* in her life. She related the final item on her list.

> The other thing is this: He always made me get money from him. I had to come home and ask him if I could buy a dress. And one time I said to him you must have somebody else. He said, "I don't have anybody else." But he lied I think because he got up and punched me in here [left side of her breast] and punched me on the arm. My arm swelled to the size of a golf ball the next day.

Mrs. Janson said that this incident of abuse was "the last straw." She went to the hospital for her injuries and a police report was filed. According to her, however, "they never did anything. They're for the birds for helping women." But reporting him to authorities "finally calmed him down a little." After she ticked off these events of suffering, she returned to the story of her life.

> I had very good parents; they took good care of us. But my father always had me jumping up and doing things. He could never let me stay seated. I think my father and my nerves had something to do with each other. I mean someone constantly having you jump up to get something. . . . He had me take up cleaning for my mother like my mother was helpless and couldn't do it. But I had to do it. My brother never had to do anything.

She traced the genesis of her "nerves" to her father's demands on her. She saw her mother as a silent partner to her father's tyranny; her brother was never the focus of his demands. She either remembered little else or did not want to say more about her childhood, which was "isolated" because of her "problems."

Mrs. Janson said that as an adult she made peace with her father although she never talked with him about the past. She said that she "wasn't that sad" when he passed away in 1957 and that after his death she "got better." Throughout the interview she stressed the link between her father and her "nervous problems," but "doesn't know" and "can't imagine" the reason why her father treated his only daughter that way.

Mrs. Janson's narrative is choppy; it is not threaded by time, but by the theme of abusive relationships. After she mentioned her father's death, she returned to her early years. As a teenager, she met two brothers who lived in the same North Philadelphia neighborhood where she grew up. She dated the older brother for a while, but decided he "drank too much," and chose to go steady with the younger brother, Ed. They married when they were both 21 years old. She described the early years of her marriage as "funny and fun," and spoke of ice cream parlors, nut shops, and movie theaters that the couple frequented when they were newly married.

Four years into their marriage, Mr. Janson found a "good paying job" in the oil burner business after a series of dead-end jobs. Mrs. Janson blames the people that he worked with, a "rough crowd of hard drinking men" for her husband's drinking problem. After their son and daughter, who are two years apart in age, started school, Mr. Janson's drinking became excessive and abuse was a regular aspect of their married life.

> By then, you never knew how he would be when he came home. The kids and I used to go in the back room and I'd hold them.

Mrs. Janson vividly portrayed the family's fear of her husband's violence. She and her children never discussed their father's behavior or what they remembered about their childhood. Although she described her marriage as "hell," she remained with her husband until she was 65 years old. She worried that her children, both married and with children of their own, would disapprove of their parents' divorce. When she finally told them she was leaving their father they were "very upset." Her husband, however, replied, "It's okay by me."

After her divorce Mrs. Janson lived alone for the first time in her life and felt that she had more time and energy to manage her "nerves." She felt "confused" after her marriage ended despite a conviction that life was "better without him." She revealed her conflict by weighing the positive and negative aspects of her life.

> I like my apartment. It's comfy. And I'm so thankful for my children. It's just a shame that the husband picture isn't in it. That gives me tears. But when I look at this little guy [points to picture of grandson on end table] it wipes it all away.

Perhaps Mrs. Janson's earlier expectations about how life would unfold contrasted with the reality of *where* she found herself at age 65. The important men in her life—her father and her husband—shared some characteristics: Both abused her, both controlled her comings and goings and her feelings about herself, and therefore one or the other defined her for most of her life. Mrs. Janson's grief for a *bad* marriage was unusual in our sample of women. Most women in the sample, such as Mrs. Brown and Mrs. Rink mentioned in Chapter 3, said that suffering due to abuse ended when they freed themselves from controlling husbands. Both Mrs. Rink and Mrs. Brown, however, described their childhood as surrounded by loving mothers and close siblings. Mrs. Janson felt lost at age 65 with no sure referent point to help her imagine the next phase of life. Despite her perplexity, she found an apartment she could manage on her disability income. When I asked her about the saddest time in her life, she named her mother's death, which occurred 15 years previously.

> My mother's death was very hard for me. It took me two long years to get over it. She had a heart attack.

When I asked her if there was a time in her life when she suffered, she answered:

> **Mrs. Janson:** I think it was the first time I went to the state [psychiatric] hospital. I was there a year.
> **Interviewer:** What made that suffering?

Mrs. Janson: Well, there were times when you really knew who you were and what you were doing. And there was other times that you didn't know nothing.

Mrs. Janson's comment reveals that for her, loss of self-awareness is suffering. Not to know yourself, your situation and your surroundings is to suffer. Her description of suffering includes a temporal component. The unremembered periods that she spent in the institution are named suffering precisely because they are unremembered; she mourns the time that she cannot recall who or where she was. Other respondents reported a similar definition of suffering. Mr. Callen, discussed in Chapter 5, defined spiritual suffering as "being lost to yourself." For many respondents, feeling bad is not necessarily suffering; apathy, numbness or loss of memory of one's own past is far worse. Mrs. Janson's comments also speak to suffering as a fragmenting of one's identity through time. How do we see ourselves as whole when pieces of our past go missing? She poignantly differentiated sadness and suffering.

With my mother ['s death], it was sad because the person you loved passed away. But being in the mental institution, that's suffering because there's no love there. No love period. Sometimes it just happens you have someone that takes care of you is nice to you but very rarely do you get someone like that. No love there. I remember though it's been a long time ago.

Perhaps for Mrs. Janson the most important aspect of self-awareness and moral agency is the ability to connect with others. The mental institution, reflective of the lack of reciprocal relationships, became a symbol of suffering. Within this bleak environment, however, she chanced upon a meeting that transformed her.

Mrs. Janson: There was a Reverend there that had me dust his desk for him. I liked him an awful lot. He kept the suffering out.
Interviewer: How did he do that?
Mrs. Janson: He was the love.
Interviewer: How was he the love?
Mrs. Janson: He made me feel big. He made me feel special. He did it on purpose.

Mrs. Janson found complex concepts, such as self, no-self, and the intentionality of love in the harsh world of the state institution, and brought them, many years later, to our interview. If the Reverend's request to dust his desk had been a random act of kindness, it would not have transformed her. He spoke to her uniqueness as a human being in order to set her apart from others; the grinding lack of individuality in the institution was integral to her suffering. She believes that his action saved her; she improved after this non-intimate, generally non-verbal relationship began. She described her feelings when she left the institution.

Mrs. Janson: It was a real joy, a real release and I'm one again.
Interviewer: What does that mean, you're one again?
Mrs. Janson: I'm my own self. I'm together.

This comment implies that suffering, according to Mrs. Janson, is a rupture of the self; she alluded to the sense of wholeness she experienced when suffering ended. Her physical fragility, evident at the beginning of the interview, was more apparent at the end. Our dialogue, which she described as "enjoyable," seemed to both energize and tire her. For Mrs. Janson, the morality of suffering is to bear it, to endure it, and perhaps most significantly, to remember it.

MR. GANS

Mr. Gans is a 73-year-old African-American man. He lives with his second wife, who works outside the home, in a row house in Northwest Philadelphia. When I interviewed him on a summer morning, the Gans' home and its furnishings looked worn and threadbare, as did Mr. Gans' clothes. At times during the interview, Mr. Gans himself seemed older than his years, and frail. When asked to tell the story of his life, he reached into the distant past.

> My father died in an accident when I was five and I was with him. He and I were very, very, very good friends. It was after midnight and we were on this lonely road and something spooked our horse. I think a spirit frightened it and it started to run. My father was holding the rein and one side burst. So there was no control over the horse. I was sitting at the back on a basket. My father misjudged the speed that the horse was going which was a terrible rate. He tried to jump off and see if he could hold its head. But he couldn't run fast enough. The wheel of the cart knocked him out and the cart passed over him, and he fell in a ditch. We got almost to the end of the road where the ocean begins, and this figure, more an image, came from nowhere. It was just like God was. . . . [crying] I always get emotional when I come to this part. That image came in front of the horse. Whoever it was put their hands up like this and the horse just . . . stopped. But my father, he died and I survived.

Mr. Gans condensed his early life into one night over 70 years ago when he lost his father and "good friend" in an accident that left him unharmed. This comment sets the tone for Mr. Gans' interview and provides a theme for his life. He believes that his father's death taught him the message of Ecclesiastes: "There is a time for every purpose under heaven." The tragedy also taught him that death was meant to miss him that night and also that "something spiritual was working" in his life. It brought him into contact with an "angel" that has followed him since his father's death.

Mr. Gans could not remember the reason that he and his father were out at midnight on this lonely road. He recalled only that spirits abounded in his childhood. His parents and their neighbors often discussed how one spirit brought sickness, another brought health, and another, death. For him, one spirit frightened the horse; another spirit saved his life, and yet another heralded his father's death. Although he believed he was touched by the mysterious hand of God and spirits, his mother introduced him to the practical value of domestic work.

> My mother taught me to sew, to cook, to do everything around the house. I love to cook; I bake every day. My wife don't have nothing to do when she comes home. I cook, I do the dishes, I sew her clothes. I do everything.

Mr. Gans gained various skills from male family members and friends of his father's. Although he never attended high school, he believed that he "knew more" than any child his age. He learned carpentry from an uncle, and as a child, assisted a mechanic "down the road" in repairing cars and trucks. Another uncle bought him "books on electronics." He assembled a radio from a kit when he was 13 years old.

Work was an important topic in Mr. Gans' life story. After he told me about the "unusual talents" he displayed as a child, he skipped to a discussion of his first full-time job. He did not mention when he married or how he met his wife, but said only that his first wife worked as a domestic early in their marriage. She asked her employer, a manager in an electronics company, if there were any openings for her husband, whom she described as "brilliant with electronics." The sole position available, her employer told her, was in housekeeping as an assistant office cleaner. Instead of refusing because he was over-qualified, Mr. Gans decided to trust his "angel." He knew that something better would come his way if he first took the humbler position in housekeeping. He described his first day on the job.

> I went in and they said, "You work with this guy." The fellow they sent me to work with said, "Look, I work here and I have no boss, nobody comes to look at me. I start work at 7 and when it's ten o'clock I go in here [a broom closet] and take a good sleep, so you can come in and sit down and sleep, too. You keep quiet and we'll be alright." We cleaned the offices together and then we cleaned the shop together. We did a little more cleaning and then we went into the broom closet and he sat down on the soft chair and closed his eyes. And I sat down on a straight chair and I watched him until he went fast asleep. And I got up; ran 'round the corridor straight into the employment office. I said, "I'm looking for employment." They said, "Yes, we're hiring." Just like that [snaps his fingers]. I fill out papers and they say, "We'll call you." I went back into the broom closet and close the door. He was still sleeping.

Mr. Gans draws a parable-like portrait of two men. Both are sent on a work assignment. One man chooses to sleep on the "soft chair" as the other hurries to find a better job. His parable portrays him as a man whose sense of responsibility matches his desire to succeed. He believed that it was his duty to find an outlet for his talent. He continued his story.

When he opened his eyes and said, "Okay it's time to go now," I didn't tell
him nothing. We went and we started to clean again. About three days later
my wife said the company called and you have an appointment. Nobody
knew I was working there as a cleaner.

A week after Mr. Gans cleaned offices for the company, he began his new job
packaging electronic equipment. His superiors noticed his self-motivation. He
was sent to school and received an electrician's license. Over the next 25 years
he was promoted into jobs that fostered his skills. He retired as supervisor of
the last department in which he worked. Mr. Gans smiled as he told this story;
he named the years that he worked for this company as the happiest in his life.

> **Mr. Gans:** Oh, I was making good money. I could send the children to
> college. My wife didn't have to go to work. I received full benefits. [Pause]
> But I made many mistakes.
> **Interviewer:** What do you mean?
> **Mr. Gans:** This interview is about suffering? [Pause] Well, I think I'm going
> through it now. I feel tense. I cannot tell my wife. I have so many bills.
> When you are owing people money they write you letters and make threats
> over the phone. They say we'll take your house.

Because Mr. Gans and his family "felt rich," during his working years they
"bought many, many things" on credit. Unfortunately, he had little understanding of interest rates and found himself in debt for "many thousands of
dollars." Mr.Gans took out a home loan in order to pay credit card bills. Although
he did not realize it at the time, this loan was actually a second mortgage on
the family's modest home, which he is still "paying off." When I asked him to
define suffering, he considered.

> I think it is regret. Sometimes all of these things come back to me at
> nights. Sometimes I just lie down and look at the ceiling for the whole night
> without a blink. Two or three months ago I started getting pain from it all
> over my body from no sleep.

Most respondents personalize their definition when asked to define suffering,
just as Mr. Gans did. One's definition of suffering is usually one's experience
of it. Yet all respondents, like Mr. Gans, spoke of suffering as an all-inclusive
experience.

> **Interviewer:** What is your regret about?
> **Mr. Gans:** My regret is for the mistakes I made about money. I cannot
> sleep. And I would say suffering has to do with loneliness, too. My wife
> doesn't know so many things. She is a person who comes home from
> work, has her dinner, and then she'll fall asleep and be gone 'til the next
> day. She don't know if Good Friday would fall on a Monday next year.
> I'm just sitting there alone with my thoughts. And I feel guilt, too. My wife
> should not have to be working, she should be home now. My children is in
> no position to help me. They depend on me even though they're married.

For Mr. Gans, suffering is both an inner and outer enemy who both is and *brings* suffering. The poignancy of his regret is its irredeemable nature; he sees no second chance to right past wrongs he believes he committed. His description of suffering as "loneliness" speaks to his unwillingness to share his worries. Perhaps he cannot give up an image of himself as his family's—even his adult children's—provider. Mr. Gans distinguished the concepts of depression, sadness, and suffering.

> They take different tolls, they give different pains. At first this [regret] didn't give me physical pain, but pain of the mind—and heart. I say to myself I should not have done it; I should not have taken the loans. It is a regret. But I cannot sleep, so my suffering becomes physical, too.

Mr. Gans cannot sleep because of his regret. Lack of sleep leads to worry and to bodily pain. Bodily pain brings further anxiety, which brings greater suffering. Suffering veers out of control and becomes a cycle of bodily, mental and spiritual pain without end. When I asked him what a picture of suffering would show, he said:

> **Mr. Gans:** It would be tension, stress, and pain from the tension.
> **Interviewer:** Is there anyone in the picture?
> **Mr. Gans:** Well, I would have to turn it on myself. I am alone in the picture.

Mr. Gans ultimately connected his financial suffering to his "turning away from the Lord's Word." He believed that while he was making "a lot of money" he "forgot the Lord." During the most financially solvent time in his life, he did not attend church or read Scripture. He was certain that neglecting his spiritual life made him vulnerable, which augered a "day of reckoning." In other words, spiritual impoverishment foreshadowed material poverty. Suffering forced him to "remember" God, and because this helped him to "save [his] soul" suffering has inestimable value.

> **Mr. Gans:** I think Biblically suffering is important. If somebody don't go through it they could lose their salvation because they would forget God. Some people can get carried away, you know.
> **Interviewer:** How do they get carried away?
> **Mr. Gans:** Well, I must say I was never a good steward. I handled the Lord's talent not in a good way. The things that he gave me, the money that I made, I didn't use it right. I suffer now because of that. I got carried away. God gives one person five talents, so I didn't use mine right. It appears as though I buried mine. So I am suffering now because of that. I blame myself.

Mr. Gans mediated the value of suffering through an interpretation of Scripture according to his religion (African-American Episcopal). Because he "lived high" in young and middle adulthood, "squandered" his talents, and mounted up bills that remain unpaid, he believes his suffering is a punishment both deserved and instructional. "With what I know now," he assures himself, "I will never stray." Mr. Gans found purpose in his suffering because it prepares him for a "changed" future. He recited the first and last prayer he offered each day: "Lord, take me out of this predicament. I will never mess up again."

Money is an overarching symbol of morality for Mr. Gans, that is, a symbol of what is right and wrong, good and bad, helpful or harmful to one's peace of mind in this life, and to salvation in the next. He believes that improper use of money led him into foolish behaviors that eventually resulted in a painful old age. Along with internalizing his religion's doctrine of stewardship, he also internalized the cultural directive for how men should react to pain.

> I'm not a talker. I'm a man to my own self. And I like doing things by myself.
> And I always find a way. But this time, I cannot find a way out of this. Life
> is not a smooth journey. Even some millionaires, I guess they have stress.

Part of Mr. Gans's suffering is his inability to "fix" his problem or "find a way out." Driving his wife to work each morning reminds him that he is not providing for her. It is not enough that he works hard in the home. For him, it remains the "man's job to earn the money."

> Yes, there's a lot of guilt. My wife would like to stay home now. She prefers
> to be a housewife. And that hurts—that I take her to work and I stay home.

Mr. Gans emphasized that his age has little to do with suffering. Although he recently tried to find a job and was unsuccessful, he did not blame his failure on old age; he believes that he is capable of "doing anything." He suspected he was viewed as a "risk" because of his "weakness." His regret causes suffering; suffering causes bodily weakness, and weakness causes his inability to reverse the trajectory of his suffering.

> **Interviewer:** Do you think being older and closer to the end of life is a form
> of suffering?
> **Mr. Gans:** No! I wouldn't exchange my age now for nothing. Because the
> times that we had before I think was better. In every stage of life there are
> insufficiencies, but this age is difficult. There is so much crime and laziness.

Although Mr. Gans admitted his "mistakes," he is convinced that he has grown in the "Lord's Word." Despite suffering, he offered proof that the Lord continues to bless him.

> I'm about the oldest member in my church. There's only four of us from
> the beginning. And one of them, she got sick, she can't move, just lying
> there, just lying there. So there's three of us. I would never, never never like
> to get in a position like that. It scares me, you know. I would like to go like
> that [snaps finger and laughs].

Mr. Gans nodded when I asked questions about the relationship between suffering and dying. To him, they are connected in a curious way.

> With suffering there is no limit. With dying, you know death is coming. You say, tomorrow is not the next day. Death is the next day. That is dying. Then it is over. But with suffering, there is no limit. It is all according to what is torturing you.

Dying has a limit; death is the end. Suffering is worse than death because of its temporal insult, and because the sufferer has no control over the event. For Mr. Gans, the end of suffering depends on the external "thing"—a lack of money—that is torturing him. Because he does not see death in his near future, Mr. Gans sees no end to his suffering.

THE HIERARCHY OF SUFFERING

A group of questions in the interview schedule asked respondents to differentiate among the concepts of depression, sadness and suffering. Some elders created a hierarchy of suffering as "first" or "worst." This hierarchy reflects a morality of suffering. To place suffering as first or worst within a group resonates to the negativity of the experience as well as to how that experience might be viewed from the outside, that is, by others in one's moral community, such as family, neighborhood, church group, or society as a whole.

Other respondents viewed depression, sadness, and suffering as linear in negative experiences, but different in cause and outcome. Respondents spoke of the internal-external nature of each concept. For many, suffering was an enemy that had its origin outside the self and threatened the self with attacks of illness, loss, or shame. Depression was "all inside"; sadness was an emotion that often resulted from experiences of grief that "everyone goes through."

Descriptions that elders give to depression, sadness, and suffering speak to a cultural change in the propriety of discussing subjects that were once taboo, such as certain physical diseases, abuse, mental illness, unalleviated grief, or alcoholism. Differentiation among the concepts also reflected respondents' self-insight. The vantage of age does not blend sorrows together or merge them in elders' memories. Each experience becomes further defined and refined with time, according to how and where it fits into the life as a whole.

The following respondent clearly differentiates the three concepts while cognitively constructing a link among them, based on her experience.

MRS. LOWELL

Mrs. Lowell is an African-American woman who lives in a subsidized apartment for seniors. She seemed younger to me than her 75 years, perhaps because she laughed often throughout the interview. Before I turned on the tape recorder, she told me that she was in good health and that she has many friends who live in her building. She also volunteers for her church; she visits parishioners who are hospitalized and other ill elders from the surrounding South Philadelphia neighborhood. When I asked her to tell me the story of her life, she laughed.

> Wow! The story of my life! Oh, brother! Well, I guess I'll start when I was a kid. There was 11 of us. And we were so happy. I guess that's why I don't have any children because I wanted 10. It was in North Carolina and we was raised on a farm. My mother would cook and bake all the time. And we came to the city when my father died. I was six! I hated it! All of us and my stepfather and three stepbrothers and one stepsister, all in this little house. I used to go crazy. I cried all the time.

Mrs. Lowell's recollection of the past is filled with exclamations and extremes. Only ten children of her own could match the happiness of her childhood. Her joy at being raised in a loving family in the open spaces of North Carolina did, however, equal her sadness when her father died and her mother and siblings joined aunts, uncles, and cousins in South Philadelphia. Her life took a drastic downturn when her mother remarried. The large family was forced to share a small row home with a stepfather and stepsiblings.

> He [stepfather] was so different from my father. He hardly even talked to us, much less play with us. My mother tried to put on a happy face, but when you love somebody you can see their unhappiness. She wasn't happy. My mother passed when I was 14, just when I needed her most. And it was hard. But my oldest brother and his wife, they had taken me in. And my oldest sister, she was married. She took my youngest sister.

Mrs. Lowell spent little interview time discussing her adolescence. She said that she would rather forget the years following her mother's death. Although her brother and his wife cared for her, he made little money as a cook in a large center city hotel and could not support her. She refused to remain on a "type of welfare" for orphaned children and left school to enter a work program.

> I love my brother and his wife. They treated me like their own. But I didn't finish school. I went to the 8th grade and I got out of school. I didn't like being on the welfare so I got a job. There wasn't no war yet, but maybe they was preparing for war so I went on a program to learn welding. I was scared to death but I said I'm going to learn that. I learned how to make tools. I stayed with it a couple of years and then the program gave out. So in the meantime I did housework, cooking and cleaning and taking care of people.

Mrs. Lowell's childhood ended with her mother's death. She described this time in her life as "scary," and admitted that she was afraid many times in her young life, such as when the welfare people came to check if you had a radio, when she left school, when she entered the government learning programs and when, because she did not attend school, she could not "find girlfriends." Despite the grief and fear she experienced in those early years, she was also proud of the "guts" it took to earn her keep at age 14.

At 18, Mrs. Lowell found work in a yarn factory in North Philadelphia, found friendships there, and made enough money to help her brother maintain their rented home. When she was 20 years old, she met her future husband. He worked as a bartender in the center city hotel where her brother worked. They were married eight months after they met. She believed that she and her new husband had many things in common, such as a sense of humor, ambition, no fear of hard work, and a strong desire for children. Unfortunately, the couple experienced three miscarriages early in the marriage.

> It was difficult because I always loved children and I wanted a big family. But then, I could say I raised about 14 children—brothers, sisters and my brothers' children. They used to come stay with me. A lot I took care of because their parents was working. So I guess I had children.

Mrs. Lowell often put a bright spin on an event or period of her life that might be considered bleak or even tragic. Although she described her marriage as "pretty good," she reconsidered her opinion later on in the interview and admitted that she left her husband after "a few years."

> I guess it could have been better without his mother interfering in his life. If we'd argue, his family always got in it. I couldn't take that. It wasn't hard for me to leave him, but he took it pretty hard because he didn't think I would do it. No matter what they doing to you they figure she'll still be there. He was unfaithful, he used to drink, he used to gamble. His gambling, his drinking, I'd put up with. But being unfaithful I won't take.

Although she believed that her husband would "never stop" his philandering, she feels remorse about leaving him. She wondered what part she played in his infidelity and if she could have avoided the "final step" of divorce.

> Looking back on it now, a lot of it could have been my fault. Because if I let him get away with so much and don't say nothing then he's going to keep on doing it. I should have talked it over with him and maybe, you know, it could have been different. I still loved him but I couldn't give in.

Mrs. Lowell refused to point a finger at her husband without turning it on herself. I could not discern whether she took responsibility for her husband's behavior because she continued to love him or whether, in viewing the marriage in retrospect, she was able to see *her* part in its disintegration. Whatever, she kept in contact with her husband and was with him "as a friend" at his death.

> He had gotten sick and I used to go see him. You know, just talk to him. But by then, it was all over.

Mrs. Lowell enjoyed "a few" romantic relationships after her divorce, but preferred to date "casually." She recalled her dating experiences with a dark humor; she realized that by the time her husband died she "didn't trust men." Her family, especially her younger sister, satisfied her need for closeness and took on the role of confidant. When I asked her about the saddest time in her life, she replied that it was *not* the loss of her parents.

> The saddest was when I lost my younger sister. She lived in this building.
> Oh, yeah, her and I would go everywhere together, do everything together.
> You know I had been with her much longer than I'd been with my mother.
> When my sister died I was 70.

The sadness that Mrs. Lowell felt when her sister died eventually led to suffering. Her sister was admitted to the hospital for a minor procedure and never returned home.

> It was late at night. He [doctor] was supposed to do some kind of test on her but he got to the hospital late and he was tired. I said, 'Why don't you wait and do this tomorrow? "No, I can do it right in her room." Then the nurse called back and said your sister wants you right away. That doctor got on the phone and said, "Oh, we have to take her to the operating room." I said, "Don't touch her 'til I'm there." She was in the operating room when we got there. Then he [doctor] comes out and says, "We're sorry but your sister passed." That was the worst moment *because it didn't have to be* [Mrs. Lowell's emphasis].

Mrs. Lowell knew that the doctor was "too tired" to perform the test and "too proud" to admit it. She believes it was ultimately his pride that caused him to "mess up" the procedure and cause her sister's death. As Mrs. Lowell relives the events preceding her sister's death, she rewrites her sister's last day. *If* Mrs. Lowell had been firmer in telling the doctor not to perform the test, *if* the doctor had not been tired and too proud to admit it, *if* she had been at the hospital instead of at home perhaps her sister would still be alive. Although her sister died over four years previously, the intensity of her shock, grief, and anger remains. She will never feel "at peace" about her sister's death because of its unfairness—her sister died in "good health" because of an arrogant doctor. Yet no one, neither the doctor nor the hospital, will be held accountable. She also worries that her sister will not find peace in the afterlife because of the untimeliness of her death.

> I had lost all those brothers, I had lost my mother, lost another sister, but this one (sister) we were so close and we had been together so long. Neither of us had children. We had each other. I miss her still. I think about her all the time. I even talk to her sometime. We did everything together and went everywhere together.

Mrs. Lowell and her sister were best friends and traveling companions; they interpreted the world for each other for the better part of each of their lives. She explained how her shock over her sister's death became suffering.

> With sadness (over her sister's death), someone else done it, the doctor done it. But then it went into suffering because I couldn't get over it. Suffering comes on you, you can't help it.

Mrs. Lowell felt that she was "being torn apart" after her sister's death. When I asked her how depression fit into this hierarchy, she replied:

Oh, depression is different altogether. Depressed mostly is when you're down on yourself. See, both sadness and depression go into suffering. Suffering is the worst. Suffering is something coming on you, like when my sister died and she didn't have to. It was wrong. Depression is something that I have done and I could have avoided, if I had done something some other way. Depression is something you have to do for yourself, the doctors cannot help you. You have to come out of it. You have to fight your way out. But once it goes into suffering, then it's hard.

Mrs. Lowell placed these negative concepts into strict categories. Sadness and depression are like tame streams which, if not handled properly, flow into a cascade of suffering. When I asked her what a picture of suffering would show, she considered.

I don't know why I keep looking at it as if something going round and round and round, getting bigger and bigger and bigger. You can't get out.

Mrs. Lowell's picture of suffering implies activity and vitality. The sufferer is trapped within the vertigo; she is dizzy from the motion but going nowhere. The core of suffering for Mrs. Lowell is being locked within a sadness that has taken on a life of its own.

Mrs. Lowell believes that suffering is a natural part of life; no one escapes it. She also believes that although "old age doesn't have to be a time of suffering," there is a suffering peculiar to old age. Old age holds the accumulated sufferings of dark memories, bodily pain, and broken or lost relationships. She described suffering in old age both metaphorically and symbolically.

Mrs. Lowell: As you grow older you have a shopping bag and every year you put a little bit more in it. The shopping bag is life, I call it. You're adding a little more onto it each year. In your old age, you add this year on and this year on; it gets heavier and fuller as the years go by.
Interviewer: What happens to the shopping bag?
Mrs. Lowell: You have to trim it down and try to empty it. Little by little, throw things out.
Interviewer: What are you throwing out?
Mrs. Lowell: Mostly the problems and the sadness. And then start over again. You have to keep emptying because as long as you live, the bigger the bag's going to get.

Mrs. Lowell attended a knitting class in her apartment building. During one session all attendees were invited to knit a carry-all tote. She noticed that although everyone was working on the same craft—a large knitted square with handles—everyone's bag was different. Some were solid in color, some had stripes, some were personalized with flowers, bows or initials. She began to call her tote, "the bag of life." Mrs. Lowell went to her bedroom and showed me the bag she designed: it was large, bright with primary colors, and knitted in a criss-cross pattern.

Interviewer: Do you carry yours with you?

Mrs. Lowell: No. I leave it at home and when I come home I throw things in there like, hey this happened to me today. You know, unpleasant things. Then when I'm alone I look at what's in here. Sometimes it's people, sometimes it's thoughts. If somebody is hindering you, you put them in the bag. Then you empty it.

Interviewer: How do you empty it?

Mrs. Lowell: Well, I get out, I walk, I do my visiting in the hospital, I go sit with them. I don't take my sadness or my depression there. I leave it in the bag. I have them laughing, you know, and kidding, so that helps.

Mrs. Lowell's bag is a repository for painful experiences and negative people. Interestingly, her bag is both packed and emptied in a similar way; hurtful relationships and regrets clutter the bag; pleasant relationships and good works empty it. Like all respondents, her depiction of old age and of suffering was complex, nuanced, and unique.

Mrs. Lowell: Old age doesn't have to be suffering. It can be a time of peace, too.

Interviewer: Which is it for you?

Mrs. Lowell: The older I get, the more peace I get. And peace is when you think calm. Because I have envisioned myself falling apart. I have two brothers out of 8 and no sisters left and I can see myself going to pieces seeing all of that, you know, the loneliness. But I choose my thoughts.

Mrs. Lowell clarified that choice and control are integral to whether a negative experience is defined as suffering or not suffering. There is a visual component to this choice; she imagined herself in two ways: as either "thinking calm" or "falling apart." She then chose what she perceived was the morally correct choice: think calm and reject suffering.

Mostly, suffering is something you can't help. But even then, if you're suffering and if you just let it sink down in you, you'll suffer more. You got to put it in that bag. Sometimes I tell myself your bag is getting full [laughter], you got to start throwing out. Get rid of this, get rid of that, get rid of this thought, if it's a person, put them on in there, too.

Mrs. Lowell's suffering is wrapped in a brightly colored bag and stowed away in her bedroom. She looks at it in the quiet of her apartment and chooses when and how to lighten it. It is up to her to control the appearance and the contents of suffering in her bag of life.

THE RIGHT AND WRONG OF SUFFERING

This chapter shows that elders frame a morality of suffering by attributing a cause and purpose to the experience. They interpret whether suffering is good, bad, worth, or worthless both by the reason it occurred and what they learned from it.

Through her time in the mental facility, Mrs. Janson defined the cause of her suffering—no love. Because she lost *time* as well as memories while living in the institution, she saw her past self as fractured. She could not remember herself as either subject or object of the occurrences there. She believed that finding love in that sterile environment repaired her brokenness and "put her back together" again. For Mrs. Janson the morality of suffering was straightforward: a lack of love ruptures the self, receiving love and responding to it mends the self.

Mr. Gans' interpretation of the morality of suffering is based on his religious beliefs; he blamed himself not simply for mounting up credit card bills, but also for being a "poor steward" of God's gifts. He failed the injunctions of Scripture. Because of this failure, he defined his suffering as regret. Although he acknowledged that he is responsible for suffering, he feels powerless to change his situation.

Mrs. Lowell's suffering is based on a regret for "what might have been." In a sense, her belief that she could have saved her sister from death keeps her sister alive. She replays in her mind what she would say to the doctor, hospital administration, and her sister if she had a second chance. Mrs. Lowell also goes over other major events in her life, trying out various scenes and different lines during a lonely childhood and a regretted divorce.

Individuals often look to a *moral community* to help decide the worth (or lack of worth) of their suffering. The moral community of the three elders discussed in this chapter lay in their pasts. They judged their present pain both by "what was" and "what could have been." The behaviors of remembered (and unremembered) selves haunted them. I did not believe, however, that their stories of suffering were stories of despair. They believe they learned, through their experiences, the "right" way to approach suffering. Mrs. Janson sought mental help; Mr. Gans remains silent, prays, but burdens no one, and Mrs. Lowell quietly fills her "bag of life" with sorrows that she eventually throws away. Each respondent reported that they had gained important lessons from suffering. Mrs. Janson learned, through *losing* several years of her life, that love repairs the self as surely as "no-love" erodes the self. Mr. Gans admitted that, "with what [he] learned, he will never stray from God." Mrs. Lowell learned that it is her choice whether her sorrows become suffering.

Elders' suffering and stories of suffering are filled with judgment and evaluation. For the most part, they assess *themselves* within the suffering experience. The morality of suffering emerged not only from the purpose and value they assigned to suffering, but to the purpose and value of their lives, because of or despite suffering.

THE NEXT CHAPTER

Chapter 8 focuses on three metaphors that can be used in any domain of suffering: Suffering as an attack, injustice, and loss. Metaphors such as these are significant in elders' stories because they help respondents *and* researchers analyze, define and describe an experience that may be considered ineffable.

CHAPTER 8

Metaphors of Suffering

Respondents used various metaphors to describe the intimate and social, common and unique aspects of suffering (Bakan, 1968). Here, I explore three metaphors that are common to this sample and classic in the history of thought on suffering (Aulen, 1951). The first metaphor is: Suffering as threat or attack. This metaphor resonates to the normative wholeness of the individual who is threatened by, for example, poor health, unfair social structures, grief or shame. The risk of personal disintegration through suffering is a significant concept in Western cultural and religious views (Cassell, 1982; van Hooft, 1998). The awareness that one's integrity, both bodily and spiritual, is in danger and that the peril may come from inside or outside the self speaks to a duality that remains a Western construct of the self (Duffy, 1992; Scheper-Hughes & Lock, 1991). This "cognitive duality" speaks to the self as a social entity who is keenly aware of others as it attends to its own inward processes. Because the self is both subject and object of its thoughts, it maintains a mental self-portrait that may differ from how it is presented to the outside world (Berman, 1999). This cognitive duality resonates to the human being as an individual who, at different times in life, is the "I am" and the "I do," and the warden as well as the prisoner of his or her fate (Sennett & Cobb, 1975).

In age, one both watches and charts the passing of the years and the changes within oneself and the world at large. Recollection and a continuing sense of self are significant in this experience of being both watcher and watched. At all times of life human beings are both actors and acted upon, but in age, this dual role is extreme and polarized because there are more accumulated years to tally up, more changes to map, and more of a continually *revising* and *revised* self to lose and less of a future in which to lose it.

In the health domain, suffering may be experienced as a physical attack, such as a virus or cancer invading the body, or as depression occupying the mind. Respondents relate that they both experience and gauge the diminishment that is wrought upon the body through illness (Kleinman, 1988). As *subject*, the sufferer views the trajectory of attack. She remembers the self before the onslaught of illness, the enterprises she engaged in, and either imagines a future of improved health, or intuits that illness will lead to death.

145

The self also regards the body or the mind that has been attacked as an *object* of betrayal. Body and mind seem both distant *to* the self and overloaded *with* the self. Although the larger world is canceled out, the pained body or mind becomes the self's sole point of focus (Scarry, 1985). Suffering sharply polarizes the inside/outside view of the self (Becker, 1997).

Suffering as an attack threatens the self in its fullness. The case that follows is illustrative of this first metaphor. It also represents both the distinctions and the commonalities of this metaphor in elders' stories of suffering.

SUFFERING AS THREAT OR ATTACK:
MR. CARSON

Mr. Carson is a 73-year-old European-American never-married man. I first interviewed him for a project concerning men's childlessness six years previously. At that time I was invited to the large, two-story row house in Northwest Philadelphia where he and his four siblings were raised by parents who emigrated from Denmark. To enter Mr. Carson's home in the mid-1990s was to step back in time. A bulky sofa suite was covered with papers, books, and unopened mail. Drawn curtains allowed little light into the living room. Mr. Carson sat on the sofa at a side angle to the card chair that he made available for me. He often looked away after I asked a question, and sometimes answered through his pets. After giving a response, he would glance at the dog at his side or the cat sitting on the stair landing and ask, "Didn't I, Shug," or, "I can't remember that, can I, Boo?"

At our first interview, Mr. Carson said that although he never changed anything in his parents' home, he accumulated a great deal since their deaths. An avid reader and avowed packrat, he parted with little that came into the house. A narrow passageway allowed him to enter each room, but separated him from the "back rows" of boxes, magazines, and newspapers stored there.

When I asked Mr. Carson to be part of a project on suffering, he seemed glad to participate. He explained that although he was "in pain" from arthritis, had difficulty walking and did not drive, he preferred to come to my office. His home was in such disarray, he explained, that he "hated" for anyone to see it. When I reminded him that I had already visited his home, he demurred. "Oh, no, it's much worse than last time."

> When I asked Mr. Carson to tell me the story of his life, he frowned.
> **Mr. Carson:** I have the same nerves as when I last saw you, was it five years ago?
> **Interviewer:** It's almost six years.
> **Mr. Carson:** I didn't think that. I know I've aged since I last saw you. When I look in the mirror I think, oh, that can't be me. That's not me. I got that Just for Men [hair coloring], but it came out jet black. I didn't have it mixed right. Oh, I had a heck of a time getting it off.
> **Interviewer:** Getting gray bothers you?

Mr. Carson: Oh, yeah, I don't like to see gray. Men on television like [a local newscaster]. Oh, he went so gray. Why doesn't he dye his hair? Oh, I get upset. I don't like to face aging. I like to see youth.

Mr. Carson was dismayed that I asked him to repeat his life story. His assurance that he was the "same person" with the "same nerves" as last time reminded us both that although he had "gone gray," he had not changed. Mr. Carson began his life story by revealing that the most important role he played in life was as a son and the happiest time in life was childhood. When I asked how he considered his life as a whole, he shrugged.

Seems like my life was just, you know, caring for my parents. I guess for a man, I guess you would say I was a clinging vine. Most people my age would have been out on their own, but I, I wasn't able to do that, I didn't find the motivation. And I had a good life here. I didn't sponge off them. I always kept myself busy at home, did things in the home. See, I was the youngest. They used to call me the baby [chuckle]. A 73-year-old baby.

In retrospect, those things which comforted him early in life, such as living with his parents, being directed by them, and helping them with house chores, now held tags of feminization and shame. For Mr. Carson, age itself was an attack on his treasured identity as son and baby of the family. In youth, his qualities of shyness and dependence were rewarded at home with security. In age, these qualities expose him as a defective male. Now, not even hair coloring can disguise his frailty and his inadequacies. Who is he to himself, with gray hair?

Mr. Carson was unable to "find motivation" to go out on his own. His belief that "someone else" did or should control his life was pervasive throughout his narrative. He told me that because schoolmates laughed at his appearance as a child, he sought refuge at home.

I had very, very light hair. I used to get kidded about that, you know. The boys would call me whitey or skinny. And I was very, very, quiet. I figured there was something wrong. It might have been a birth injury or something hereditary, I don't know. My mother was 37 when I was born so maybe, you know, some unhealthy condition with her, maybe it showed in me. One doctor thought I had a type of aphasia. That would be like a blank mind. I had to force myself to talk and I felt I could lick it through reading. I persevered.

Mr. Carson wondered if his mother's "advanced" age when she bore him was the cause of his "problems." It was interesting that he called his aphasia "like a blank mind." Mr. Carson depicted himself as an empty shell that was missing inner content but was ready to be filled—with reading. Because classmates tormented him at school, he was allowed to be silent at home. He named the happiest time in his life as the Sundays of his childhood, when his parents took him and his siblings on "country" drives. He sat in the backseat of their station wagon, an observer from whom nothing, not even speech, was expected or demanded. His family of origin unconditionally accepted his silence.

Mr. Carson persevered with reading and graduated near the top of his high school class. Although he was considered very bright, he had no desire to "prolong the agony of a school setting" and refused a partial scholarship to a local college. Shortly after graduation he found a job near his home as a proofreader. Despite that fact that he "never earned much," the solitude of his workspace satisfied him. Although he had several chances to advance, he refused promotions because he was "afraid of change," and "couldn't handle responsibility, like supervising." He considered the rote of proofreading a type of "therapy." Mr. Carson remembered this period of young and middle adulthood as "almost perfect. We all got along great."

One by one, his siblings married and moved away. Mr. Carson remained with his parents in their large row home. He did not learn to drive because he accompanied his parents on their outings. Besides, he liked staying close to the neighborhood; he named a few of his former neighbors as his best friends.

During the late 1950s Mr. Carson's life changed. His parents' health declined and *his* life narrowed even further. He was proud that he was his parents' sole caretaker before their deaths and described caretaking as a skill that came naturally to him. When I asked him if there was an event, incident or time in his life when he suffered, he hesitated, then offered a memory that captures that moment. It occurred in 1967, shortly after the death of his mother and several years after his father died.

> **Mr. Carson:** I guess I shouldn't even talk about it. I started spending money. I shouldn't have. Every time I passed a state store I went in. And I didn't buy the lowest priced ones. First it was wine, then after several times I got so deathly sick from that. I don't know why I was doing that. It went down so easily.
> **Interviewer:** What makes that memory suffering?
> **Mr. Carson:** It's hard to say. I guess there was, I guess a floodgate opened up and it rushed through and I was trying to fill in some of the emptiness with alcohol.

As a child, Mr. Carson filled his "blank mind" with reading. After his parents' deaths, he filled his loneliness with alcohol. No longer needed as a caretaker and alone in the large home, Mr. Carson became confused, insecure, began to drink heavily and experienced significant depressions. Although he described himself as "always indecisive," he began to make "dangerous" choices concerning money and friends without the guidance of his parents. This period was not only the saddest in his life, it was also a turning point. After his parents' death, the neighborhood changed; the "old" neighbors either died or moved away. He continued to frequent the corner bars but met "bad companions" there. He believed that he was often "rolled" during periods when he "blacked out" from drink. He had no idea how much money he lost during these episodes.

> I couldn't seem to get myself to stop [drinking]. See, I couldn't get myself to do things unless somebody was working along side with me. And that sort of motivated me. But like by myself, there was nothing to motivate me, to drive me or lead me or get me to stop.

Mr. Carson related that he must be activated by someone in order to move forward, yet failed to find that important other. The sense that he experienced suffering at the same time that he witnessed the downward slide of his life speaks to the cognitive duality of the self that both watches and experiences suffering.

Mr. Carson continued to drink heavily for about ten years. When various health problems emerged he feared that alcohol was shortening his life. During this period he also became addicted to several anxiety-reducing medications. Although alcohol and drugs did not cause him to miss work, it did affect how he presented himself. One of his coworkers commented that he "looked real bad," after a weekend binge.

> Sometimes I would get deathly sick. The girl I worked with, she was a proofreader, too. One day she said, "You look awful." She was a very nice person. So I told her. And she said, "Well, I guess you should be commended for just making it to work." I said, "Well I just made up my mind that I wasn't going to use that for an excuse." I thought no, I can't let that alcohol control me like that. But she spotted it on me.

I wondered if Mr. Carson was moved to take control of his life because of his coworker's comment. Attuned to being directed by others, Mr. Carson needed an external push to "get away" from alcohol and drugs. Although he admitted that it was "almost impossible to stay away from liquor," he believed that death was imminent if he continued. By the time he reached his mid-fifties he felt compelled to find another way to "fill the emptiness." During a period of enduring severe headaches and depression, Mr. Carson "chose life."

> One day, I was so depressed I poured out about 15 of my pills. I had reached that point. Then I thought, gee, there's got to be some other answer for me. So I put the pills back in the bottle. I never even told my family doctor that. So the next day I kept thinking, what could I do? I got to make a big, big change in my life. So I went down to the SPCA and I looked over different dogs and I found Pee-Wee [prior dog]. So then I took her home and I felt good for about six months after having the dog and then all of a sudden the depression started to hit me again. So then I went back, yeah, the next day again, and I got Cubby [prior cat]. I mean I still had my ups and downs, but they needed me. And then with these two [current cat and dog], I think about that in the morning. If I wasn't here, who would feed them?

Mr. Carson's attachment to his pets was profound and poignant. Several times during our first interview, he sat on the floor with his pets, grooming, petting, and talking to them. When I knelt in front of my chair and petted each of the animals, he made eye contact with me.

Shortly after he won his battle with alcohol and drugs, he was felled by another blow. In the late 1970s, Mr. Carson lost his job. After 27 years of service, he was caught in the publishing company's downsizing.

> This was very difficult. I had nothing to do for the last few months. And I thought oh, boy, I wonder, will they put me on the night shift or will they let me go? And then finally one day they let some fellow on the midnight shift, they let him go. And then another fellow had 32 years. They let him go. And then they called me into the manager's office and let me go.

I pictured Mr. Carson watching a parade of coworkers march into the manager's office to hear their fate as he waited, outside the door, to learn of his own. He regretted his decision to stay on at the company despite "having nothing to do." He thought perhaps that his inability to leave before he was terminated showed weakness. He also linked this perceived weakness to his parents' deaths. After they died, his lack of energy, difficulty in dealing with adversity, and a greater reluctance to make decisions had long-lasting ramifications on the second half of his life.

> The death of my parents really changed my life. So many times I wished I had pulled myself together, and been stronger, you know, had moral fortitude. I wished I did more things for them. Or even now, for me. I wished I could have pushed myself to get away to a newer neighborhood. Geez, its hard for me sometimes to talk about it, to go back. But sometimes it's better to talk about, to get it out of your system.

Mr. Carson named his "lack of strength" as a moral failing that was prompted by an external event—the deaths of his parents. His emotional, physical and spiritual suffering came together as shame for the life he continued to live. Although he regretted some of the actions and omissions of his life, it seemed more that he was ashamed of who he *was* and *is*. His pain was not only that he felt inadequate, but also that his inadequacies had hurt those closest to him— his parents. In the shadow of his shame even the happiest time in life—his childhood—came under scrutiny. His fondest memories became tainted because his childhood foretold a "wasted" future.

> I had. . . . A doctor told my father that I had a sheltered life. I guess I did. But we had good times together. We took day trips. We had good times. I was like leaning on my parents. Like these druggies today.

Despite his age, Mr. Carson identifies more readily with the young and aimless "druggies" than the elderly retirees in his neighborhood. Although his story portrays an ongoing internal struggle, when I asked him what a picture of suffering would look like, he named something external to himself.

Hmmm. Well, I would say it would be like a picture, an oil painting coming to life or possibly the tentacles of an octopus reaching out. I would be watching it, trying to keep my distance from those tentacles getting close to me or grabbing me. Yeah, I think that would be it. [Pause] I remember a movie years back, the "Picture of Dorian Gray," I believe it was called, and the picture, the oil painting started to move. Ooohhh, I heard one woman let out a yell, and I thought that was the way I felt, too. I didn't let out a yell as she did, but ooohhh, I don't know if I stayed to watch the end.

The two pictures show Mr. Carson's fear of attack and self-disclosure. In the first, the octopus, as an external demon, disarms and engulfs him. He is just shy of it, but it is always gaining on him. Its proximity results in cognitive paralysis concerning decisions he "should be making" in life, such as cleaning his house, moving from a "rotten" neighborhood, and finding friends who are not addicts. The second picture shows the real Dorian Gray as aged and twisted by deeds of cruelty and spite while the living Dorian remains young and handsome. Perhaps this picture reveals what Mr. Carson thinks he would find if he could look inside himself.

Mr. Carson suffers as a child might—from lack of guidance. To him, the cause and resolution of his problems are external. He believes that someone (he does not know whom) might direct him in the "way to go," but cannot find anyone to fill this protective and supportive role. He told me that he was estranged from his only remaining sibling, an older sister. He hesitated to contact her because she "becomes short-tempered" when asked for advice. Also, he sees her as a poor resource because she is preoccupied with her own health and family worries. He therefore remains mired in his own questions—What should I do and who will help me? When I asked Mr. Carson if he thought suffering was a normal part of growing older, he answered without hesitation.

Parts wear out. Just like my house is 66 years old and this and that started to go. And with Gus [cat] he's old. He's wearing out. I don't think he can hear any more. So, it's just like the human body, parts wear out and they have to put another, you know, you need some other parts. When I was a young boy, doctors couldn't do that. If parts wore out, that was it.

Just as a new part might fix his home, so might some outside agent, such as hair dye, a sweet tempered sister, or a new friend, fix *him*. His comment also shows that Mr. Carson strongly identifies with his home and pets. Throughout our interview, Mr. Carson was the most animated when he nuzzled his dog or stroked his cat. Unfortunately, his sources of contentment—his home and pets—have become situations of distress. Worry about the upkeep of his home overwhelms him. He cannot afford to make minor repairs and does not have the wherewithal to "get rid of stuff" or stop bringing in additional clutter. Also, two of his neighbors have threatened his dog because of her barking. The haven of his home has become like a prison. The assaults against him, his home and his pets symbolize Mr. Carson's suffering.

> Interviewer: How would you define suffering?
> Mr. Carson: Well, I think myself, now, I could take physical suffering, like when I had the pains from hernia and ear aches, and swollen glands. I learned to adapt to that type of suffering. But the mental, I think that's, for me it was worse.
> Interviewer: How would you describe mental suffering?
> Mr. Carson: I would say frustration and running away from different problems I had, putting things off. And I can't ride elevators unless somebody is with me. I just can't. And fearfulness and lack of confidence, and apprehension. Am I going to keep running away from these problems as long as I can until there's no more time to run? Then I have to face them.

Although Mr. Carson runs from the octopus with tentacles and hides his eyes from the "living" picture of Dorian Gray, he imagines a future confrontation with them. His experience with therapy gives him insight into himself. Although health care no longer pays for therapy, he remembers receiving help from a psychiatrist during the "hard times" in life.

> Sometimes when I would leave his [psychiatrist] office I felt better. I felt more clean. But then that wouldn't last very long. And then I would have a weakness on the way home from work.

Mr. Carson uses morally charged words, such as "clean" to describe how he felt after seeing the psychiatrist and "weakness" to describe his need for alcohol. His "weakness" occurred in body and spirit; both were addicted to alcohol and both were being destroyed by it. His desire for atonement, which he could not find through religion, was realized during sessions with the psychiatrist. The psychiatrist became, at least for a while, a confessor for Mr. Carson. Throughout his narrative, issues of trust and fear, health and illness, cleansing and weakness, and life and death come together at the place where these dichotomies competed for preeminence, and created suffering.

> Mr. Carson: When I think of myself I think of that old southern song: Afraid of Living and Scared of Dying. And I think that's what it is with me.
> Interviewer: What do you mean?
> Mr. Carson: With living it's the uncertainty, not knowing what the next day will bring.
> Interviewer: Why are you scared of dying?
> Mr. Carson: I don't know. My parents wouldn't like the things that I think now. See, I read different things over the years that maybe all those things in the Bible, like an afterlife, maybe all of it's a fairy tale. Like they said, nobody came back to tell us.
> Interviewer: Do you think there is an afterlife?
> Mr. Carson: I'd like to think it, and then I hear things that people say like, hell is right in this life. Maybe that's true—it's right here.

Mr. Carson's many retrospective "shoulds" make life in the present especially stressful. If hell is indeed "here," there is little that he can do to "make it better." At the end of the interview he told me that he was "unable to take "that first step." He cannot move from his private hell toward self-redemption because both states of mind are mired in the mundane affairs of everyday life.

SUFFERING AS INJUSTICE: MRS. BILLINGS

The second metaphor discussed in this chapter is: Suffering as injustice. In old age, suffering as injustice may be felt as a profound disappointment that life did not turn out the way that one anticipated, and that hard work is not rewarded by contentment and success. The following case concerns Mrs. Billings, who speaks eloquently to this unjust nature of suffering. She is a 75-year-old African-American woman who lives in a subsidized apartment in South Philadelphia. She learned several years ago that her only son, aged 54, has AIDS. He now lives in a rehab center in West Virginia. His wife was recently killed "by a drug dealer." Their four children, Mrs. Billing's grandchildren, live with various relatives on their mother's side.

Mrs. Billings described her present life as "very good," despite her own health problems, such as severe arthritis, the illness of her son, and worries about the way her grandchildren are being raised. Because she feels "financially secure" due to rent subsidies, SSI, and Medicaid, she "can't complain." The physical and emotional *place* she now finds herself, however, is different from where she imagined she would be in older age. When young, she cared about having "nice things," living a "respectable" life, and had dreams of "doing well." When she met her husband, whom she described as "good looking but full of bull," she thought her dreams would materialize if they "worked together." Unfortunately, Mr. Billings often gambled away his paycheck, was unfaithful, and the couple lived their short married life in poverty. Mrs. Billings left her husband soon after their second anniversary. She returned with her infant son to her father's home.

> Pop kept us and fed us. But the toilet was outside in the yard, and we bathed in a tin tub in the kitchen. We always kept ourselves clean but it was rough.

The outhouse symbolized poverty for Mrs. Billings. It represented the backwardness of her childhood and the years that she depended on her father's support after her son was born. If the pervasive symbol of her life during these years was the outhouse, her pervading dream was to escape the life that this symbol represented. Mrs. Billings explained that although her father was "content" with his life, her mother instilled "higher" notions of success in her three children. When her parents separated her mother moved to a nearby apartment with "indoor plumbing." Her brother found a "good" job. Her sister married "well."

> Mom got herself a beautiful place on L. Street. Herman [brother] did great
> and Louise [sister] married a man with money. I was the only one who had
> it hard. [Pause]. I mean to think I'd be so bad, not being able to go to church
> because I didn't have anything to wear.

Mrs. Billings would not go to church dressed poorly; she would not show the
world how she had *failed*. Her comment shows the social nature of suffering
and the morality she imputes to it. Her self-description as "so bad," holds a moral
reproach against how poverty "looks," such as living in a place with an outhouse,
or "not having anything to wear." Her mother succeeded by setting out on her
own, her brother "got good money," and her sister "dressed nice for church."

Mrs. Billings inability to improve her own life intensified her dreams for her
son. She believed that by "giving him up" to her former in-laws when he was
three years old he could get a head start on the "good life." She did not regret
her decision.

> He had a better life there. See they (in-laws) lived a different lifestyle
> from me. My mother-in-law never had to work. And don't forget—we had
> outdoor plumbing.

Any home, even one away from her, was preferable to one without a bathroom.
Although she remained a force in her son's life, she never again lived with him.
Her synopsis of his youth highlighted his potential, his father's unwillingness
to help him achieve it, and her son's eventual downfall.

> He went to G. School. Now when I was coming up that was one of the best
> schools in the city. He did very, very well in school. He was a basketball
> player and when I look at his trophies I think—You could have been some-
> thing. I think if his father could have just helped out, but he never did.
> And even though it was Vietnam time, he didn't have to be in the war. He
> was in the finest department in the Air Force. All he did was go from country
> to country to play basketball, he was on the all-star team. And I think
> about those things and I think my God, why did you waste? . . . But I
> certainly did my best. See, when he went to Japan, he sort of changed. I
> think that's where he got hooked on drugs. Now, many a days I didn't
> know whether I would get a call that he would be dead or not. With the
> drugs, that's how he got the AIDS.

Mrs. Billings addressed herself, her son, and me in the editorial of her son's
life. Her disappointment with him seems to mime regrets about her own past.
She identified with her son's inability to reach his potential, and is experiencing an anticipatory grief for his imminent death. She clarified, however,
that even though he had not "made something" of himself, he should "always
carry himself well." When he recently showed up in her apartment lobby looking
"fat and nasty from drugs," she told him not to come back until he "cleans
himself up." Just as the outhouse symbolizes poverty to her, "carrying yourself
well" represents success.

After she gave up her son, Mrs. Billings fell into a kind of haze. Her mother died from a painful cancer and shortly afterward she ended a "heartbreaking affair." She "could not work." Although she said that she was not depressed during this time, she admitted that she could not "get herself together." After about a year, at age 35, Mrs. Billings experienced an epiphany. She found a job, moved into a "nice little apartment," began to date, and cultivated friendships with several "good, church-going women". She worked in various chains of ladies' dress stores that were popular during the 1960s and 1970s.

> I worked at Silver Lining and the Chic Shop. I even worked at D's, that was an exclusive women's store on B. Avenue. Oh, I always dressed nice and looked good.

Mrs. Billings enjoyed this period in her life. Despite limited wages, discounts on clothes helped her to "look good." Her social life was "very active." Unfortunately, because many of the chain dress stories closed during the late 1970s, she found herself unemployed at age 55 and worried about her future. Unsuccessful in her search for work, she did not turn to her sister, whom she believes "never liked her," but to her sister's daughter, Corinne. Corinne asked her father, a prominent city official, to employ Mrs. Billings in the organization where he enjoyed VIP status.

> My niece went to her father and said, Aunt Ev cannot make it with the job that she got. You can find something for her to do at the Company.

Mrs. Billings was given the job of business manager in the financial office. She acknowledged that getting this position . . .

> . . . had nothing to do with me. No, he (brother-in-law) was crazy about his kids; did anything they asked.

The "great" salary she received ended her nightmares about poverty and helped her achieve one of her dreams—she bought a home. Mrs. Billings spent a portion of interview time discussing the furniture and custom-made curtains, bought originally for her home, which now decorate her tiny apartment.

> I just wanted a job with a decent salary, but oh, it was a nice job. I had about 16 girls under me, but I felt like I was one of the workers because the girls, they treated me so nice and they kept me in the mainstream of things. Those girls, I must say, they were the ones that helped me do the job.

Mrs. Billings gave credit for her job success to her employees. She preferred to think of herself as "one of the girls." Perhaps in retrospect she did not want to be thought of as an authority figure—like her brother-in-law. She stressed that her brother-in-law's power in the Company was absolute. She came to realize that her "great salary" exacted a stiff emotional price.

But it was a stressful job. (Pause). It was because of my brother-in-law. See, he was running the place. And he would pass by the door of the office and he would never act like I was his sister-in-law. Not that I wanted him to do anything special, but he just acted like I was nothing. Even the girls would notice, they said, "He don't say nothing to you." See, when he came around everybody would cringe, all of us, because you never know what he was going to say or do.

Mrs. Billings portrayed her brother-in-law as unpredictable. Although she did not want special treatment from him, she did not expect to be ignored. She began to suspect that what was given to her as a favor—the job—could just as easily be snatched away. She recalled the day her suspicions came true.

My girlfriend and I were in the lunchroom. His [brother-in-law's] sister was in there. So she called me over and she said, "Who are those people over there talking about Melvin [brother-in-law]? Do you know them?" I said I don't know them personally. She said, "Well you sure you don't know them?" Then I said, "Why do you keep questioning me? You're the one that heard them [talking about Melvin]. Why don't you go and tell them I don't like the way you're talking about my brother? Or go get your brother, go get somebody, but don't get me!"

Mrs. Billings, who presented herself as a non-combative person, explained that worry made her angry and suspicious. She felt that this trivial incident was a bad omen. A phone call that evening justified her "funny feeling" about the conversation.

The phone rang and it was my sister. "Did you hear anybody talking about Melvin today?" I said, "No, I didn't." So then he [Melvin] came on the phone. And he said, "I need loyalty in my place of work." I said, "Listen Melvin, you're talked about every day." [Pause] There was silence. Oh, my gosh. I should never have said that, but it was true. See, he *was* talked about every day. Then my sister got back on and said, "You better tell who it is." And finally I said, "If you think for one minute that I'm going to tell a lie on somebody, I will not do it!" I could not do it! After that I said to myself, I got real bad vibes [Mrs. Billings' emphasis].

The next day, Mrs. Billings was on edge. At quitting time, she learned first-hand about the fickleness of those who hold absolute power.

The personnel officer called me and said, "Miss Billings, could you come down a minute?" I went down there and she gave me the letter: Mr. C. terminates Mrs. Billings as of now. No reason. Well the personnel lady said, "We were all shocked. Mr. C. just told us to do it." Oh, I almost died. I started to cry, then I said, get yourself together. When I got upstairs to them girls, oh, we all had a crying session.

The sympathy of her co-workers did not lessen her brother-in-law's cruelty or help her find a new job. It did support her self-view as a good person and made his actions seem all the more unjust.

> It was the most disturbing thing in my life because I was going to be 60 years old in two months. What can I live on? How can I get another job? And I had bought a home. Oh, I almost died.

Another aspect of Mrs. Billings' suffering was feeling betrayed by her own family. She was devastated by her father's, brother's, and sister's reaction to the fact she had been fired.

> When I come home I called my father. He said, "I'm on my way." I told him what happened. And I've never been one to lie and make up stuff because I'm too scary and too timid. I said, "Papa, what in the world will I do?" See, two or three of my friends said, "Why don't you take him [brother-in-law] to a court of law and make him take you back. He got to give you a valid reason for firing you." But my father begged me, "Don't do it. How will your sister take it?" So I listened to him. Sometimes I rue the day I did it. I wonder what my mother would have said.

Mrs. Billings told me that her mother, long ago, urged her to give her son away so that he might have a better life. Taking her father's advice to "do nothing" followed her theme of getting counsel from authoritative others before making a decision. It also fortified her self-portrait as "too timid" to maneuver through the harsh ways of the world. Her brother advised her to "forget the whole thing" because he was "intimidated" by his wealthy brother-in-law. Her sister never mentioned the incident." Although Mrs. Billings' brother and father helped her pay some bills, she ultimately lost her home. Losing her job at the hands of her brother-in-law not only changed her living arrangements, but also the future of their family.

> **Mrs. Billings:** This man [brother-in-law] has really tore up our family. I don't bother with my brother. I don't go to my sister's. Like we used to have Thanksgiving and different things. That is what he did. And it could be so different. [Pause] I asked his daughter, "Corinne, maybe one day your father will apologize." She said, "I wouldn't bank on it."

Perhaps an apology would force Mrs. Billings' brother-in-law to acknowledge his misuse of power. Part of her pain over this incident is that she believes she was never *real* to him. Because he saw her as a non-entity, he did not worry about the consequences of *his* actions on *her* life.

> To me, he more or less didn't really didn't care what he was doing to me. See, I knew who was talking about him. I knew their names all the time. The next day I went in that department. They said, "Oh, Miss Billings." I said, "I couldn't name you guys." They said, "We're just so sorry you lost a job." Aaahh! That was the only decent job I had in my life that I was

> making a decent salary, that I'd been able to have a nice pension, a nice social security. If I wanted to take a little trip or something, I'd been able to do it. And he cut it off just like that (snaps fingers). It affected so much of my life.

Mrs. Billings matter-of-factly conveyed that she knew "all the time" who had spoken against her brother-in-law, but her own commitment against wrong-doing did not allow her to name them. "See, I always prayed, Lord, don't let me be no party to no evil." Although she paid the high price of unemployment for her refusal to "speak up," she also believed that being a "party to evil" demands a stiff price. She "always knew" that her brother-in-law eventually would pay for his actions against her. It is here that the metaphor of injustice comes alive in Mrs. Billings' narrative and completed, for her, the loop of cruelty, unfairness and eventual justice. The perpetrator of a wrong must pay for his misdeed at some point in his life. For justice not to occur was unthinkable to her; it offended her worldly as well as spiritual idea of fair play.

> I said to my sister that day, "He's going to pay for everything he did to me." And he did. See, there was a discrepancy in the funds [of the Company]. He went to jail for three and a half years. I never dreamed *that* was going to happen. [Pause]. But I did tell her, "Your husband is going to pay for everything he did to me" [Mrs. Billings' emphasis].

For Mrs. Billings, the idea of immanent justice was applicable in this case because justice usually does not occur with *equal payment.* Mrs. Billings' brother-in-law did not recompense *her,* but he *was* forced to "settle up" for his fraud against others. When I asked Mrs. Billings to define suffering, she graphically defined its core.

> Suffering is want, things that you actually need to survive and you don't have. I don't think of my pain as suffering. I mean you can take something to alleviate that. But being in want really to me is suffering. Like in them early years when we [she and her son] were with pop, and I didn't know what I was going to do. I was at my wits end. I felt like killing myself. That was a suffering time in my life. And then later with Melvin [brother-in-law]. Oh, it hurts. It hurts. Because you can't undo. . . . See, both times, I didn't know where to turn. When you go to bed at night, you know if you wake up in the morning, you would go through the same thing. Over and over and over.

Mrs. Billings' description of suffering is hellish—interminable days of repetitive motions that lead nowhere. Childhood deprivation paralleled material loss in old age. While her early years spoke to the dehumanization of poverty, her later years spoke to the depersonalization of cruelty. When I asked Mrs. Billings what a picture of suffering would look like, she drew a nightmarish image of "not being real."

Well I think it would be a person. And your eyes would look drawn and you look like you're worn out. Like nobody cares nothing about me. They're like a robot, wondering around with no place to go. That's it—a robot with no place to go.

A robot usually performs repetitive actions, has no control over itself, and has "nowhere to turn" unless directed by another. This robotic picture of suffering spoke poignantly to another aspect of suffering as injustice—there is a lack of authentic relationship when one person treats another unjustly. In Mrs. Billing's picture, the robot is not "real," which is how she believes her brother-in-law saw her. Because a robot is without a "self" it cannot encounter and be encountered by other human beings.

Mrs. Billings' mix of the past and present tense, as well as a mix of pronouns, such as you, me and they to describe the person in the picture revealed at least two of her theories about suffering: 1) that anyone could be the subject of such a portrait, and 2) to be a "nobody"—whether through the dehumanization of poverty or the depersonalization of cruelty—is to suffer.

The belief that her son would soon die did not cause Mrs. Billings suffering, perhaps because she believed that she "did her best" concerning him. For Mrs. Billings, the corrosive nature of powerlessness and injustice came together under poverty's paralyzing umbrella. Her symbols of suffering were an outhouse and her brother-in-law's capricious act of cruelty. These symbols point to what made suffering tragically real to Mrs. Billings—poverty—as a condition she was born into and the person she believed thwarted her escape from it.

SUFFERING AS LOSS:
MR. BANKS

The metaphor of suffering as loss reveals the contingency of life. Elders' awareness of finitude affirms that, at any moment, they may lose those significant others who help them interpret the world and themselves, such as their children, spouses, or a sibling. The metaphor of suffering as loss exposes a deeper contingency. As the next respondent, Mr. Banks, eloquently discloses, the ground on which he was firmly rooted suddenly gave way, revealing the abyss that was always underfoot.

Mr. Banks is an 82-year-old European-American man and retired newspaper journalist. He lives with his wife in a luxury apartment in a Philadelphia suburb. For our interview we sat in a spacious dining room filled with artifacts from the Banks' many travels, and scores of graduation, wedding and "new" baby pictures. The couple has three children whom Mr. Banks described as "all successful, much better off than me." When I asked him to tell me his life story, he began:

I came from a middle class background. My father had come from a rather wealthy family. He was 50 years of age when he married for the first time.

My mother was 26. My mother came from the same kind of upper middle class background. My father was 52 when I was born. My father was the least achieving of his brothers and sisters. One brother was a doctor; another was a lawyer. Two sisters married men who were quite wealthy. My father, as a politician in city government was, as I said, the least achieving of the brothers and sisters [chuckle]. Still, he managed to leave a small estate.

To describe his father as the "least-achieving" in the family put Mr. Banks' own life in a historical context concerning "doing well." It placed his father's wealth and his own achievements at a respectable point on a continuum of family success. Financially, he did better than his father and his children are "better off" than he. He remains linked to his father through their maverick ways. Like his father, he was expected to attend college but chose another route to learning.

I was in high school when I got a job as a copyboy at the R. Newspaper. I was making 9 dollars when the NRA went into effect and they raised my wages to 15 dollars a week. Somebody told me when I was still a copyboy that you could get a good education in the newspaper business because the only thing you could learn in college was how and where to get information. So I was copyboy, then head copyboy, and two years later, in 1935, they sent me up as a police reporter. And I worked there for two years and then went to the E. Newspaper where I had a similar job as police reporter. And I was getting more money all the time. I had an automobile, a little series of cars actually. Everything, you know, everything was fine. I really had a charmed life.

Mr. Banks used the phrase, "I had a charmed life," throughout his narrative. It was a metaphor for the way windows of opportunity slid open before him. This metaphor culled together significant components that make up a life, such as work, personal finances, living conditions and social relationships, and it became his life long theme. He paints an idyllic picture of himself as a young man who "held the world in [his] hands."

I was drafted in 1942, five months after Pearl Harbor. I became an instructor of airplane mechanics. Later I became editor of the newspaper there. So I never heard a shot fired in anger and was in no danger. And I led a pretty good life in the service. I always had enough spending money. So, I really had a charmed life.

Even the negatives of life, such as being drafted during wartime, fell under the spell of a "charmed" life. Mr. Banks, like most men interviewed, told his life story chronologically.

Mr. Banks: I came out of the Army and in the latter part of 1947 I met my wife [begins to cry].
Interviewer: Where did you meet your wife?
Mr. Banks: She had worked at the R. Newspaper and I had worked there. There was a reunion a year after it folded. And somebody introduced me to

Belle [wife] who worked there at exactly the same job. I was a copyboy, she was a copygirl. So we met and a couple months later we were married [crying]. I think we probably had a charmed life together.

Did the "charm" that watched over him, whether it was coincidence, fate, or Providence, allow their lives to parallel, and bring them together? His wife expanded Mr. Banks' charmed life with one son, two daughters and a beautiful home. Advanced education and hard work were stressed in the Banks' household and all three children did well. They became a stockbroker, a bank vice-president, and a financial consultant. All married, raised children of their own, and although they live far from Philadelphia, remain emotionally close to their parents.

> **Mr. Banks:** After the third child we moved to the suburbs. We were able to buy a two story stone house and had a good living there. We lived there 44 years. We came here this year.
> **Interviewer:** Why did you move?
> **Mr. Banks:** [long pause] I really had a charmed life [crying].

Mr. Banks was overcome by emotion. He pointed to the living room where his wife watched a large-screened television. His sadness was triggered by conflicting emotions: gratitude and grief for the longest chapter in his "charmed" life—his marriage. Uncertainty about his wife's health and their future together prompts this "great sorrow." As Mr. Banks continued, I suddenly understood that his story thus far was a preamble for what was to come.

> February 5th (of the current year) changed my life greatly. My wife had a heart seizure and cardiac arrest while we were playing bridge, and she passed out. By the time the medics got there her brain had been deprived of oxygen for 7 minutes. It left her with severe brain damage. So she has no memory. She can't remember anything more than five minutes. So whatever memory she has is of her childhood. She thinks of her mother and father as being alive. She still remembers all our friends, but she can't associate them with anything. If we're driving she'll look in the back seat and say, "Where are the babies?" She confuses these [non-existent] babies with our children. And our youngest is 36.

Mr. Banks divided his life into before and after his wife's heart seizure. "Before" was filled with the riches of love and work—a good marriage, successful and devoted children, and "talented, high-energy friends." "After" is a period of struggling along—alone. He prays for his wife's death because he worries that if he dies first, his children will be "forced" to put their mother in a nursing home. Because he believes that his wife lost her identity along with her short-term memory, he feels that "for all intents and purposes, she *is* dead." Mr. Banks' own existence parallels his wife's liminal state—she is betwixt and between life and death and he is betwixt and between knowing "where" his wife is.

Mr. Banks' narrative reflected the notion of time and space in suffering—he spoke of his wife in the past tense—yet his waking hours are filled with taking care of her. She follows him from room to room in their spacious apartment while repeating conversations that she "just had" with her deceased parents. She often threatens to "take a walk by [her]self." He wonders what she knows of herself and of him without short-term memory. Does she suffer through lack of memory? Perhaps because he is unwilling to "let her go," yet believes "much of her" is already dead, he is convinced that she has "earned life everlasting" through her past "good thoughts."

> **Mr. Banks:** My wife was a very generous person. I think that in the past six months, I have had a sort of confirmation of what you might think of as a stupid theory of life after death. I think that as we go through life our brains are sending up some kind of electrical signals. Whatever you do in life and whatever you think are being pushed out in brain waves just like radio waves that go off into space and go on forever. And you have life everlasting. Because all each of us consists of are brain waves and perceptions. And the fact that my wife, except for her body, much of her died on February 5th, but I think her old perceptions are still out there in space. So, she has earned eternal life.
> **Interviewer:** Do you find that comforting?
> **Mr. Banks:** Yes I do. She was a very generous person. Maybe in effect she is gone, her soul is off in space now and she's leaving her body here. But she's continuing her existence.

As a Jew, Mr. Banks described himself as prayerful but not religiously observant. His religious philosophy is exemplified by the words of the Biblical prophet, Micah. But because Judaism did not provide him with a comforting picture of the afterlife, he created one. Mr. Banks' likens his wife's brain waves to radio waves—unseen but proved by science to exist. This proof fits his need for rational confirmation of her existence after death. Her "continued existence" in this liminal state allows him to "try on" mourning before she actually dies. Both Mr. and Mrs. Banks dwell in a kind of purgatory—a shadow world where life and death complement and explain each other.

> My wife has a perception now. She sometimes really knows that her mother and father talk to her, like this morning. She said, "My mother is talking to me, she was here this morning. I say, "No, that's not reality, that's your imagination." But in her mind it's true. Maybe in effect she is gone already, her soul is off in space now and she's leaving her body here. She's continuing her existence. But I don't know if its communication or perception. I don't know where the receptor would be to connect. After all, what we're saying to each other now are generated in my mind and yours. I'm talking and you're listening and it's being processed in your mind. But I don't know if after death I might see somebody like you, but I don't know if you'll be there.

If human perception continues after death it affirms that his wife is "living" despite her loss of memory. His thoughts stumble on the link between perception and receptors, and whether one person's perceptions can communicate with another's. Although he is comforted by the thought that his wife's perceptions keep her alive, it is little comfort when his wife asks him, for the hundredth time in a day, "Where did we meet?" or Why didn't you tell me [our daughter] lives in Chicago?" Perceptions of her are no match for the capable, humorous, flesh and blood woman he has loved for over 50 years.

Based on his unique notion of individual perception, he concluded that he does not know whether all people suffer in the same way. When I asked Mr. Banks if he thought suffering was a "normal part of life" he answered:

> I don't know, I think it depends on your perception. You know, this building is peopled with old folks in wheelchairs and I guess there are more wheelchairs and walkers here than there are people. I realize that they are probably suffering and I don't know how you change the perception of people. I wonder if they are suffering or even if they enjoy their suffering—I mean there's a social aspect to suffering. They might want to make somebody suffer along with them. Or maybe they find happiness in what is given to them. I see people with horribly mangled bodies and they keep a sunny outlook. I wonder if they are suffering or if their perception is, well, this is the way it is for me. I don't know. I think of that. Often.

Mr. Banks admits that his "thinking has been transformed" by his wife's memory loss. He began to ponder subjects he seldom considered, such as "life everlasting." Because of his wife's illness, he felt pushed into another realm of consciousness—where things unseen and unproved are necessary subjects for contemplation.

During our interview, Mrs. Banks entered the room several times. Each time she looked at me quizzically but cheerfully; each time I introduced myself anew. Mr. Banks suggested that she "keep her eye on the stock market quotes" on television to see if they were "making money." She assented and walked away. As he watched his wife leave the room he commented:

> I don't think death is. . . . Had she died at the bridge table that night, it probably would have been better for her. However, right now in the state that she's in, she still is happy. She's cheerful, not depressed, so I feel that I'd like. . . . I realize that she's not ever going to be better but I do everything I can. But if she should have another cardiac arrest, I hope it's God's will that she pass away.
> **Interviewer:** Is what you're going through suffering?
> **Mr. Banks:** I don't know. I think suffering would be if I had another outlook, if I felt sorry for myself, if I were to say, why did God do this to me?

Mr. Banks treads carefully around the subject of suffering. He debates whether his wife is dead or alive, and whether he is or is not suffering. This unique status—moving in and out of belief and of suffering—allows him to be both subject and object of suffering. His ability to both watch and experience his feelings transforms raw, mute pain into a rational, though emotional discussion about it. Feeling and reason come together at the site of suffering. This synergy permits him to see his own sorrow within a vast well of human suffering.

Mr. Banks' narrative speaks to a core dimension of suffering, which includes at least two components: 1) a personal perception of suffering due to 2) an inability to control or escape a negative event. This core dimension was a pattern in all respondents' narratives. Yet, the uniqueness of experiences of suffering and respondents' reactions to them are based on respondents' personal characteristics and history.

Mr. Banks' hesitancy to name his current situation "suffering," led me to ask him if there was ever a time in life when he felt he *was* suffering.

> Gee, no. I think I've lived a charmed life. I think God has been very good to me. Maybe if you come back five years from now I might give, I probably would give different answers. I don't consider I'm suffering now. I think I'm going through a period of. . . . I think God gives you some strength and you can cope with things. I think maybe if you're. . . . If people are under tremendous stress. . . . I mean if I was in a foxhole someplace, gunfire going off all around me and so forth, I think that might be suffering.

Mr. Banks' demeanor indicates suffering—he displays deep sorrow, strong emotion, and worry about the future. Yet he is aware of the *fluid* nature of suffering. "In five years I may define suffering differently," which is a sentiment repeated by many respondents. According to Mr. Banks his current situation does not fall under the category of "tremendous stress," and therefore "falls short" of suffering. I asked Mr. Banks what a picture of suffering might look like.

> **Mr. Banks:** A picture of suffering? [long pause] I guess parents standing over the caskets of their children. Yes, a parent standing over the coffins of their children because of their own [parents] negligence or something like that. I think that would be real suffering [crying].

I could only wonder what memories this picture represents for Mr. Banks, or what part of his psyche it draws upon. In Mr. Banks' mind, being responsible for a dependent other's death evokes anguish, just as working to alleviate a dependent other's suffering, such as his wife, carries a reward. When I asked him if he ever wondered why God permits suffering, he answered through tears:

> I think of people who ask that question, "Why me, God? Why are you doing this to me?" I think I've asked that question. "Why me, God? *Why have you been so good to me?* [crying]." What I'm going through now, it's not a hardship; it's a challenge. I'm sure that there are other people who have gone through much more [my emphasis].

Throughout his narrative, Mr. Banks did not give up his theme of a charmed life. It knitted his present sorrow to his "wonderful" past and "uncertain" future. He assimilated his wife's liminal status between life and death, his need to believe that her identity is somewhere intact, and his undetermined status as husband or widower into this lifelong theme. He controlled what remained in a life irrevocably reduced by his wife's illness by believing in the continued existence of her "good thoughts" and his "charmed life." In order to retain these beliefs, he did not ask only: Why me, God? but also added, Why have you been so good to me?

OTHER METAPHORS OF SUFFERING

The metaphors of attack, injustice and loss provide rubrics under which I placed elders' stories of suffering. Of course respondents' stories rarely fit any category so neatly. Several metaphors were apparent in each of the three cases, and metaphors other than attack, injustice, and loss were used by all respondents.

Suffering as an attack has many dimensions. Mr. Carson was attacked by shame; he perceived himself as defective and inadequate in his humanness. His feelings of inferiority, emotional instability and aging came together in his story of suffering. The accumulation of shame over the decades became an unbearable burden in old age.

Perhaps the overarching nature of suffering as attack resonates to Cassell's definition of suffering as a threat to the integrity of an individual. The many colloquialisms for threats against integrity, such as "falling to pieces," "losing it," or "blowing up," or external attacks to wholeness, such as [something] "tearing me apart," "eating my heart out," or "making me crazy," are graphic representations of the perceived loss of control that comes in the wake of suffering as threat or attack.

Suffering as injustice reflects the unfairness prevalent in life whether through social disparity or through random accidents of birth. Mrs. Billings' narrative illustrates that suffering through injustice means that the sufferer is under another's control, and has little say over the duration, intensity or outcome of her experience. Feelings of anger, hurt, surprise and powerlessness combine in the experience of suffering as injustice.

None of the elders I spoke with expected to escape earthly suffering and some elders believed that present suffering was "my own fault." Perhaps to view suffering as merited removes it from randomness and frees it from the "whim of the gods"(Kliever, 1989). Certainly, an individual can always find a cause or genesis for *deserved* suffering if the net is cast far and wide enough to embrace the distant past. Still, elders wondered if the "non-escape" quality of suffering in old age could ever be considered "deserved." Popular adages heard often during interviews, such as "old age stinks" or "old age is not for sissies" implies that: 1) elders require personal strength to face the losses and declines of old age; 2) in old age personal strength is at both a minimum and a premium; and 3) most elders were surprised by the quality of suffering that they saw and experienced in old age. That is, it is not so much that elders perceived suffering to be underserved, although this might be the case, it is that the intensity of suffering occurs at a time when resources have diminished and there is a chance that life will end before suffering. This inverted relationship between "more suffering-less fight" refutes all notions of fair play. Did God or nature ignore the Golden Rule that most elders tried to follow all their lives?

It is important to note that most respondents believe that even unmerited suffering could teach a lesson about life or unearth personal attributes heretofore undiscovered. Although this did not make the suffering seem *more just,* finding a *reciprocal reward* granted meaning to suffering. In other words, if meaning can be applied to suffering, it seems less unjust (Frankl, 1959).

Although Mr. Banks' wife had not yet died, he intensely mourned her loss. His suffering carried a three-fold grief—for the wife he perceived as already gone, for the identity he assumed in relation to her, and for the unlikeliness that he would take on that role with another. His suffering showed a poignancy peculiar to the irretrievable past, yet his daily life was tortuously focused on the present. His future was both uncertain and certain to fall short of his beloved memories.

Suffering as loss refers to depletion from within. As respondents in this chapter have shown, suffering as loss also challenges a sense of self-depletion. Suffering became, to the elders discussed, an *addition* to an already fashioned identity. Elders: 1) accommodated their suffering by altering roles with new "jobs" that more appropriately "fit" the suffering experience, and 2) assimilated their suffering into an existing theme. To alter an identity or maintain an existing theme in the face of suffering requires a diligence that often buffers respondents against despair (Luborsky, 1994).

Although metaphors of attack, injustice and loss allowed me to elaborate and dramatize respondents' narratives, elders used various metaphors to represent themselves and their experiences of suffering. It is the work of the listener to tease out the metaphor that best captures this representation. For example, an 84-year-old respondent eloquently described herself and her experience of suffering.

> I'm like a cast away button. A button you have no use for. The color's not right; the size isn't right. It's old and worn. Bent out of shape.

This metaphor cannot fit into anyone else's story. It springs from her sense of uselessness, and also from the fact that she worked for over 50 years—from the time she was 17 until she was 73—as a sewing machine operator. She reiterated that she "would have kept right on working," but the numbness in her hands from arthritis caused her to worry about "not feeling it" if her fingers "got pricked" by the sewing machine needle. Her multi-layered metaphor for suffering—the cast away button—stands alone. Its appropriateness *and* poignancy to *her* story of suffering lay in its uniqueness, its fluidity, and its ability to translate the ineffable—suffering—into the describable.

Elders used metaphors to discuss another ineffable—death. These metaphors gave respondents a *safe* way to imagine impending death. An 82 year-old European American woman confided: "I feel like I'm empty inside, like I'm already dead. I feel like I'm just a shell of a person." On a follow up call, this respondent felt much better. She had been taken to the hospital after a fainting spell. There, she learned that she was bleeding internally due to a stomach lesion and was given several blood transfusions. The wisdom of her body provided a metaphor—that it was "just a shell"—that both heralded death and protected her from it.

THE NEXT CHAPTER

Chapter 9 discusses how activity helps alleviate or even stave off suffering. Elders use various mental, physical and spiritual activities to control or understand experiences of suffering.

CHAPTER 9

The Activity of Suffering

The primary activity of suffering may be the self's focus on the experience. Although respondents might desire to *get away* from the experience, *where* is uncertain. It might be an irrational desire to get away from oneself, like Mrs. Kean mentioned in Chapter 4, or to go back in time when one was not suffering, like Mrs. Rickman mentioned in Chapter 2. Unlike Mr. Wickers, mentioned in Chapter 5, most elders did not seem patient during suffering. Perhaps the primary activity of suffering is to *actively* wait for its end by re-binding or re-constructing the self broken by suffering. Although reintegration might be accomplished in several ways, narrative may bring together these broken parts. An elder presents a narrated, unified self in the life story and story of suffering. Some respondents might discover a value for suffering as they recount the experience.

The activities involved in telling a story about suffering presuppose another important activity of suffering: finding meaning in suffering that can be connected in a reasonable and rational way to one's self, past and present circumstances, and worldview. Relating the suffering story to a professional stranger in the forum of the interview is an important activity of suffering. An elder may find meaning in suffering by being the author and interpreter of her own story.

Related to the activity of suffering is the fact that, to many respondents, inactivity results in suffering. Likewise, engaging in an activity that shows no product or result can be a source of suffering because failure to produce demoralizes. Prevalent cultural, social and religious messages inform us that productive activity is necessary and good, but only if the product is useful. Elders in this study reported that not working, being unproductive, or engaging in purposeless activity results in suffering. Mrs. Kean, mentioned in Chapter 4, believed that her son might be suffering because of his lack of engagement in productive labor. Hobbies or avocations could not be enough, according to her, to bring him satisfaction.

In the first two cases I introduce elders who counter their suffering with the talents and tools they employed to "succeed" at life. They defy suffering, however, by immersing themselves in the details and events that caused their suffering in the first place.

MR. SPARKS

Mr. Sparks is a 73-year-old European-American widower. I interviewed him over seven years ago for another project. When Mr. Sparks called to request participation in the present study, I was not at my desk. When I phoned him, his voice on the answering machine told this brief story: "This is Hal, husband of Rose and father of Hal, Jr., who are both in heaven. God bless them. God bless you. Leave your message." When I last saw Mr. Sparks his wife and son were alive and well. He told me later that their recent deaths influenced his desire to be part of the study.

Although I interviewed Mr. Sparks last time in his row home, this time he preferred to come to my office. He explained that he likes "to drive" and "get out of the house." Mr. Sparks lived alone since his wife's death two years previously.

I waited for Mr. Sparks in the lobby of my office building. His appearance had changed dramatically in seven years. Where once he stood tall and straight, he now looked stooped. Formerly rather husky, he seemed frail due to loss of weight. A nagging cough punctuated his sentences and a raspy voice made it difficult for me to hear him. This is the way he began his life story:

> I was born and raised in Germantown. I went to elementary school, junior high, then S. High. I met my wife over in England in 1945. Yeah, I was in the army over there. They would switch me around, take me in the Air Force, put me in the infantry, then in the Air Force, and that's where I met my wife, at the Air Force dance. She was the best. We got married there, September 25, 1945.

Mr. Sparks began his life story chronologically, but moved quickly to the theme that granted him a binding identity—his marriage. The significance of family, especially his wife, loomed large in his life story and in his definitions of both happiness and suffering. He recalled "their early years" when he worked as a mechanic and their five children were "all at home."

> We were always going here or there, piling in the station wagon and singing all the way up to the mountains or down the shore. We used to go all over. Oh, we had a good time. You know, I had the best wife in the world. She won't be replaced.

The loss of Mr. Sparks' greatest treasure, his wife, causes him suffering. The death of the Sparks' oldest son from cancer at age 49 presaged his wife's death.

> I don't think my wife ever got over it [son's death]. She passed out when we were going to the cemetery. Passed right out, scared everybody. And it was only six months that she lived on. She was in a lot of grief and you couldn't do nothing with her.

In the months after their son died, Mr. Sparks and his wife went through periods of depression. Although he "came out of it," his wife "really took it hard."

She suffered a stroke a month after their son's death. When I asked him to name an event, incident, or time in his life when he suffered, he answered without hesitation:

> When my wife passed on, that was suffering. There couldn't be no worse. She come down that Sunday morning and I said, "What do you want, hon?" She says a cup of tea and toast. After that, she says, "I think I'm going upstairs and lay down." A little later, I call up. No answer. So I yell, "Yo, hon, you want to go for a ride?" No answer. And I go up, and looking up there, I say, "Oh God, no!" So I started mouth to mouth, but she didn't come around. Oh, man, I don't know what I'm doing there. I go downstairs, call my oldest daughter, then I call 911. Well, anyway, too late, she was gone.

Mr. Sparks merged the facts of his wife's death with past and present feelings. His wife's death remains the emergency it was the morning she died; his frenzy at seeing her dead is a present frenzy. The way in which he recounted her death was similar to the way Mrs. Billings, in Chapter 5, relayed her disappointment with her son. This manner of narration shows that he: 1) remains emotionally rooted in the events that are being recalled; 2) has unresolved feelings about the events; and 3) feels betwixt and between the past and present, emotion and rationality, remembering and actually reliving those events.

Mr. Sparks relives, through memory and narration, each second that led to her death. Despite his wife's illnesses, such as diabetes, several heart by-pass operations, and a recent stroke, he said that part of his suffering results from shock—he was surprised that he "lost her." He retained a sense of control over the event by forbidding the paramedics to take her to the morgue.

> I said, "Oh, no, you're not taking my wife to the morgue, no way." They said that's the law. I said, "I don't give a damn about your law, mister, if you take her out it's over my dead body." My son even said, "When my father says no, he means no!" Then I said, "Now get out of my house, you didn't do me no good." Then they left her lay on the floor, and that was worse yet. Because I wouldn't let them take her to the morgue, they left her laying on the floor.

Rage was one antidote to suffering for Mr. Sparks; it kept him from succumbing to a paralyzing grief. His anger fought against quietism, passivity, and depression. It also spoke to a masculine expressiveness—rather than cry, he became furious with the men who tried to remove her body from their home. "Everything" has changed since her death.

> I don't go out like I used to. The kids keep on me, "Dad, you've got to get out." Like I used to go around to the taproom, maybe 3 or 4 times a week. Now, maybe for 2 or 3 weeks they won't see me. Then they start calling, "Where you been, Hal, you all right?" No desire. No desire for that.

Mr. Sparks' family and friends construed his lack of desire to "go out" as depression. He views it as a choice. He chooses to stay home alone with his memories and gains a special status in his own eyes by nurturing his grief.

> Everybody's different than me. I said I had the greatest wife in the world. That's the way I always felt and I always will feel until I go. And when I go I know I'll be with her.

Mr. Sparks' primary activity is keeping his wife "alive." For example, his daily routine includes visiting his wife's grave. On the day of our interview he described the busy afternoon ahead of him:

> **Mr. Sparks:** After we're done here, I'm going to the cemetery. I've got the rake in the car and I'll do some raking because I know there's going to be leaves all around. So I know it's going to be clean for Thanksgiving. Yeah, I got a little fence around it and plants all in there. And I sit and I talk with her.
> **Interviewer:** What do you say?
> **Mr. Sparks:** Oh, different things about the family, what's going on, how much I miss her. I pray to her every night. Because we were married 53 years when she passed on. Oh, we were real close.
> **Interviewer:** How did you manage after her passing?
> **Mr. Sparks:** Well, right away I was under the doctor's care. Then I come around and I guess I was all right. But then I had that slight heart attack.

Both Mr. and Mrs. Sparks' grief translated into bodily sickness. Mrs. Sparks' grief for her son, along with the gravity of her illnesses, resulted in death. Mr. Sparks channeled his loss into the busyness of mourning. He transformed his own life through the reality of his wife's death. He did not view himself as a victim, however, *keeping her death alive* became his primary activity. In fact, her death gave him a renewed reason for living—he tends her grave and recounts her virtues to anyone who listens. His children's closeness with him and each other resulted from his wife's diligence as a mother. The day after our interview was Thanksgiving; his children planned an elaborate dinner.

> It's going to be nice tomorrow because they're all going to be in the one house. I have 19 grandchildren; 3 great grandchildren. My kids got it all figured out. I give my wife all the credit. She was the best in the world. She was there for everybody. I don't know what to say because she meant so much.

Just as Mr. Sparks' wife will be *present* at Thanksgiving dinner, she was present at our interview, and central in his answers to most of the interview questions. When I asked him what a picture of suffering would show, he hesitated.

> **Mr. Sparks:** It may sound silly but I had a picture taken of my wife in the casket and I still got it at home to remember how she looked before

they closed it. Oh, yeah, I kiss that every night. I got it up in my bedroom.
Interviewer: Does it hurt you to look at that picture?
Mr. Sparks: I have to. I have to. I have to look at it as far as I'm concerned.
I figure she's with me that way. And I always carry pictures of her right
over my heart [Mr. Sparks retrieved pictures from his shirt picket and showed
them to me].

Mr. Sparks' griefwork is all-consuming. He displays pictures of his wife at
various stages of their married life throughout the house. He tucks a few into the
bathroom mirror so he can "watch her" while he shaves; he sleeps with one under
his pillow. Pictures keep Mrs. Sparks close to her husband, but her nearness
is more than symbolic. He affirmed the compelling nature of his suffering by
his answer to the question: Does suffering have any value?

It has value to me. As long as I can think about her I know she's with me.
Like I say I dream about her and I thank God I wake up every morning. See,
I like waking up because that's when I look at the picture of my wife. She
went up there to go to sleep and I didn't get a chance to say goodbye. That's
my biggest regret that I never had a chance to say goodbye. That final kiss.
Just went up and that was it. Biggest shock of my life.

Mr. Sparks feels gratitude for each new day because it gives him another
chance to "go over her life." His review becomes a myth of origin and destiny
that speaks of virtuous women, relationships between genders, and how human
lives should unfold. Like a sacred narrative, he finds a new exegetical meaning
with each review of his memories. Because of constant probing, his grief remains
open and expectant.

Although suffering may be thought to deplete energy, Mr. Sparks is ener-
gized by his grief. Since his wife's death, he is aware of the value of each day.
Although he defines grief as suffering, he actively chooses to grieve for the
rest of his life. He considers his wife's death a tragedy in which they both
play the lead. Unlike Mr. Wickers mentioned in Chapter 5, or Mrs. Billings
discussed in Chapter 8, the core of Mr. Sparks' suffering is not loss of control or
knowing which way to turn, but a continuous and deliberate mulling over the
event of his wife's death.

I tell them [his children], there's nothing nobody can do, it's [grief] going
to be with me as long as I'm here. That's it. 'Til the day I die. If it wasn't
left to me, both my son and my daughter, they'd have me living with them.
Get rid of this and get rid of that? I said no! I got pictures of my wife over
the mantelpiece and I got pictures in the basement. It might sound crazy
to some people.

Toward the end of the interview Mr. Sparks mentioned another period of life
when he "might have suffered a little." He recalled the emotional and physical
pain "we all endured" during and after the Second World War.

Mr. Sparks: I had frostbite up to my hips when I was in the army and they were going to take my legs off, but back in '44 they started with spinal blocks and nothing was really known about that then. So, there were quite a few of us and we said, "We don't care, save our legs." And thank God they saved mine. Oh, yeah, I seen all my buddies coming back, legs off, heads blown off, what have you, because I was in the Battle of the Bulge. I lost a lot of buddies.

Interviewer: Your experiences in war was suffering.

Mr. Sparks: [Pause] Well, you look back on it and you remember some of the guys. See, we always thought this would be the end of wars. That's what we fought for so that our children would not have to go. We figure well, we get it done and over with, and that will be the end of war. But it didn't come about that way.

Mr. Sparks' memory of active duty held a double-edged suffering. It was anguish enough to be wounded and to witness the violent deaths of buddies. To learn later that one of the reasons he fought—so that his children "would never have to go"—did not come to pass, brought added pain. Two of his sons served in Vietnam; one is psychologically disabled because of combat experience. Still, for Mr. Sparks, the reality of war rested on the periphery of suffering. He emphasized that it was only with his wife's passing that he experienced *real* suffering.

No, war is just something. . . . You just got to go through it. I just happen to be lucky. I could have not been here, I mean like the other guys. But I just happen to be lucky. I mean, if you would have asked me these questions [about suffering] five years ago, I wouldn't give you the same answers. It [suffering] only came with the loss [of wife].

Mr. Sparks' comment speaks to a temporal component in elders' accounts of suffering. There is an irretrievable nature to loss in old age, whether it is the loss of a significant other, bodily strength, cognitive function, or faith. The sense of irretrievability is connected to an elder's perception that they have little energy to change external circumstances, or little hope that bodily strength, cognitive function or faith will return in the time left to them.

Although Mr. Sparks' major responsibility was that of devoted husband even after his wife's death, his role as veteran helped him with his griefwork. He remains active in several veterans' organizations; he emphasized that he is not "just a member," but holds influential positions, such as commander and representative, in veterans' posts around the city.

I've been in the legion for 43 years. I went through every chair from chaplain right on up to Commander. When you're commander you got to go all over the state, you're kept on the go. I give each post a report every month. You got to get up and read it out to your comrades. We call each other comrade. If everybody would make a report like you, Hal, we'd be all right. You make the best. Membership is important. It gives you your body, your strength, that's why I believe in membership. That's why I belong. Costs me in dues every year, but it's worth it. A lot of people say you only have to belong to one [veterans' organization], but I belong to them all.

These comments show at least two major themes in Mr. Sparks' narrative: 1) the importance of belonging, and 2) his whole-hearted commitment to his chosen and designated roles. The positions he assumed in life, such as husband, father and World War II veteran, demand lifelong allegiance. He performs the duties required by these roles even after the "contracts" have expired, and he gains self-esteem by continuing to honor them. He unites his major roles by the themes in his narrative.

Up there in the cemetery I got American flags and I put the prettiest flag right on the front, right in the middle, and that's for my wife. And there's still a flag that flies all the time, too, in front of my house. That's my wife's flag.

There is a religious quality to Mr. Sparks' activity with the American flags. He hangs flags on his front porch and stakes them at his wife's gravesite. They are symbols of active devotion to wife and country. After our interview, Mr. Sparks asked me to walk him to his car so he could give me something. In the trunk of his car lay dozens of tiny American flags. He offered me one, and then as a gesture of warmth and connection—handed me another.

MR. BRYAN

The case of Mr. Bryan shows that just as activity mitigates suffering, as it did for Mr. Sparks, who chose to be "active" in his grief, inactivity in itself can be defined as suffering. Mr. Bryan is an 80-year-old African-American man who lives with his second wife in a federally funded apartment for low-income seniors. He has many health problems, including partial blindness and severe arthritis, and seldom leaves his apartment. His wife, who is ten years younger than he, "goes out a lot." He began his life story this way:

When I was a kid there was a kid over on the other side of the lot and he shot a rubber band and it went right into my eye. So I went to the hospital and they operated on it and fixed it up so I could see out of it. And it wasn't until I started getting old that, just like that, the sight just went out. But the other eye is good. And maybe the sight went out of that one and went in the other one because I see good out of this one. It made it stronger. Just like when a person gets an arm cut off, they get strong in the other one.

With this account, Mr. Bryan introduced his life's theme—a theory of compensation. Individuals are entitled to a certain amount of sight or strength, so vision or strength lost in one eye or arm goes into the other. In other words, he views any loss as offering a reciprocal gain. When I asked him about his early life, he said:

> Well, it wasn't too bad. I know I had a lot of brothers. I had one sister, but she died. I grew up in Maryland. My father, I can't remember him because I saw him but one time. But my mother, she raised us the best way she could.

Mr. Bryan's short-term memory is failing. He also cannot remember his long-term past—when specific events in his life occurred. He recalled that he went as far as the sixth grade in a small schoolhouse in rural Maryland. He began working when he "was around 11 or 12 years old."

> I used to do people's kitchens and their porches and steps, like scrubbing them down. Then I worked with this lady, I used to help her clean the house and take her two little kids to the park. I did work like that.

Mr. Bryan enjoyed domestic work as a child, because he "played with the kids who lived there (the homes where he worked)." When he reached his teenage years he thought that he ought to find "strong work" because he had been "born with large bones." At 16 years of age he accompanied an uncle to Philadelphia to find work. He was interested in construction, but because it was part-time and seasonal, he chose a steady, year-round job at Horn and Hardart's.

> **Mr. Bryan:** I stayed there [H&H] for about 4 or 5 years and they said, well, if you just hang in there you'll get a gold watch [pulls a face and laughs].
> **Interviewer:** You didn't want the gold watch?
> **Mr. Bryan:** No, just to have your name engraved in that? No, no [laughter].
> **Interviewer:** What did you want?
> **Mr. Bryan:** Well, when I was coming up I could tap dance pretty good. I used to win all kinds of amateur nights. So somebody was talking to me about getting a break on dancing. I had an audition with Duke Ellington. But I messed up. I was out the night before, and when I got up that next morning, he had gone. I was good. But I messed around and then I couldn't get into show business. I just didn't get up there on time.

Mr. Bryan's comment brought to mind a hypothesis I had when beginning this research—that "dreams denied" might be salient in elders' stories of suffering. Most respondents, however, spoke of long-held dreams with humorous or nonchalant quips: "Dreams are dreams—living is for real." "Those kinds of things (dreams), I don't worry too much about them now. I have too much else to worry about." "What's then is then. I can't bring it all back. So I just look forward."

Although Mr. Bryan's dream was a career in dance, he realized after he became a husband and father that "dancing was young man stuff." He eventually found a job in construction, which offered him security, self-satisfaction and a decent wage. He worked as an unskilled laborer for 30 years and retired with a pension and benefits. He was proud of the work he did because he used natural talents, such as strength and endurance, and learned skills, such as pouring concrete in the foundations of new buildings and spreading tar on roofs.

Still, the fact that Mr. Bryan brought up his "lost career" in dance showed that he felt some regret about it at this stage of life. Is the memory of dance important because he can no longer walk? Or, perhaps because he cannot remember much of his past, the "dancer" is the clearest picture of his past self. When I asked him bout the saddest times in his life, he answered:

> My wife died before my mother. She died of cancer. I was there to see her [in the hospital] and she died right in my arms in the bed.

Mr. Bryan could not remember how long he was married to his first wife, but he described the moment of her death and the grief he felt. He also recalled they she had borne children, but he could not tell me how many. He knew that he had not seen his children for many years, but could not remember why they were estranged. Perhaps because of the haziness of his past, Mr. Bryan told me he prefers "not to look behind," but to live in the present and anticipate the future.

Mr. Bryan brought up a "problem" that makes him "angry and sad." Some of the seniors who live in his building are more mobile than others; some drive but most do not. The elders who drive charge their less ambulatory neighbors for taking them to the supermarket or bank. Although Mr. Bryan has not driven for several years, he acted as chauffeur to many frail elders in the past without charging them. Because he is disgusted by the "drivers'" lack of charity—"senior charging senior to go to the food store," he waits for his wife's daughter to take him shopping. He feels angry because he cannot drive. *He* would run errands for his neighbors "for nothing." When I asked Mr. Bryan to define suffering, he answered:

> Well, it feels bad not to work. I used to want sometimes to go and do a little something but I can't go and do what I want. Oh, I keep busy. I do the vacuuming in here and the cleaning up.

To work—to be defined by what you do and how well you do it, was an important component of identity for both male and female respondents. But as Mr. Bryan clarified, "keeping busy" is not the same as work. "Work" uses unique talents; one's "specialness" emerges through labor. Work holds the essence of being human. "Keeping busy" may mean engaging in unproductive labor for the sake of "busyness," and may itself cause suffering.

Suffering, as an inability to work, overwhelms Mr. Bryan. Work presupposes independence, productivity and choice, which are signposts of moral worth in Western society. He often feels useless, trapped inside his apartment, and tired of watching television or cleaning. Yet, he clarified that he is the final judge of whether he currently suffers. The last bastion of choice and freedom is his own mind.

> **Interviewer:** Is this (not to work or be active) suffering?
> **Mr. Bryan:** It depends on you. It's how you got it in your mind. See, you make yourself hurt. But you can be hurt and don't be suffering.

Mr. Bryan's complex comment about the sufferer's role in suffering speaks to two components of suffering in elders' accounts: 1) An event, incident or time in life is considered suffering if the elder perceives it to be so, and 2) As long as an elder feels some control over a negative experience, he usually described himself as "not suffering."

Mr. Bryan said that feelings of discouragement and frustration "are always with [him]" because his physical condition "will not get better." Yet his portrait of suffering did not include his body.

> **Interviewer:** If you were going to take a picture of suffering, what would it look like?
> **Mr. Bryan:** Your mind.
> **Interviewer:** Your mind?
> **Mr. Bryan:** Yeah. You would be your own suffering. You make it [suffering] yourself. You're doing it with your own mind. So you got to get rid of it yourself.

Mr. Bryan's remarks reveal the cultural notion that the moral worth of the sufferer and the value of suffering are measured by the sufferer's ability to "get rid of it." Mr. Bryan affirms the Western concept of the individual as master of his fate. To suffer is to be a victim of a mind "out of control." As the interview progressed, he recalled another time in his life that might be called suffering.

> **Mr. Bryan:** One time 5 guys jumped me. They robbed me. I did what I could but it was five guys. They cut me here and they cut me there [shows me his arm with a scar from his elbow to the palm of his hand].
> **Interviewer:** That's some scar. What made that incident suffering?
> **Mr. Bryan:** Because I couldn't do what I wanted to do after they cut me. I couldn't do work; couldn't do nothing for a while.

Mr. Bryan was hospitalized for three days and out of work for several weeks. When he returned to his job he was forced to work part-time because he had minimal feeling in two fingers. He described this incident as suffering because, along with money, the men stole his ability to be productive. They robbed him of the dignity and security of going to work and earning a paycheck. When I asked him if he still felt angry about this incident, he shook his head and explained that at this stage in life, "nothing" worried him.

> **Mr. Bryan:** I seen so many people go out of this building foot first, it wasn't even funny. Sometimes I think about them, but it doesn't get to me. Cause if I'm not careful, I'd be jumping out the window for sure.
> **Interviewer:** Does anything "get to you"?
> **Mr. Bryan:** Nothing. No, nothing.

Mr. Bryan, like Mrs. Lowell mentioned in Chapter 7, recognized that the result of regret, sorrow or worry *could be suffering*. Mrs. Lowell *could* "fall to pieces," and Mr. Bryan *might* "jump out the window" if they allow themselves to dwell on the hurts of the past or the fears of the present and future. Mr. Bryan mentioned a more productive way to react to suffering.

> You only suffer so much until you just give up. See, you hurt yourself by not giving up, so you give up.

Although surrender might be construed as passivity, Mr. Bryan clarified that surrender is a choice to the individual who suffers, and choice represents control. His comment resonates to that of Mr. Wickers discussed in Chapter 5, who spoke of "waiting it out" while suffering.

> Sometime I think when I used to be in good shape and I used to work and do what I want to do. And now I can't do what I want to do. What I got in mind to do, I can't do. I mean some things you can't even do because your body won't let you. Like your legs won't let you.

Mr. Bryan has become both the animator and observer of his own body. He watches himself "push" his body into activity. Because his body feels as though it has a "life of its own," he feels disconnected from it and from his younger, physically integrated self. He offered advice on handling suffering.

> Well, if you're suffering too much, you just pray to God to help you to stop suffering.
> **Interviewer:** Is prayer the key?
> **Mr. Bryan:** If you believe, it probably is.
> **Interviewer:** Is it for you?
> **Mr. Bryan:** Well, for me, I just don't let things get to me. You have to be careful the way you live and you have to be careful the way you think.
> **Interviewer:** What do you mean?
> **Mr. Bryan:** [With a smile] Just be careful.

Mr. Bryan guards this important locus of activity—his mind—because this is the place where secrets are kept, personal battles are fought, choices are made, suffering takes place, and decisions about the existence of God play out.

Mr. Bryan answered many interview questions with a quiet but firm indirectness that left little room for probing. These words of counsel—be careful—might have sprung from many sources—worry about forgetfulness, estrangement from children, feeling surrounded by "mean, unfriendly" neighbors, or perhaps being interviewed by a white female stranger. Whatever his reasons, Mr. Bryan stitched a theme of *carefulness* into his life story, his story of suffering, and even his relationship with God.

Perhaps Mr. Bryan compensated for his memory loss by limiting the information he shared about himself. If or when he surrenders to suffering, however, it will be on his terms, and will thus show his ability to control his physical or psychic pain.

MRS. SANDS

Mrs. Sands is a 74-year-old European-American woman. She lives with her husband in a large home in the suburbs of Philadelphia. For our interview, she half sat, half reclined on a chaise lounge in a small den that she described as: "a room of my own." She explained that lack of energy was one side effect from the medicine she takes because of a heart condition. She reported that she seldom goes out by herself, but when she does, she is aware not only of her physical weakness, but also of her emotional frailty in the midst of a world that "seems to be created for healthy young people."

> You're invisible once you get to be a certain age. It's lonely and it's strange. I think they're not trying to be rude but there will be young people walking toward you and I just stand still and they'll just crash right into me. I'm braced; I'm over as far as I can go to the wall and I have learned to wait. "Oh, I'm sorry," they'll say. Because I used to say I'm sorry to them, because *I* was in the way. Do you know what I mean?

Mrs. Sands began her life story with an anecdote in which she describes herself as invisible and draws me into her narrative with a question. She wondered if I understood the profundity of what she was telling me about herself—that she was "in the way"—and her place in the world—"braced, close to the wall"—as an older woman. She continued with the story of her life.

> I grew up in a small college town in Ohio. Oh, I had a great-great grand-mother who was a feminist back in 1840. She left England on a sailing vessel to teach school in India. Only a third of the shipload was alive by the time they got to the Indian Ocean.

Unlike most of the respondents I interviewed, Mrs. Sands knew her ancestors' names and reveled in their adventures. She was proud of her foremothers and the fact that they survived much adversity—from braving the Atlantic to the boredom of residing in a small college town. She remembered the maxims that they passed down to her.

> My great grandmother told my mother to grasp life, it is precious, say yes to life. And my mother did, and of course she preached that to me. My mother was a surgical nurse during World War I. My father was a college President in Ohio. But I don't think they were happy [laughter]. I think my father would rather be a janitor at Princeton than President of this little college.

Mrs. Sands glossed over her parents' dissatisfaction with their lives and focused on the treasures they bequeathed, such as common sense and a love of learning.

> I guess I agree with many things they [parents] thought. I mean there's a certain sanity to life with an excellent education. Of course, my mother was a snob. She was embarrassed to live on Iris Street in Ohio. When someone would ask her where she was from she would say Massachusetts [laughter].

In retrospect, Mrs. Sands understood both the elitism and poignancy of her mother's yearnings. She used her own perspective of late life to paint her mother's life with pathos.

> If there was a storm, she would find some excuse of why she had to go back into the garden, really race out in the garden. Oh, I left something outside, she'd say. Because just being out in a storm gave her some kind of. . . . She needed to live more vitally then being a professor's wife and have two children to raise. [Pause]. I regret I wasn't more of a comfort to her.

Mrs. Sands offered no clear picture of her father or younger brother and said little else about her childhood. She did not speak about the members of her family again except to tell me that "they are all dead now."

> It was just a family of four in a little house in Ohio. I was the first faculty child ever to go away to college.

After her brief reminiscence about childhood, she jumped to the magical world of the "first rate woman's college" she attended in a neighboring state. There, her sense of adventure was sparked because of the vitality of her teachers and classmates and the demands of the curriculum.

> I remember my first class in Zoology. We were to draw the paramecium so I had my pencil there and I was looking at it through the microscope. I had never seen live forms like this before and it was such a moving experience about the beginnings of life. When I lifted my head I had tears running down my face.

Intellectual curiosity erased any shyness she felt as a child. At school, she initiated meetings with well-known writers and passionately engaged them in subjects of their choice.

> I was just a freshman when I heard that Robert Frost was going to be in the area. I wrote to him and told him I had a poetry group. And he came! There has been so much written about the dark side of him, but I hate to hear that. I was riding at that time and I was trying to describe the exhilaration I felt flying along on the horse. At any rate, he was terribly interested in what it felt like.

Mrs. Sands sat upright in her chaise when she talked about "the girl [she] used to be." She seemed to be describing an *old* friend she admired and remembered as innocent and even foolish in her enthusiasm. Just as she drew a portrait of her mother in a rainstorm that captured her mother's longings, she painted a portrait of herself with unlimited potential. Mrs. Sands had dreams of attending medical school. One teacher's unprovoked cruelty changed her career path.

> Long after, I would still be having nightmares about a teacher there, Miss Dell. I have no idea what I did to offend her, but apparently she sort of picked out a person to. . . . Well, she picked people that were sort of innocent.

She did me great harm and I had never experienced this before. I had done a very comprehensive paper with footnotes and everything. And she gave me an F on it. And that would have meant I would not have graduated. Fortunately, members of her department, all of whom needed their jobs badly said they would all quit and they took the paper with the F on it to the Dean of women. I got an A. But nothing was done to punish her. She also accused me of being a communist, and this was done during the McCarthy era. So that mark was on me. She really affected my life. I still feel bitter about it.

Because this teacher gave her a poor reference, Mrs. Sands did not receive a scholarship. Her parents paid her brother's way to medical school; they could not afford to send both children. She decided to attend a graduate program in Illinois. She talked about some of the people that she met in the program, including "the only genius I ever knew," and a teacher who "had something to do with creating the atomic bomb." She also met her husband there.

Everything sort of falls apart here. There was this handsome young man that I had gone out to coffee with. And he said, "Would you mind if Bud came along?" And there was Bud coming down the stairs in the main hall. He was not nearly as good looking as the boy I had been having coffee with, and I know this is irrational, but I wanted to know his last name because I was wondering what my last name was going to be [laughter]. So, we were married between semesters. But my mother was hoping I would go into politics or do something interesting with my life.

Mrs. Sands did not explain why "everything fell apart" after she met her husband. Her dreams were forced off course due to marriage; she stopped pursuing an academic career. Perhaps she worried that her mother would be disappointed, or that she herself would be forced to run outside during rainstorms to find excitement in life. After her husband received his doctorate, the couple settled in Philadelphia. Mr. Sands became a professor of Literature at a nearby university. Mrs. Sands described this time as "extremely pleasant." She was working as a research assistant when she became pregnant. She planned to return to work after a short maternity leave. The birth of her first son, Joseph, changed her life.

He was almost a month late. I kept telling the doctor I'm in labor. But it was the doctor's error. Afterward, he needed 24 hours care. I wanted to give this baby the best chance in the world before I even got pregnant. But then he was born and it was an ordeal. At first I wasn't told anything and I couldn't seem to find any doctors around. Finally we found out what was wrong with him. One doctor said, "He's just a vegetable. He won't live past three."

Joseph was born with cystic fibrosis. Along with the doctors' grim prognosis, he was a difficult baby who "cried all the time." Mrs. Sands described this period in her life as "just too much." She remembered the night that she accepted the fact that even if Joseph grew to adulthood, he would never be a *normal* person.

Joseph was three months old. In one vividly recalled moment, Mrs. Sands stopped believing in God.

> I didn't believe the doctors. I thought I could pray him well. Well, that night, he was crying and I was crying. And I was standing at his crib praying like crazy. [Pause] Then I realized that nobody was listening.

The desperation with which she prayed equaled her sudden certainty that no one heard her. After that night, she experienced peace about Joseph's condition. She would offer no more pleas to a silent God, and would spend no more time waiting for an answer. She explained how she overcame suffering during the first two years of Joseph's life.

> **Mrs. Sands:** I started to learn calculus after that.
> **Interviewer:** Why calculus?
> **Mrs. Sands:** It makes you focus. You know word games? One time someone said when you hear the word beauty what do you think of? I said, Math. Then I suddenly realized I truly feel that way.

When Joseph was almost three years old the Sands placed him in an institution where he remains. At the time of my interview with Mrs. Sands, Joseph was a 44-year-old college graduate who outlived all of his doctors' predictions. His mother revealed, with pride, how he had completed his college curriculum.

> It took him twenty years but he got his Bachelor's degree. The reading was no problem; he has great comprehension. And he typed his school papers by using a stick on his head—he typed with that stick. But it's not just that, that makes him amazing. I think somewhere in the damage to his brain they damaged what makes most of us human, which is a certain meanness. He is loved by everyone who knows him.

The Sands' second son, James, was born five years after Joseph. Mrs. Sands told me, with laughter, that Joseph refers to him as "my so-called normal brother." She revealed that although James was "physically perfect," he had "his share of problems."

After James reached school age, Mrs. Sands returned to a nearby university to earn a master's degree. Although she lost her faith the night she prayed at Joseph's bedside, she recognized a need for "some absolute" and found it in the study of Mathematics. She reported that she "trusts the elegance, precision, and infiniteness of numbers". When I asked Mrs. Sands to tell me about a time in her life when she was suffering, she answered:

> Oh, there were so many of them. With Joseph, knowing he was so sick and so brave. And still knowing that. And still not knowing what's down the line for him. And James. He had a bad marriage and dropped out of school. There was a drug problem too. I would see youngsters his age lying on the street and almost being afraid to look. I thought I might see him there.

She mentions James' "drug problems" almost nonchalantly in her story of suffering, but offers no details. Joseph made "wonderful progress" at the institution; James enrolled in a rehab program, went back to school, graduated, and remarried. After Mr. Sands retired the couple traveled, took classes together, and visited their sons frequently. While on a "working" vacation, Mrs. Sands was struck by a sudden illness.

> I was on a trip. I flew down to Guadalajara to take a watercolor class, and I became very sick. It was congestive heart failure. It was almost as if I went from being one person to another. But it wasn't just the heart failure, there's an enormous amount of data on congestive heart failure. It was the depression. Everything lost its color.

Mrs. Sands had never experienced depression, and had no idea what befell her. Although mental and physical illness disrupted her life, they became markers for personal growth. She described negative events in her life as bridges from one way of life to another, as well as bridges for being one "kind" of person to becoming another. The birth of Joseph and her illnesses were watershed events; she and the world, quite literally, never looked the same as they had before the events occurred. She questioned whether depression "hit [her]" because of age, illness, and thoughts of finitude.

> I had absolutely no energy. I thought maybe it was religious. You know, maybe it's your soul. You're unhappy, you're old, you're not going to live that much longer. I was trying to write a mystery story and all that was out. I found that playing the piano was too tiring; even painting was too tiring.

With therapy and the proper medicine, "color" flooded back into Mrs. Sands' life, but not energy. She remains too weak to continue social and artistic activities that she enjoyed before her diagnosis. She described her current condition as suffering because she believes she will soon die. Although no doctor told her that death is imminent, she senses its nearness. Her mind constantly turns to thoughts of death. Questions to her therapist are urgent.

> She [therapist] said, "What is your main question?" I said, "Well, it's the universal one—What is it all about? What am I doing here? You're born alone, you die alone and you can keep the idea of death away so long but then when you get this close to it you begin to think."

Mrs. Sands said that she has asked the "universal questions" since childhood and believed, until Joseph's birth, the answers given by her Methodist religion. Her experience of depression caused her to revisit those beliefs, but she failed to find solace in them. Now, she no longer looks to religion or God to provide answers. When I asked how she thought the concepts of depression, sadness and suffering were different from one another, she explained:

> When the depression hit I was yearning for death. I kept trying to figure out ways of doing suicide so it wouldn't seem like suicide and the family

wouldn't be hurt by it. That's when I sought therapy. Suffering is a constant search for solutions; it's positive. I mean it hurts a lot but you're looking for solutions. Like with Joseph, or with James' drug problems. Even with Miss Dell. You're busy. Whereas depression is total hopelessness. Sadness—well, I think I'm not a sad person but I cry easily. I cry when I see a painting in the Art Museum. But I'm not sad. Or maybe crying makes sadness easier to bear.

For Mrs. Sands, mental activity controls and counters suffering. Learning about Joseph's condition, trying to understand the causes and outcomes of James' drug addiction, and reading "everything [she] could get her hands on" about depression and heart failure, helped her to stay on top of situations that might have overwhelmed her. When I asked her what a picture of suffering would show, she considered.

The idea of drawing suffering would be totally beyond me. I immediately think when you said that I would try to recreate the Pieta. I think suffering has to do with a mother and child. In fact I think Michaelangelo thought the Pieta was the greatest thing he had ever done. It was the only thing he signed because it represented true suffering—suffering and the mother who knows.

Mrs. Sands mentioned earlier in the interview that she "trusts the elegance, precision and infiniteness of numbers." Although the perfection of numbers cannot hurt her, neither can it give her comfort. To portray suffering she turned not to math, nor to God, but to the Mother of God depicted in the Pieta, who holds her grown child's lifeless body in her arms. The grief that Mrs. Sands feels for her son, still alive, may be deepened by her grief for the God in whom she no longer believes. Her picture of suffering shows the Mother of God mourning the loss of her child.

Mrs. Sands viewed our interview as a way to take stock of her life. She weighed her mother's boredom with life against her own academic success. She placed herself as a college girl, full of promise, alongside a picture of herself as a young mother who pleaded with God to make her son well. Each fine memory had a corresponding sorrowful one. Mrs. Sands made it clear that each sad recollection, especially about her children, offered a matching scene of their unimagined achievements.

Although Mrs. Sands could not walk out of the "room of her own" without exhaustion, she countered her suffering by remaining busy with her faculties of memory, discernment, and a "rational expectation" of "somewhere" finding answers to the "universal questions."

THE FUNDAMENTAL ACTIVITIES OF SUFFERING

Perhaps the fundamental activity of suffering is to find meaning in the experience. To view the self as growing in old age rather than stagnating or deteriorating requires a non-materialistic notion of growth. For some, the quest to find meaning in negative experiences in old age takes on a significance that is inherently sacred.

Mr. Sparks and Mrs. Sands chose activities with which they were comfortable, identified strongly, and held the potential for answering questions about the meaning of suffering. Mr. Sparks' activity level may have increased after his wife's death. He continued in his role as husband by organizing his time around the memory of his wife. This activity answered some of his questions about life's meaning after her death.

Mrs. Sands found meaning for her sufferings through the power of her intellect. To her, suffering means mental activity—to find solutions for each of her son's tragedies and answers to the age-old question of "What's it all about?" in the face of finitude. During our interview, she catalogued the accumulated sufferings of life and cross-referenced them with periods of joy. She tallied, in a spiritual accounting system, the positives and negatives of her life.

Mr. Bryan's narrative illustrated how a lack of productive activity could be suffering, but only if he allowed it to be so. For him, knowing the time to surrender to suffering demonstrated that even in suffering, there is choice.

For the respondents discussed here, the activity of suffering, which includes mourning, questioning, and choosing to surrender, is synonymous with vitality. How each finds meaning in suffering is connected to the way and the why each found meaning throughout life. Mr. Sparks lived his live through his wife's eyes. Mr. Bryan was forced, throughout life, to surrender to jobs and roles that matched his skills. Mrs. Sands used her intellect to internalize the majesty and silence of nature, and of suffering.

"The work that man [sic] does must be essential to his being" (Marx, 1975, p. 328). In our society, work helps individuals transcend themselves by experiencing fulfillment in the work activity itself (Weber, 1958). Respondents' "chosen" activity countered suffering with *work* that was unique to their life and experience of suffering.

THE NEXT CHAPTER

Chapter 10 is the concluding chapter. In it I ask a final question: Who is the self that suffers? This question is integral to an examination of the "lived experience" of suffering.

CHAPTER 10

Who is the Self that Suffers?

At some point on the continuum between muteness and easement, suffering demands language. Language is integral to the "progress" of suffering. To remain speechless in suffering—"that is death" (Soelle, 1975). Through language, an elder names her suffering, describes the circumstances that led to it, discerns its fit within the context of her life, and imbues it with value or rejects value. The men and women I interviewed were not mute in the face of suffering. They eloquently demonstrated that language is integral to the movement of suffering from silence to, possibly, transformation.

Respondents did not need me to define suffering for them because they already had defined it through personal experience. Mrs. Inglund described suffering as: "a hurt that never goes away," which resonated to lifelong illnesses and decades old grief for her oldest son. Mr. Callen defined suffering as a "hurtness" that he later refined to: "being lost to oneself through drunkenness." Respondents personalized broad cultural concepts—illness, pain, loss—of suffering and posited a personal theory of suffering's cause and effect.

Within the parameters of grief, illness or tragedy that is part of every human life, elders made sense of suffering. They did so through at least two lenses: their unique personal history and the shared knowledge they held as members of a cultural, ethnic or religious group. One of the most important activities in suffering was to find meaning in the experience. Respondents often imputed meaning to suffering through a non-material or spiritual lens. But secular and spiritual aspects of life were not easily separated; they were all of a piece in elders' stories of suffering. Finding meaning in life and in suffering connected sacred and profane enterprises. Meaning in life was found in the minutiae of everyday along with life's climactic moments. Finding meaning in suffering often depended upon whether elders gleaned moral or spiritual rewards from the experience. According to elders, there was a mystery to the why of suffering that could not be tapped cognitively; an acceptance of suffering fell out of the lines of reason. While discussing this mystery, elders viewed suffering within the context of concrete and spiritual worlds, and experienced it as universal and contingent, unique and comparative, mundane and transcendent. Suffering connected them to both the banal and distinctive aspects of being human.

Despite the uniqueness of elders' stories of suffering, patterns emerged across the sample. An overarching theme in respondents' narratives was: suffering is a lack of control over one's self, one's body, or the circumstances of life. The theme's pervasiveness in elders' accounts shows that suffering is experienced and expressed culturally. Suffering in its many aspects—illness, loneliness, being grief-stricken or in pain or feeling shamed, challenges the American model of the person as autonomous. An individual's ability to direct her comings and goings remains a benchmark of contentment and maturity. Respondents said that suffering *may or may not be* connected to old age, but it *is* connected to the challenge to personal agency in everyday life that comes in the wake of suffering.

Elders also revealed, through their narratives, the incomparability in quality and meaning of suffering in old age to other stages of life. This distinction resides in a persistent awareness that time is running out; finding meaning in suffering and in life has a particular urgency. Because of this, issues of suffering are issues of identity of self and important others in the face of finitude.

Respondents' stories of suffering were filled with a second pattern that mimes the first—that of suffering as loss, because lack of control is a particular kind of loss. Elders grieved when they lost a significant other. When ill, they mourned the loss of mobility or stamina. Thoughts of death posed its own loss: loss of the joys of this world, leaving beloved others behind, and loss of certainty about the future. Stories of suffering as loss showed that elders believed that something precious was gone and could not be regained—it was irretrievable. Present life was lived in the shadow of "what was" or "what might have been."

According to elders, suffering as loss was ultimately relational. And like any current or past relationship, suffering as loss was multi-layered and multi-faceted. Respondents' narratives included the accumulated losses that elders endure through a lifetime, as well as the multiple meanings that elders attribute to a particular loss. If loss captured the experience of suffering in elders' narratives, it did so with the caveat that loss was different to each elder because it was based on losing individually named treasures.

Patterns in respondents' stories did not mean stereotypes. There were no stereotypes in elders' narratives because there are no stereotypical elders. For example, several men in the sample had been loving caretakers for parents and spouses; several women interviewed did "men's jobs" inside and outside the home. A lack of stereotypes was illustrated by the singularity of each elder's life story as well as by the paradoxes that emerged in elders' stories of suffering, even when similar themes, such as lack of control and loss, occurred. As Mrs. Janson indicated through her narrative of suffering in the mental institution, there must be a sense of self to suffer, yet to have no self *is* to suffer. Mr. Callen showed through his narrative that respondents place suffering in both local and larger contexts. He stated that all African-Americans know the concept of suffering because of their situatedness in the local and larger world, yet it was his entry into the dream world of drunkenness that resulted in suffering. Mr. Inglund described suffering as "physical agony," yet his narrative showed that the brokenness of his body in and of itself was not suffering. It was to a *fuller* brokenness (itself, a paradox) of body, roles and identity that his suffering spoke. Both Mr. Wickers and Mr. Danders suffered due to individual and collective discrimination. Mr. Wickers continues to suffer from his "fall through the cracks" of the American Dream; the price Mr. Danders paid for achieving the Dream was an intense suffering that he fought against and eventually overcame. Respondents named "having a choice" as significant in whether an experience was named suffering. Mrs. Billings had little choice in her brother's-in-law decision to fire her from a "good paying" job, plunge her into poverty, and thus into suffering. Mr. Carson perceived that the choices he freely made throughout his life caused suffering in old age. Elders' choices were often shaped by accidents of birth or powerful others. Most respondents, however, reported that they could choose how to react to a negative situation, or even to name a loss or tragedy "not suffering."

Patterns and themes in stories of suffering emerge from respondents' common humanity as well as through their shared time and place in a cohort history. Yet, states of being, such as chronic illness or poverty, and components of identity, such as class, ethnicity and gender, result in unique reactions to negative experiences as well as in dissimilar experiences of suffering from similar causes. Elders narrated a common take on the commonplace of suffering. Yet, each respondent's uniqueness of perception precluded stories from sounding or "being" the same.

So who is the self that suffers? Among many definitions, a self may be considered a process or an object, an entity, essential core or an "indeterminate capacity to engage the world" (Csordas, 1994). Metaphors symbolize the self, places represent the self. The body may be the first boundary of the self; relationships may construct the self; introspection may realize the self. Through certain cognitive illnesses peculiar to age, such as Alzheimer's disease, the self might be considered lost, missing, or even destroyed. In a previous chapter, we saw Mr. Banks struggle with just such a question as he wondered "where" his wife "existed" after she sustained brain damage. Although he believed that she died the day she lost her memory, he was convinced that her generosity of spirit kept her "somewhere intact" through her brain waves. According to him, something essential had gone missing from his wife, but something essential also remained. Although her mind, as the medium by which she discovered herself and the world seemed to him, lost—her body, as the medium by which she disclosed herself to others, and her spirit, as the medium by which she, according to him, transcended her *missing* self—were intact. Mr. Banks preserved his wife's self through his love for her, his knowledge of her personal history, and his hope that she would somewhere "persist." For Mr. Banks, his own suffering demanded that he continue to interpret his wife's self, which was rendered ambiguous by the effects of her illness. Mr. and Mrs. Banks illustrate the concept that the cognitively lost or missing self may be defined, interpreted, maintained and *hoped for* by another, and considered eminently worthy of love and honor.

It is to this sense of maintaining the self (one's own or others) through suffering that I return to the definition of suffering that I offered in the Preface—as a visceral awareness that humans are vulnerable to being broken at any time and in many ways. Colloquialisms of suffering—"coming apart," "falling to pieces," "spurting from the guts," and "my insides dropping out of me," portray the *breaking* or *broken* self in suffering. The brokenness usually occurred through disconnection—itself a break—self from self, self from others, self from God.

In elders' narratives, both the self and suffering were contextual. The self is constructed from an individual and communal history, memories, traditions, and beliefs about what constitutes the self, such as cognition, relatedness, the spirit or the breath of life, the body, free will. The experience of suffering is constructed from extreme distress as well as from beliefs about the purpose and value of suffering, and whether the self is annihilated upon death or endures.

In elders' narratives, there is a strong sense of hope to be reconnected, after brokenness, with self, others, and God, and ultimately to remain oneself. In respondents' stories, the opposite of suffering is integration. Because of this, the various aspects of the self—cognitive, embodied, situated, social, inspirited—sometimes falter, break apart, go missing, die, but according to elders, hopefully, ultimately reintegrate.

Appendix
(Partial Questionnaire)

1. Would you tell me the story of your life? Start where you like and take as much time as you need.
2. Would you describe an event or period in your life when you felt that you were suffering? What happened? How was it resolved?
3. How would you define suffering?
4. If you were going to draw a picture of suffering, what would it show?
5. How do your past sufferings influence the present quality of your life?
6. Do you think suffering is a "normal" part of life? A "normal" part of growing older?
7. Do you suffer when you experience certain feelings, such as regret, remorse or guilt over things that you did nor did not do in your life?
8. What do you think is the purpose of your suffering?
9. What does your religion say about suffering?
10. Why do you think God allows us to suffer?
11. Do you think that being older and closer to the end of life is a form of suffering?
12. Do you think older people suffer more than younger people?
13. Do you ever think about suffering in relation to dying?
14. What do you think happens after we die? Do you think we still might suffer then?
15. Can you think of anyone—a particular person or a group—who has suffered for a cause?
16. Is there such a thing as quiet or silent suffering or is suffering always expressed in some way through words or cries or gestures?

References

Ahola, A. (1992). Gender Differences in Revealing Psychological Symptoms. *Psyykkisen Orienilun Sukupolieroista, 29*(1): 23-34.

Alexander, B., Rubinstein, R., Goodman, M., & Luborsky, M. (1992). A Path Not Taken: A Cultural Analysis of Regrets and Childlessness in the Lives of Older Women. *The Gerontologist, 32,* 618-626.

Allen, L. (1999). Personal correspondence.

Amato, J. (1990). *A History and a Theory of Suffering.* New York: Praeger.

Aulen, G. (1951). *Christus Victor: An Historical Study of the Three Main Types of the Idea of Atonement.* New York: Macmillan.

Austin, W. (2001). Nursing Ethics in an Era of Globalization. *Advances in Nursing Science, 24,* 1-18.

Bakan, D. (1968). *Disease, Pain and Sacrifice: Toward a Psychology of Suffering.* Chicago, IL: Beacon Press.

Baltes, P., & Smith, J. (1999). Multilevel and Systemic Analyses of Old Age: Theoretical and Empirical Evidence for a Fourth Age. In V. L. Bengston & K. W. Schaie (Eds.), *Handbook of Theories of Aging* (pp. 153-173). New York: Springer.

Becker, E. (1972). *The Denial of Death.* New York: The Free Press.

Becker, G. (1997). *Disrupted Lives.* Berkeley, CA: University of California Press.

Beecher, S. (1957). *Measuring Pain.* Cambridge: Cambridge University Press.

Bellah, R. N., Madsen, R., Sullivan, W. M., Swidler, A., & Tipton, S. M. (1985). *Habits of the Heart.* New York: Harper & Row.

Belsky, J. (1997). *The Adult Experience.* St. Paul, MN: West.

Berger, P. (1967). *The Sacred Canopy.* New York: Anchor Books.

Berman, H. (1999). Paper presented at the 52nd Annual Gerontological Society of America, San Francisco, CA.

Bianchi, E. (1982). *Aging as a Spiritual Journey.* New York: Crossroad.

Birren, J. E., & Cunningham, W. R. (1985). Research on the Psychology of Aging. In J. E. Birren & K. W. Schaie (Eds.), *Handbook of the Psychology of Aging* (1st ed., pp. 3-38). New York: Van Nostrand Reinhold.

Black, H. (1996). "Wasted" Lives and the Hero Grown Old: Personal Perspectives of Spirituality by Aging Men. *Journal of Religious Gerontology, 9,* 35-48.

Black, H. (2001). Jake's Story: A Middle-Aged, Working Class Man's Physical and Spiritual Journey toward Death. *Qualitative Health Research, 11,* 293-307.

Black, H. (2002). She Cried, He Cried? Gender Differences in Experiences and Expressions of Suffering. Annual. Address presented at the College of the Holy Cross,
February 11, Worcester, MA.

Black, H., & Rubinstein, R. (2000). Old Souls: Aged Women, Poverty and the Experience
of God. Hawthorne, NY: Aldine deGruyter.

Boddy, J. (1991). Body Politics: Continuing the Anti-Circumcision Crusade. *Medical
Anthropology Quarterly, 5*(1), 15-17.

Bourdieu, P. (1993). *The Weight of the World: Social Suffering in Contemporary Society.*
Stanford, CA: Stanford University Press.

Bowker, J. (1970). *Problems of Suffering in the World's Religions.* Cambridge: Cambridge
University Press.

Bradley, E. H., Fried, T. R., Kasl, S. V., & Idler, E. (2001). Quality-of-Life Trajectories of
Elders in the End of Life. In M Powell Lawton (Ed.), *Focus on The End of Life:
Scientific and Social Issues* (pp. 97-119). New York: Springer.

Brannon, R. (1976). The Male Sex Role: Our Culture's Blueprint of Manhood, and What
It's Done For Us Lately. In D. David & R. Brannon (Eds.), *The Forty-Nine Percent
Majority* (pp. 1-45). Reading, MA: Addison-Wesley.

Bregman, L. (1999). *Beyond Silence and Denial.* Louisville, KY: Westminster John
Knox Press.

Bregman, L. (1987). Models of Suffering. *Religion and Intellectual Life, 4,* 78-91.

Brennan, P. U., Moos, R. H., & Kim, J. Y. (1993). Gender Differences in the Individual
Characteristics and Life Contexts of Late Middle Aged and Older Problem Drinkers.
Addiction, 88, 781-790.

Brodwin, P. (1992). Symptoms and Social Performances: The Case of Diane Reden. In
Mary-Jo DelVecchio Good, Paul E. Brodwin, Byron J. Good, & Arthur Kleinman
(Eds.), *Pain as Human Experience: An Anthropological Perspective* (pp. 67-99).
Berkeley, CA: University of California Press.

Brody, H. (1987). *Stories of Sickness.* New Haven, CT: Yale University Press.

Browning, D. (1966). *Atonement and Psychotherapy.* Philadelphia, PA: The Westminster
Press.

Bruner, J. (1990). *Acts of Meaning.* Cambridge, MA: Harvard University Press.

Cannon, K. (1995). *Katie's Cannon.* New York: Continuum Press.

Cassell, E. (1982). *The Nature of Suffering and the Goals of Medicine.* New York: Oxford
University Press.

Cassell, E. (1992). The Nature of Suffering: Physical, Psychological, Social and Spiritual
Aspects: The Hidden Dimension of Illness and Human Suffering. *National League
of Nursing Publication, 15*(2461), 1-10.

Cassidy, J., & Mohr, J. (2001). Unresolvable Fear, Trauma and Psychopathology. *Clinical
Psychology: Science and Practice, 8,* 275-298.

Charmaz, K. (1995). Identity Dilemmas of Chronically Ill Men. In D. Sabo & D. F.
Gordon (Eds.), *Men's Health and Illness: Gender, Power and the Body* (pp. 266-291).
Thousand Oaks, CA: Sage.

Charmaz, K. (1999). Stories of Suffering: Subjective Tales and Research Narratives.
Qualitative Health Research, 9, 362-382.

Cherney, N. (1996). The Problem of Inadequately Relieved Suffering. *Journal of
Social Issues, 52,* 13-30.

Chopp, R. (1986). *The Praxis of Suffering.* Maryknoll, NY: Orbis Books.

Collins, S. (1988). Women at the Top of Women's Fields: Social Work, Nursing, and Education. In A. Statham, E. M. Miller, & H. O. Mauksch (Eds.), *The Worth of Women's Work: A Qualitative Synthesis* (pp. 187-204). Albany, NY: SUNY.

Cone, J. (1970). *A Black Theology of Liberation.* Philadelphia, PA: Lippincott.

Connolly, W. 91996). Suffering, Justice and the Politics of Becoming. *Culture, Medicine and Psychiatry, 20,* 257-277.

Coyne, W. (2001). Lecture given at Polisher Research Institute. Philadelphia, Pennsylvania.

Cristofalo, V., Tresini, M., Francis, M., & Volker, C. (1999). Biological Theories of Senescence. In V. L. Bengtson & K. W. Schaie (Eds.), *Handbook of Theories of Aging.* New York: Springer.

Csordas, T. (1994). *The Sacred Self.* Berkeley: University of California Press.

Cumming, E., & Henry, W. (1961). *Growing Old: The Process of Disengagement.* New York: Basic Books.

Daniels, A. K. (1987). Invisible Work. *Social Problems, 34*(5), 403-415.

Davis, A. (1981). *Women, Race, and Class.* New York: Random House.

Das, V. (1997). Sufferings, Theodicies, Disciplinary Practices, Appropriations. *International Social Science Journal, 49,* 563-572.

Das, V. (2000). *Violence and Subjectivity.* Berkeley: University of California Press.

Das, V., & Kleinman, A. (2001). *Remaking a World: Violence, Social Suffering and Recovery.* Berkeley: University of California Press.

Dass, R. (2000). *Still Here.* New York: Riverhead Books.

Drazen, r. (2002). *Frankl's Choice.* Documentary produced for WHYY TV 12.

Duchan, J. F. (2001). *Learning Leveling and Leveling Learning.* Paper presented at the University of Buffalo.

Duffy, M. (1992). A Theoretical and Empirical Review of the Concept of Suffering: The Hidden Dimension of Illness and Human Suffering. *National League of Nursing Publication, 15*(2461), 291-303.

Eisenhandler, S. (2003). *Keeping the Faith in Late Life.* New York: Springer.

Estes, C., Swan, J., & Gerard, L. (1982). Dominant and Competing Paradigms in Gerontology: Towards a Political Economy of Ageing. *Ageing and Society, 12,* 151-164.

Farley, W. (1992). Tragedy and the Compassion of God. *Second Opinion, 18,* 23-29.

Fernandez, J. (1974). The Mission of Metaphor in Expressive Culture. *Current Anthropology, 15,* 119-145.

Fetzer Institute Publication. (1999). *Multidimensional Measurement of Religiousness/ Spirituality for Use in Health Research,* Kalamazoo, Michigan.

Fischer, L. (1994). Qualitative Research as Art and Science. In J. Gubrium & A. Sankar (Eds.), *Qualitative Methods in Aging Research* (pp. 3-14). Thousand Oaks, CA: Sage.

Francis, D. (1990). The Significance of Work Friends in Late Life. *Journal of Aging Studies, 4,* 405-424.

Frank, A. (1992). Illness and Self-Knowledge. *Second Opinion, 18,* 31-41.

Frank, A. (1995). *The Wounded Storyteller.* Chicago: University of Chicago Press.

Frank, A. (2001). Can We Research Suffering? *Qualitative Health Research, 11,* 353-362.

Frankl, V. (1959). *Man's Search for Meaning.* New York: Washington Square Press.

Freud, S. (1920, 1966). *Introductory Lectures on Psychoanalysis* (J. Strachey, Trans. and Ed.). New York: Liveright.

Fromm, E. (1947). *Man for Himself.* New York: Rinehart and Company.

Geertz, C. (1973). *Religion as a Cultural System.* New York: Basic Books.

Gergen, M., & Gergen, K. (1993). Narratives of the Gendered Body in Popular Autobiography. *The Narrative Study of Lives, 1,* 191-218.

Glaser, B., & Strauss, A. L. (1967). *The Discovery of Grounded Theory: Strategies for Qualitative Research.* Chicago, IL: Aldine.

Goffman, E. (1963). *Stigma.* New York: Simon and Schuster.

Good, B. (1992). A Body in Pain. In M. J. DelVecchio Good, P. E. Brodwin, B. J. Good, & A. Kleinman (Eds.), *Pain as Human Experience: An Anthropological Perspective* (pp. 29-47). Berkeley, CA: University of California Press.

Good, B., & Good, M. J. (1981). The Meaning of Symptoms: A Cultural Hermeneutic Model for Clinical Practice. In L. Eisenberg & A. Kleinman (Eds.), *The Relevance of Social Science for Medicine* (pp. 165-196). Dordrecht: D. Reidel.

Goodman, M., Black, H., & Rubinstein, R. (1996). Paternal Bereavement in Older Men. *Omega, 33*(4), 303-321.

Graneheim, U. H., Lindah, E., & Kihlgren, M. (1997). Description of Suffering in Connection with Life Values. *Scandinavian Journal of Caring Sciences, 11,* 145-150.

Grant, J. (1989). Womanist Theology: Black Women's Experience as a Source for Doing Theology. In G. S. Wilmore (Ed.), *African American Religious Studies* (pp. 208-227). Durham, NC: Duke University Press.

Grant, J. (1997). The Sin of Servanthood. In E. M. Townes (Ed.), *A Troubling in My Soul: Womanist Perspectives on Evil & Suffering* (pp. 199-218). Maryknoll, NY: Orbis Books.

Gubrium, J. (1993). *Speaking of Life.* New York: Aldine deGruyter.

Gutierrez, G. (1987). *On Job: God-Talk and the Suffering of the Innocent.* Maryknoll, NY: Orbis Books.

Hall, E. T. (1959). *The Silent Language.* Greenwich, CT: Fawcett Premier Book.

Harper, A. (1990). *The Theodicy of Suffering.* San Francisco, CA: Mellen Research University Press.

Harrison, B. (1985). *Making the Connections: Essays in Feminist Social Ethics.* Boston, MA: Beacon Press.

Hauerwas, S. (1990). *Naming the Silences.* Grand Rapids, MI: William B. Eerdmans.

Hauerwas, S., & Jones, L. G. (1989). *Why Narrative? Readings in Narrative Theology.* Grand Rapids, MN: Eerdmans.

Heath, C. (1989). Pain Talk: The Expression of Suffering in the Medical Consultation. *Social Psychological Quarterly, 52,* 113-125.

Heidegger, M. (1962). *Being and Time.* J. Macquarrie & E. Robinson (Trans.). New York: Harper & Row.

Heitman, E. (1992). The Influence of Values and Culture in Responses to Suffering. *National League of Nursing Publication, 15*(2461), 81-102.

Hick, J. (1990). *Philosophy of Religion* (4th ed.). Englewood Cliffs, NJ: Prentice Hall.

Hillman, J. (1983). *Healing Fiction.* Barrytown, NY: Station Hill.

Holstein. J., & Gubrium, J. F. (1997). *The New Language of Qualitative Method.* New York: Oxford University Press.

Huyck, M. (1990). Gender Differences in Aging. In J. E. Birren & K. W. Schaie (Eds.), *Handbook of the Psychology of Aging* (3rd ed., pp. 124-132). San Diego, CA: Academic Press.

Kahn, D., & Steeves, R. (1986). The Experience of Suffering: Conceptual Clarification and Theoretical Definition. *Journal of Advanced Nursing, 11*, 623-631.

Kales, H., & Valenstein, M. (2002). Complexity in Late-Life Depression: Impact of Confounding Factors on Diagnosis, Treatment, and Outcomes. *Journal of Geriatric Psychiatry and Neurology, 15*, 147-155.

Katz, S. (1996). *Disciplining Old Age: The Formation of Gerontological Knowledge.* Charlottesville: University Press Virginia.

Kaufman, S. (1980). Cultural Components of Identity in Old Age. *Ethos, 9*, 51-87.

Kaufman, S. (1986). *The Ageless Self.* Madison, WI: University of Wisconsin Press.

Keyes, C. (1985). The Interpretive Basis of Depression. In A. Kleinman & B. Good (Eds.), *Culture and Depression.* Berkeley: University of California Press.

Kimmell, M. (1995). Introduction. In D. Sabo & D. F. Gordon (Eds.), *Men's Health and Illness: Gender, Power and the Body* (pp. 139-157). Thousand Oaks, CA: Sage.

Kleinman, A. (1980). *Patients and Healers in the Context of Culture: An Exploration of the Borderland between Anthropology, Medicine, and Psychiatry.* Berkeley: University of California Press.

Kleinman, A. (1988). *The Illness Narratives.* New York: Basic Books.

Kleinman, A. (1992). Pain and Resistance: The Delegitimation and Relegitimation of Local Worlds. In M. J. DelVecchio Good, P. E. Brodwin, B. J. Good, & A. Kleinman (Eds.), *Pain as Human Experience: An Anthropological Perspective* (pp. 169-197). Berkeley, CA: University of California Press.

Kleinman, A. (1996). Suffering, Ethics, and the Politics of Moral Life. *Culture, Medicine and Psychiatry, 20*, 287-291.

Kleinman, A. (1997). Intimations of Solidarity? The Popular Culture Responds to Assisted Suicide. *The Hastings Center Report, #27*, pp. 34-37.

Kleinman, A., Brodwin, P. E., Good, B. J., & Good, M. J. (1992). Pain as Human Experience: An Introduction. In M. J. DelVecchio Good, P. E. Brodwin, B. J. Good, & A. Kleinman (Eds.), *Pain as Human Experience: An Anthropological Perspective* (pp. 1-28). Berkeley, CA: University of California Press.

Kleinman, A., Das, V., & Lock, M. (1997). Introduction. In *Social Suffering* (pp. ix-xxvii). Berkeley, CA: University of California Press.

Kliever, L. (1989). Dax and Job: The Refusal of Redemptive Suffering. In L. D. Kliever (Ed.), *Dax's Case: Essays in Medical Ethics and Human Meaning* (pp. 187-211). New York: Springer.

Koenig, H. (1994). *Aging and God: Spiritual Pathways to Mental Health in Midlife and Later Years.* New York: The Haworth Pastoral Press.

Krause, N. (2003). Religious Meaning and Subjective Well-Being in Late Life. *Journal of Gerontology, 58B*, S160-S170.

Langer, L. (1997). *Social Suffering.* Berkeley, CA: University of California Press.

Lawton, M. P. (2000). *Annual Review of Gerontology and Geriatrics: End of Life Issues.* New York: Springer.

Lawton, M. P. (2001). Personal correspondence. Philadelphia, PA, July 18.

Lawton, M., Moss, M., & Hoffman, C. (1999). Health, Valuation of Life, and the Wish to Live. *Gerontologist, 39*, 406-416.

Lawton, M., Moss, M., Hoffman, C., Kleban, M., Ruckdeschel, K., & Winter, L. (2001). Valuation of Life: A Concept and a Scale. *Journal of Aging and Health, 13*, 3-31.

Lazare, A. (1992). The Suffering of Shame and Humiliation in Illness. *National League of Nursing Publication, 15*(2461), 227-244.

Lieberman, M., & Peskin, H. (1992). Adult Life Crises. In J. Birren, R. Sloane, & G. D. Cohen (Eds.), *Handbook of Mental Health and Aging.* New York: Academic Press.

Lipton, J. A., & Marbach, J. J. (1984). Ethnicity and the Pain Experience. *Social Science and Medicine, 19,* 1279-1298.

Lightner, J. (1993). Lecture given at LaSalle University. Philadelphia, Pennsylvania.

Livingston, J. (1989). *Anatomy of the Sacred.* New York: Macmillan.

Lorde, A. (1980). *The Cancer Journals.* San Francisco, CA: aunt lute books.

Lutzky, S. M., & Knight, B. G. (1994). Explaining Gender Differences in Caregiver Distress: The Roles of Emotional Attentiveness and Coping Styles. *Psychology and Aging, 9,* 513-519.

Mark, N. (1997). A Perspective on Jewish Healing. *Sh'ma, 28,* 4.

Martin, E. (1987). *The Woman in the Body.* Boston: Beacon Press.

May, W. (1989). Dealing with Catastrophe. In L. D. Kliever (Ed.), *Dax's Case: Essays in Medical Ethics and Human Meaning* (pp. 131-150). New York: Springer.

May, W. (1991). *The Patient's Ordeal.* Bloomington, IN: Indiana University Press.

McFadden, S. (2003). Older Adults Religious Emotions. In M. Kimble & S. McFadden (Eds.), *Aging, Spirituality and Religion* (Vol. 2, pp. 47-58). Philadelphia: Fortress Press.

McGoldrick, M. (1996). Irish Families. In M. McGoldrick, J. Giordano, & J. K. Pearce (Eds.), *Ethnicity and Family Therapy.* New York: Guilford Press.

Migliore, S. (2001). From Illness Narratives to Social Commentary: A Pirandellian Approach to "Nerves." *Medical Anthropology Quarterly, 15*(1), 100-125.

Miller, S. (1985). *The Shame Experience.* Hillsdale, NJ: The Analytic Press.

Mirowsky, J., & Ross, C. E. (1995). Sex Differences in Distress: Real or Artifact? *American Sociological Review, 60,* 449-468.

Mischler, E. (1986). *Research Interviewing: Context and Narrative.* Cambridge: Harvard University Press.

Moltemann, J. (1969). *The Crucified God.* New York: Paulist Press.

Morse, J. M., & Field, P. A. (1995). *Qualitative Research Methods for Health Professionals* (2nd ed.). Thousand Oaks, CA: Sage.

Moss, M., Moss, S., Rubinstein, R., & Black, H. (2003). The Metaphor of "Family" in Staff Communication about Dying and Death. *Journal of Gerontology, 58,* 5290-5296.

Mowsesian, R. (1986). *Golden Goals, Rusted Realities: Work and Aging in America.* New York: Macmilllan.

Moyers, B. (2000). *On Our Own Terms: Moyers on Dying.* Produced by E. Owen for WHYY, PBS, New York.

Mutran, E. (1987). Family, Social Ties and Self-Meaning in Old Age: The Development of an Affective Identity. *Journal of Social and Personal Relationships, 4,* 463-480.

Murphy, R. (1987). *The Body Silent.* New York: W. W. Norton.

Mussat, D. (2000). Regional meeting of American Academy of Religion, Chadds Ford, Pennsylvania.

Myerhoff, B. (1979). *Number Our Days.* Chicago: University of Chicago Press.

Nathanson, D. (2003). *Shame and Pride Affect, Sex, and the Birth of the Self.* New York: W. W. Norton.

Neugarten, B. (1977). Personality and Aging. In J. E. Birren & K. E. Schaie (Eds.), *Handbook of the Psychology of Aging* (pp. 626-649). New York: Van Nostrand Reinhold.

Niebuhr, H. R. (1989). The Story of Our Life. In S. Hauerwas & L. G. Jones (Eds.), *Why Narrative? Readings in Narrative Theology* (pp. 1-22). Grand Rapids, MI: William B. Eerdmans.

Neuhaus, R. (2000). *Eternal Pity: Reflections on Dying.* Indiana: University of Notre Dame Press.

Pan, C., & Meier, D. (2000). *Clinical Aspects of End-of-Life Care.* In M. P. Lawton (Ed.), *Annual Review of Gerontology and Geriatrics* (Vol. 20, pp. 273-308). New York: Springer.

Parkin, D. (1985). *The Anthropology of Evil.* Oxford: Basil Blackwell.

Perakyla, A. (1997). Reliability and Validity in Research Based on Transcripts. In D. Silverman (Ed.), *Qualitative Research: Theory, Method and Practice* (pp. 201-220). Thousand Oaks, CA: Sage.

Picard, C. (1991). Caring and the Story: The Compelling Nature of What Must Be Told and Understood in the Human Dimension of Suffering. *National League of Nursing Publication, 15*(2401), 89-98.

Pirandello, L. (1990). *One, No One, and One Hundred Thousand.* Boston, MA: Eridanos Press.

Polkinghorne, D. (1988). *Narrative Knowing and the Human Sciences.* Albany: SUNY Press.

Rawlinson, M. (1986). The Sense of Suffering. *The Journal of Medicine and Philosophy, 11*, 39-62.

Reich, W. (1987). Models of Pain and Suffering: Foundation for an Ethic of Compassion. *Acta Neurochirurgica, 38*(Suppl), 117-122.

Reich, W. (1989). Speaking of Suffering: A Moral Account of Compassion. *Soundings, 72*, 83-108.

Remen, R. (1999). On Defining Spirit. *The Park Ridge Center Bulletin, Issue #7,* January-February, p. 4.

Reissman, C. (1997). *Narrative Analysis.* Newbury Park, CA: Sage.

Ricoeur, P. (1986). Life: A Story in Search of a Narrator. In M. C. Doeser & J. N. Kraay (Eds.), *Facts and Values: Philosophical Reflections from Western and Non-Western Perspectives.* Norwell, MA: Martinus Nijhoff.

Ring, N. C., Nash, K. S., MacDonald, M. N., Glennon, F., & Glancy, J. A. (1997). *Introduction to the Study of Religion.* Maryknoll, NY: Orbis Books.

Robinson, A. (1993). Attitudes toward Nursing Home Residents among Aides of Three Cultural Groups. *Journal of Cultural Diversity, 1,* 16-18.

Rosen, E. J., & Weltman, S. F. (1996). Jewish Families: An Overview. In M. McGoldrick, J. Giordano, & J. K. Pearce (Eds.), *Ethnicity and Family Therapy.* New York: Guilford Press.

Rosenwald, G., & Ochberg, R. (1992). *Storied Lives: The Cultural Politics of Self-Understanding.* New Haven, CT: Yale University Press.

Rosenthal, G. (1993). Reconstruction of Life Stories: Principles of Selection in Generation Stories for Narrative Biographical Interviews. *The Narrative Study of Lives, 1,* 59-91.

Rubinstein, R. (1989). The Home Environments of Older People: A Description of Psycho-social Processes Linking Person to Place. *Journal of Gerontology: Social Sciences, 44,* S45-S53.

Rubinstein, R. (1992). Anthropological Methods in Gerontological Research: Entering the World of Meaning. *Journal of Aging Studies, 6,* 567-576.

Rubinstein, R., & Black, H. (1998). *Native Theories of Suffering.* Research funded by The Fetzer Institute, Kalamazoo, Michigan.

Rubinstein, R., Goodman, M., & Black, H. (1993). *Older Men: Caregiving, Generativity and Narcissism.* Paper presented at the NIA sponsored conference, Men's Caregiving Roles in an Aging Society, Washington, D.C.

Rubinstein, R., Kilbride, J., & Nagy, S. (1992). *Elders Living Alone.* New York: Aldine deGruyter.

Rubinstein, R., & Lawton, M. P. (1997). *Depression in Long Term and Residential Care: Advances in Research and Treatment.* New York: Springer.

Rudnytsky, L. (1993). Lecture on the Ukrainian Holocaust. LaSalle University, Philadelphia, PA, September 25.

Sabatino, F. (1992). Aids as a Spiritual Journey. *Second Opinion, 18*(1), 94-99.

Sabo, D., & Gordon, F. (1995). Rethinking Men's Health and Illness. In D. Sabo & D. F. Gordon (Eds.), *Men's Health and Illness: Gender, Power and the Body* (pp. 1-21). Thousand Oaks, CA: Sage.

Sacks, O. (1984). *A Leg to Stand On.* New York: A Touchstone Book.

Sajatovic, M. (2002). Aging-Related Issues in Bipolar Disorder: A Health Services Perspective. *Journal of Geriatric Psychiatry and Neurology, 15,* 128-133.

Sarbin, T. (1986). *Narrative Psychology: The Storied Nature of Human Conduct.* New York: Praeger.

Schaie, K., & Willis, S. (1999). Theories of Everyday Competence and Aging. In *Handbook of Theories of Aging* (pp. 174-195). New York: Springer.

Scarry, E. (1985). *The Body in Pain.* New York: Oxford University Press.

Scheper-Hughes, N., & Lock, M. (1991, Spring). The Message in the Bottle: Illness and the Micropolitics of Resistance. *The Journal of Psychohistory, 18*(4), 409-432.

Scheper-Hughes, N., & Lock, M. (1987). The Mindful Body: A Prolegomenon to Future Work in Medical Anthropology. *Medical Anthropology Quarterly, 1,* 6-41.

Schneider, C. (1992). *Shame, Exposure and Privacy.* New York: W. W. Norton.

Schussler-Fiorenza, E. (1989). In Search of Women's Heritage. In J. Plaskow & C. Christ (Eds.), *Weaving the Visions: New Patterns in Feminist Spirituality* (pp. 29-38). San Francisco, CA: HarperSanFrancisco.

Schwarz, E. (1992). Stories that Heal, Wheel Within a Wheel. *Second Opinion, 18,* 90-93.

Schweizer, H. (1995). To Give Suffering a Language. *Literature and Medicine, 14*(2), 10-21.

Sennet, R., & Cobb, J. (1974). *The Hidden Injuries of Class.* New York: Vintage Books.

Simeon, D., Guralnik, O., Schmeidler, J., Sirof, B., & Knutelska, M. (2001). The Role of Childhood Interpersonal Trauma in Depersonalization Disorder. *American Journal of Psychiatry, 158,* 1027-1033.

Smith, B. (1997). *Belief and Resistance.* Cambridge: Harvard University Press.

Smith, R. (1996). Theological Perspectives. In B. R. Ferrell Sudbury (Ed.), *Suffering* (pp. 159-172). Massachusetts: Jones and Bartlett.

Soelle, D. (1975). *Suffering*. E. R. Kalin (Trans). Philadelphia, PA: Fortress Press.

Sontag, S. (1978). *Illness as Metaphor*. New York: Farrar, Straus & Giroux.

Soskice, J. (1985). *Metaphor and Religious Language*. Oxford: Clarendon Press.

Spalding, H. (1999). Personal correspondence. Philadelphia, Pennsylvania.

Spradley, J. P. (1979). *The Ethnographic Interview*. New York: Holt, Rinehart & Winston.

Stewart, A. (1994). The Women's Movement and Women's Lives: Linking Individual Development and Social Events. *The Narrative Study of Lives, 2,* 230-250.

Stillion, J. (1995). Premature Death among Males. In D. Sabo & D. F. Gordon (Eds.), *Men's Health and Illness: Gender, Power and the Body* (pp. 46-67). Thousand Oaks, CA: Sage.

Strauss, A. L., & Corbin, J. (1990). *Basics of Qualitative Research*. Newbury Park, CA: Sage.

Sullivan, L. (1996). Coming to Our Senses: Religious Studies in the Academy. *Journal of the American Academy of Religion, 66*(1), 1-11.

Surin, K. (1986). *Theology and the Problem of Evil*. New York: Basil Blackwell.

Svenaeus, F. (2000). The Body Uncanny—Further Steps Towards a Phenomenology of Illness. *Medicine, Health Care and Philosophy, 3,* 125-137.

Tellis-Nyak, V., & Tellis-Nyak, M. (1989). Quality of Care and the Burden of Two Cultures. *Gerontologist, 29*(3), 307-313.

Tornstam, L. (1994). Gero-Transcendence: A Theoretical and Empirical Exploration. In L. E. Thomas & S. A. Eisenhandler (Eds.), *Aging and the Religious Dimension*. Westport, CT: Auburn House.

Townes, E. (1997). Living in a New Jerusalem. In E. M. Townes (Ed.), *A Troubling in My Soul: Womanist Perspectives on Evil & Suffering* (pp. 78-91). Maryknoll, NY: Orbis Books.

Turner, T. (1996). Anthropology and Multiculturism. In D. T. Goldberg (Ed.), *Multiculturalism: A Critical Reader* (pp. 406-425). Cambridge, MA: Blackwell.

Uehara, E., Morelli, P., & Aba-Kim, J. (2001). Somatic Complaints and Social Suffering among Survivors of the Cambodian Killing Fields. *Journal of Human Behavior in the Social Environment, 3,* 243-262.

van Hooft, S. (1998). The Meaning of Suffering. *Hastings Center Report, 28*(5), 13-19.

Verhey, A. (1992). Compassion: Beyond the Standard Account. *Second Opinion, 18*(2), 72.

Wandel, L. (1996). Defining a Life: The Western Tradition. In H. Spiro, M. McCrea Curnen, & L. Wandel (Eds.), *Facing Death*. New Haven, CT: Yale University Press.

Weber, M. (1958). *The Protestant Ethic and the Spirit of Capitalism*. New York: Scribner's Press.

Webster's New World Dictionary. (1972). Wm. Collins and World Publishing Co., United States of America.

Weil, S. (1951, 1973). *Waiting for God*. New York: Harper & Row.

Weiss, R., & Bass, S. (2002). *Challenges of the Third Age: Meaning and Purpose in Later Life*. New York: Oxford University Press.

Widdershoven, G. (1993). The Story of Life: Hermeneutic Perspectives on the Relationship between Narrative and Life History. In R. Josselson & A. Lieblich (Eds.), *The Narrative Study of Lives* (pp. 1-20). Newbury Park, CA: Sage.

Wiesel, E. (1961). *Night.* New York: Avon Books.

Wiesel, E. (1990). *The Night Trilogy.* New York: Hill and Wang.

Williams, B., & Healy, D. (2001). Perceptions of Illness Causation among New Referrals to a Community Mental Health Team: Explanatory Model or Exploratory Map? *Social Science and Medicine, 53,* 465-476.

Young-Eisendrath, P., & Miller, M. (2001). *The Psychology of Mature Spirituality.* London: Routledge.

Zborowski, M. (1969). *People in Pain.* San Francisco, CA: Jossey-Bass.

Zussman, R. (1993). *Intensive Care.* Stony Brook: SUNY Press.

Index